MANAGING THE AGEING

EXP...

Le...ning from... people

Denise Tanner

90 0888512 X

KT-524-543

This edition published in Great Britain in 2010 by

The Policy Press
University of Bristol
Fourth Floor
Beacon House
Queen's Road
Bristol BS8 1QU
UK

t: +44 (0)117 331 4054
f: +44 (0)117 331 4093
tpp-info@bristol.ac.uk
www.policypress.co.uk

North American office:
The Policy Press
c/o International Specialized Books Services
920 NE 58th Avenue, Suite 300
Portland, OR 97213-3786, USA
t: +1 503 287 3093
f: +1 503 280 8832
info@isbs.com

UNIVERSITY OF PLYMOUTH

9 00888512 X

© The Policy Press 2010

British Library Cataloguing in Publication Data
A catalogue record for this book is available from the British Library.

Library of Congress Cataloging-in-Publication Data
A catalog record for this book has been requested.

ISBN 978 1 86134 885 2 paperback
ISBN 978 1 86134 886 9 hardcover

The right of Denise Tanner to be identified as author of this work has been asserted by her in accordance with the 1988 Copyright, Designs and Patents Act.

All rights reserved: no part of this publication may be reproduced, stored in a retrieval system, or transmitted in any form or by any means, electronic, mechanical, photocopying, recording, or otherwise without the prior permission of The Policy Press.

The statements and opinions contained within this publication are solely those of the author and not of the University of Bristol or The Policy Press. The University of Bristol and The Policy Press disclaim responsibility for any injury to persons or property resulting from any material published in this publication.

The Policy Press works to counter discrimination on grounds of gender, race, disability, age and sexuality.

Cover design by The Policy Press
Front cover: image kindly supplied by www.alamy.com
Printed and bound in Great Britain by Hobbs, Southampton

The Policy Press uses environmentally responsible print partners.

Contents

List of figures

Notes on the author

Denise Tanner is a lecturer in social work at the University of Birmingham. She is a registered social worker and has extensive practice experience in social work with adults as well as many years' experience as a lecturer and researcher. She has a particular interest in service user and carer involvement in social work education and research.

Acknowledgements

This book would not have been possible without the willingness of the older people, whose stories form the central thread of the book, to take part in the research. I am immensely grateful to them for welcoming me into their homes, giving their time generously and opening their lives to me with such warmth, humour and fortitude.

Other people who have helped in various ways and at different times include Joan Forbes, Barbara Walters, Paul Bywaters and John Harris.

My thanks to Judith Phillips and staff at The Policy Press for their patience, understanding and support during the writing and production period.

Finally, my love and thanks to Jessica, Charlotte and Eleanor, for sustaining me through difficult times.

Foreword

Judith Phillips

Managing the ageing experience analyses the strategies used by older people to manage the changes that accompanying ageing. The book is well grounded in the experiences of older people themselves, and provides us with the views of 12 older people and their practical strategies for managing change as well as the wider context of gerontological social work and social care. Taking a lifecourse perspective it connects current processes with values, goals and past experiences of dealing with loss and change. Themes discussed in the book illustrate the resilience, creativity and resourcefulness of older people in their attempts to sustain themselves and to engage in the social environment.

The themes within the book address theoretical frameworks for making sense of change as well as providing the voices of older people to illustrate the key issues. Students, academics, professionals and policy makers will find this text of particular value with its synthesis of current research and fresh analytical lens on how older people develop strategies for change.

Introduction

> The way people perceive their lives is of vital importance, not only as a means of exploring the aging process but also as a guideline for social policy and the delivery of care in an aging society ... an understanding of the phenomenon of growing older can only be fully shaped through an investigation of personal meanings of aging, which are expressed in metaphors, images and life stories. (Ruth and Kenyon, 1996, p 2)

The central aim of this book is to learn from the ways in which older people manage the experience of ageing. An overview of research projects commissioned by older people as part of the Joseph Rowntree Foundation's Older People's Research Programme between 2000-04 highlighted the need for policy and practice to start with an understanding of older people's lives, in all their richness and diversity, and then, based on that understanding, to consider how services can support older people to live the lives they choose (Older People's Steering Group, 2004). This reflects the ethos of this book, which aims to develop understanding of older people's lives, as illuminated by research based on their experiences and perceptions, and to consider what this means for the development of services and strategies to support their well-being.

As argued by Ruth and Kenyon (1996), understanding of the process of managing ageing can only be acquired through uncovering the experiences of older people and the meanings they give to these experiences. Central to this book are the experiences and perspectives of 12 older people who participated in a three-year research study (2000 to 2003). The study explored how the older people managed difficulties for which they had been refused help by social services on the grounds that their needs did not meet eligibility criteria. In order to keep the research anchored as closely as possible to older people's experiences, the research used approaches that sought to promote the active involvement of older people as research participants. Although the older participants have not been directly involved in writing the book, it is hoped that its content and messages are firmly rooted in their understandings and experiences. Direct quotations from their interviews feature prominently in an effort to project their own voices as far as possible.

In addition to exploring what can be learned from close attention to the experiences of these 12 older people as they endeavoured to manage the ageing experience, this book also seeks to connect these experiences to wider research about older people's needs, preferences and experiences, to themes and debates in gerontological theory and to recent and current developments in social policy and practice.

It is apparent through this process that older people's understandings are not simply isolated, individual phenomena; rather, they are negotiated within a social and cultural context that both shapes and is shaped by individual meanings. In this way, investigating personal meanings goes beyond merely uncovering subjectivities at an individual level; it also reveals relationships between individual meaning and 'collective subjectivities', that is, the broader social context (Ruth and Kenyon, 1996, p 4). Recognising the dynamic between older people's experiences and perspectives and the broader social and cultural context, there are a number of key questions that serve as ongoing threads throughout this book:

• What factors influence older people's ability to manage loss and change?
• How do older people maintain a sense of 'personhood' when faced with assaults on their personal and social identities as competent and independent adults?
• How do the views and understandings of older people 'fit' with professional discourses about 'need' and 'services'?
• When we talk of care, support and services, what determines whether the help received is experienced by the older person as helpful and supportive?

I see the 'knowledge' arising from the research presented in this book as jointly created by the older people who participated in the research and myself, as researcher. Our respective roles, identities and the stories told were jointly constructed during our research encounters (Holstein and Gubrium, 1997). Chapter One therefore focuses on introducing the older people who took part in the research and myself. This chapter also presents a rationale for starting from older people's lives when seeking to understand ageing.

Chapter Two outlines the policy and practice background to the research and provides the context for discussion in subsequent chapters of the extent to which policy and services support or undermine older people's efforts to manage the experience of ageing. It also describes the research processes and relationships that have generated the understanding the book seeks to convey.

Chapters Three, Four and Five discuss different aspects of older people's experiences of negotiating and managing difficulties in later life. Chapter Three focuses on older people's efforts to 'keep going' by using practical or 'doing' strategies. Chapter Four examines the cognitive processes or 'being' strategies through which they strive to preserve a positive sense of self. Chapter Five explores the resources and threats that comprise 'the slippery slope' of later life and influence older people's capacity to withstand or negotiate successfully the difficulties they encounter. All three chapters draw heavily on the views and experiences of older people themselves, with direct quotations from participants used to develop and illustrate key themes.[1] These views and experiences are discussed in the context of other relevant research findings and wider theoretical perspectives.

Chapter Six takes forward the issues raised in the previous three chapters, presenting a model of managing later life that integrates the 'keeping going', 'staying me' and 'the slippery slope' themes. The proposed model is compared with other psychological and social models of ageing. A core theme of sustaining the self is discussed in the context of theories of identity and ageing.

The final chapter discusses the implications of the issues highlighted for social policy and social work and social care practice and suggests directions for policy and practice that are consistent with the messages contained in previous chapters.

Note
[1] Quotations are identified by participant pseudonym and interview number (1-5).

ONE

Starting from lives

The greater the distance between direct experience and its interpretation, then the more likely resulting knowledge is to be inaccurate, unreliable and distorted. (Beresford, 2003, p 22)

This chapter begins by introducing the older people whose experiences and perspectives form the central thread of the book. I then introduce both myself and the research, aiming to make as transparent as possible the research relationships and processes through which understanding of older people's strategies for managing ageing has been generated. The final part of the chapter considers the rationale for starting with the experiences of older people in order to understand ageing. This encompasses discussion of theory, epistemology, values and policy.

Introducing the older participants

As mentioned in the Introduction, I wanted to 'get close' to older people's experiences, not only by using methods that helped them to talk openly about their experiences, but also by trying to involve them in some of the research processes. To promote their involvement and also to present them as 'whole people', rather than a series of dissected quotations, I invited them to write, or help to write, their own 'pen picture'. Most said they wanted me to write it, but that they would like the chance to read and amend it, so this is the process we followed. All names are pseudonyms, in most cases as chosen by participants.

Alice

Alice is in her mid–80s. She lives in a detached, owner-occupied house at the end of a quiet no-through road in a small village. The house is shared with her sister but it is divided into two separate units. They have lived in the house for 17 years, purchasing it together after Alice's husband died. They each have a separate entrance and living accommodation but there is a communicating door between the two halves of the house and they share a kitchen. Alice has difficulty climbing the stairs so her bedroom and bathroom are both on the ground floor.

Alice was widowed 19 years ago. Her husband was a headmaster and they had an active social life together following his retirement. Several of the school staff and former pupils are still in touch with Alice. She has one daughter who lives locally but her daughter's husband has a debilitating illness so this limits the amount of contact between them. The sister with whom she lives has an extensive family, including 11 grandchildren, so there are always people visiting the house. As well as this sister, Alice has another sister and a brother, both living locally, and they meet up regularly. She has always lived in the West Midlands, knows many people in the area and has a number of friends with whom she is in frequent contact.

Alice has osteoarthritis in her spine, shoulder, arms, knees and feet. She walks with sticks in the house and uses a wheeled trolley with a basket to carry things. She takes painkillers at night to ease the pain. She had an operation for breast cancer eight years ago. She also has bowel problems that mean that she has to wear incontinence pads all the time. She has learned to manage this herself and none of her family or friends are aware that she has this problem. She has a commode in the bedroom that she empties herself each morning. She follows a careful diet. She still drives, although getting in and out of the car is becoming increasingly difficult. She uses the local volunteer driver service for longer journeys. She is able to do things like getting her own shopping as the supermarket will provide an assistant to push her in a wheelchair and help load the shopping into her car. She and her sister remain fairly independent of each other, but will do little things to help each other out. For example, Alice's sister will buy things for her at the shops, collect her pension, hang out her washing and sometimes they share a meal. Alice has a lifeline alarm system. She has ready-prepared frozen meals delivered for times when she does not feel like cooking. Her nephew maintains the garden and will do small maintenance jobs around the house, although she does not like having to ask him. She has her hair washed and set once a week by a woman who lives a few doors away as she is not able to lift her arm high enough to wash or tend her hair herself.

As well as her retirement pension, Alice has some income from property and receives Attendance Allowance. She feels that she is comfortably off and she is able to buy certain private services such as hydrotherapy and other forms of natural healing.

Alice is active in the local community. She attends church regularly and supports church events such as coffee mornings. She likes making things, such as knitted teddies, which are sold at such events in aid of church funds, and she manages the church bookkeeping. Once a year she goes on holiday with a group of people from the church. She is also a member of the Women's Institute, attending their fortnightly meetings and going on some of their outings. She is a volunteer at a local private nursing home, helping to run their shop. She feels that she is always busy and never has time to do all the things she would like to. This is partly because her deteriorating mobility means that it now takes her longer to do basic things such as getting washed, dressed and ready to go out.

Alice had received help with bath aids from social services in the past, but these are no longer of use as she is not able to get in and out of the bath, even with this equipment. The district nurse referred her to social services for help around the house. She was sent a list of private agencies but when she tried to contact these she was unsuccessful in finding someone who could give the help she wanted. The agencies either did not cover her outlying rural area or charged an exorbitant amount in travel costs. She was eventually successful in finding a private cleaner through her informal contacts in the village. Towards the end of the study, she was referred to social services again by her doctor and began receiving daily help from the council's home care service.

Barbara

Barbara lives alone in a ground floor privately owned flat which has warden facilities. She was aged 82 when the research period started. She had been widowed for five years. Prior to that, she cared for her husband, who had Alzheimer's disease, for 10 years. Her husband spent the last three years of his life in a local authority residential home so Barbara had some contact with social services at this time. She has a son and daughter who both live in the local area and do little things to help her out. However, both work and she is careful not to put upon them.

When younger, Barbara used to work as a telephonist, but she loved children and eventually trained as a teacher and taught infant children, which she loved. As well as her retirement pension, she receives a small teacher's pension as well as a small occupational pension from her husband's employment. She has some savings but this money is tied up and finances are a bit of a worry for her.

Barbara has a number of health problems. She has angina, has had two hip replacement operations and is partially deaf. She has also received treatment for depression and feels she tends to worry about things. She is reasonably mobile but cannot walk far or bend down, which makes some household tasks difficult or impossible. Keeping the house clean is important to her and it gets her down if she is not able to maintain her normal standards. She still drives a car and describes this as her lifeline, although she drives less often than she used to and only when weather conditions are good. She is able to walk to the local shops using a trolley, but is nervous of falling after she had a nasty fall caused by uneven paving stones. She is still awaiting the outcome of a compensation claim against the council for this injury.

Barbara has a good friend (aged 94) who lives in the same accommodation block. They meet for morning coffee and/or afternoon tea and a chat most days and Barbara takes her friend shopping once a week. She also has a male friend who often visits, takes her out and for whom she sometimes cooks a meal. She attends parchment craft lessons once a month and spends a lot of time at home producing intricate parchment work. This hobby has introduced her to new friends. She also attends a nearby club at the local Methodist church.

The warden made the referral to social services that triggered Barbara's involvement with the study. Barbara had been ill with a virus and the warden contacted social services on her behalf to ask about obtaining help with cleaning. She was sent a list of private agencies but she did not at that time pursue this. After her fall, when she had difficulty getting around, she did contact a private agency and for a while they visited once a fortnight to do the heavy cleaning. However, she was not satisfied with their work (two cleaners came each time) and she cancelled this help. Some months later, her daughter arranged for her to have help again from a private agency and this time she liked the cleaner and was satisfied with the service provided. She finds it very expensive, however.

During the course of the study, Barbara obtained a hearing aid, sustained another fall in which she fractured her wrist and underwent a quadruple heart bypass operation. This operation was very successful and she now feels better than she has for years, as though she has been given a new lease of life.

David

David is 88 years old. He is Scottish and moved from Glasgow a year ago to his present home. This is a privately rented first floor flat that is part of a sheltered housing scheme. There is a resident on-site warden and all of the flats have an alarm system installed. The flat is in the centre of a town.

David moved to be nearer to his daughter, who lives in a village a couple of miles away. He has another daughter and also a son. His son lives in Canada. His family was worried about him living far away in Glasgow and persuaded him to move here. The rent is expensive and his son, who is quite well off, pays half. David only has his retirement pension and a small occupational pension and would not be able to afford to live here otherwise.

David feels quite healthy but he has arthritis in his legs. He has trouble bending and things like cutting his toenails are difficult. This, in turn, can make walking painful. A few months ago he had a cancerous growth removed from his face. He is hard of hearing but does not get on with his hearing aid. He tends to forget things and can get a bit muddled.

He enjoys learning new things and at the moment is trying to master Dutch and Welsh. He enjoys sketching and painting in watercolours and can spend many hours at this, oblivious of time passing. He likes to give his pictures to people. He also enjoys music and plays an electric organ. He loves dancing and used to dance regularly but since he moved to England he does not know anyone he can ask to be his partner. He has always enjoyed female company and misses this. He likes to keep fit and is worried that he has put on weight since moving to the flat. He does exercises and tries to go for a walk most days.

His daughter helps with cleaning and large laundry items. He does his own shopping as the supermarket is only across the road. Shopping is a chance to meet people and he is quite friendly with one of the girls on the checkout. He has given her one of his paintings.

David gets lonely. Although he passes the time of day with other people in the flats, he has not really made any friends. He does not feel he has settled into his new home and he would like to move. He used to be a postman and misses walking and being outdoors. He does not like being in the centre of a town or in a flat and would like to live somewhere where he can see the sky when he looks out of his window. He would like to return to Glasgow, but his family does not think this is a good idea. They are going to help him look for somewhere else in the area.

When trying to telephone David to arrange the third interview, I could obtain no reply to his number and I was unsuccessful in finding out what had happened to him. He may have moved to a different address.

Elsie

Elsie was aged 91 at the start of the study and nearly 94 by the time it concluded. She lives alone in a bungalow in a small village in a rural location. The council owned the bungalow, but a few years ago it was transferred to the management of a housing association. It has an alarm system installed with pull cords in each room so that Elsie can summon help in the event of an emergency. She has not yet had occasion to use this. Her main source of income is her retirement pension, topped up with Income Support. She has a small amount of savings but these are dwindling as she has to draw on them for expenses such as clothes and holidays. She used to work as a children's nanny. Her husband was in the Royal Navy so was often away from home for long periods. They were never very well off as her husband gambled. He died some years ago and Elsie points out that she has now been widowed longer than she was married. She had two daughters, but one daughter died at the age of 32 from a brain haemorrhage. In later years, Elsie played a significant part in the upbringing of this daughter's three children after their father remarried and they had a poor relationship with their stepmother. Each granddaughter eventually left home to live with her.

She has a wide and supportive family, encompassing her surviving daughter and son-in-law, five grandchildren and nine great-grandchildren. Most of these live locally and are in frequent contact with her. One granddaughter lives in Portugal but arranges for Elsie to have holidays with her and also spends part of the year in England. Most support is provided by Elsie's daughter and son-in-law, who telephone every day and visit often. Her son-in-law refitted the kitchen for her and will do any maintenance jobs. She feels very lucky in her family and although she does not want to rely on them, she knows they would give her any help she needed.

Elsie has lived in the village most of her life apart from a period living away during her married life. She has many friends who call round or telephone and she is often invited out. She has been an active member of the local community and attends church regularly. She used to give talks about local history to visitors at the church, deliver church leaflets and until recently helped to clean the church and decorate it with flowers.

Elsie likes to keep herself active both mentally and physically. She does not see herself as 'old' and much prefers the company of younger people. She enjoys travelling and in recent years has enjoyed hot air ballooning and piloting a helicopter. She has many interests including writing articles for *Country Living* magazine, doing crosswords, reading and sewing and knitting for the many new additions to her family. She also likes to raise money for charities by making crafts to sell at sales. She enjoys her garden and has an arrangement with a local man that he maintains her garden; in exchange, he has most of the produce from the vegetable garden. She does all her own cleaning and cooking, including making jam, chutney and pickles, most of which is given away to family, friends and charitable sales. Her daughter washes large items of laundry (for example, bed linen) for her and in exchange she does the ironing.

She has maintained very good health and, until only a few years ago, regularly walked long distances and cycled. However, this is now restricted by arthritis in her back, neck, knees and feet. She also has angina and gets dizzy spells. Her request to social services was for the installation of a walk-in shower following a fall that fractured her femur and made getting in and out of the bath difficult. She was sent a questionnaire to complete and the response from this was that she was not eligible for a shower installation as she did not have specific health needs that required regular showers. During the study period, the housing association fitted a shower as part of refurbishment of the bathroom, but this was a shower fitted inside the bath so it did not address Elsie's difficulty in climbing in and out of the bath. The council said they would fit a grab rail but this did not materialise and eventually her son-in-law fitted one for her.

Gerald

Gerald is 85 years old. He was widowed five years ago. At the time the study started, he was living alone in a privately owned bungalow in a small village. During the period of the study, he moved to a privately owned warden-controlled ground floor flat in the centre of a town 10 miles away.

Gerald is partially deaf and has damage to his hand and legs as a result of war injuries. He can only walk short distances and tends to lose his balance easily. He finds it difficult to grip things in his right hand. He is taking various sorts of medication and is prone to adverse side-effects so this is another potential cause of health problems for him. He is awaiting an operation on his Achilles tendons but is putting this off as it will mean his feet will be in plaster for several weeks and he is not sure how he will manage to look after himself during this time.

Gerald was self-employed all his life. He used to work in the motor trade but had a range of other business interests as well. When living in his bungalow he enjoyed attending car rallies, doing up rally cars and collecting china plates, but he gave up these hobbies when he moved as he lacked the space to continue them. He had to sell or give away many of his things when he moved to the much smaller property.

Gerald made the referral to social services himself. As he lives alone, he was concerned how he would manage if he did need help, so he called in to ask them what help he would be able to get. He was taken aback to find that this was very little! He was given a list of private home care agencies. He already employed a private cleaner and has continued to do this at his new address. There are laundry facilities and an emergency alarm system in the accommodation complex and he often goes out to eat. He drives his car locally and there are a few shops directly across the road from his flat.

Gerald has no close family. He and his wife chose not to have children and his only relative is a second cousin's child (on his wife's side of the family). He has one or two close friends, including a man he worked with for many years and a woman who lives in the same accommodation complex. One of the reasons Gerald moved was to be nearer to her and they spend a lot of time together. She is not so well off financially so Gerald often takes her out for meals to local pubs and supermarket cafes. She has a serious heart condition so is also quite restricted in what she can do. Gerald sometimes attends the weekly residents' committee meetings. Apart from going out for meals and to medical appointments, he does not go out much.

Gerald considers himself quite well off financially. He has savings, receives a war pension as well as his retirement pension and also receives Attendance Allowance. He belongs to a private health scheme. He has purchased special equipment to help with his disabilities, for example, a hearing aid and special built-up shoes. He knows that he has enough money to buy any help he needs, although he does not feel he knows much about what help is available or how to get it.

Harriet

Harriet lives in a privately owned semi-detached house near the centre of a small town. She is aged 82 and was widowed 12 years ago. She has one daughter, who is disabled with rheumatoid arthritis. Her daughter has a live-in carer, who helps Harriet with odd jobs around the house and garden. However, she is very careful not to ask too much of him as he is occupied with looking after her daughter. Harriet also has one son and a grandson who live in a neighbouring town. Her son is divorced and works long hours so the help he is able to give her is limited. Harriet has a number of health problems. She has rheumatoid arthritis and irritable bowel syndrome (triggered by medication she has taken long-term for the arthritis). She had a mastectomy 18 years ago and this operation has left her with weakness in one arm, causing difficulty in lifting things. A few months before the study started, she started getting dizzy spells and on one occasion collapsed and had to be taken to hospital. As a result of the dizzy spells and blackouts, Harriet had to give up driving. She felt this was a major loss of her independence. It meant that she had to rethink many of the activities and ways of managing that she had taken for granted. The dizziness has given her a fear of falling and also a feeling of disorientation and loss of confidence about going out.

Harriet likes to keep busy and to maintain a routine. She has many hobbies. She loves her garden and still does as much of the work involved in maintaining this as she can. She also enjoys craft activities such as sewing, quilling and parchment. She used to make clothes for family and friends but now just makes them for herself although she still does mending jobs for the family. She has a number of friends who live locally and she is involved in various social activities and clubs, some of them based around her craft interests. Public transport is limited in the area in which she lives so she has to rely on friends to offer her lifts. Keeping a clean and orderly house is very important to her, because this is something she has always done and also because she believes this is important in preventing falls and keeping healthy.

Harriet had cared for her husband for many years after he suffered two strokes. During the latter few years, she received some help from the social services home help service. When her own health deteriorated, she contacted social services again to see if they might be able to give her help or offer advice about where she could get help. They sent her a list of private home care agencies but she was unable to find anyone who would help with cleaning (as opposed to providing personal care). She was eventually able to find a private cleaner through a recommendation from a friend.

Harriet has a lifeline alarm pendant that she wears around her neck so that she can summon help if she falls or has warning of a blackout. She does her own cooking, shopping and laundry and she has learned various ways of adapting how she carries out these activities in order to get around her physical difficulties (for example, doing things on her hands and knees to avoid bending). However, she is finding these jobs more difficult and exhausting to accomplish as time goes on. She is aware that her memory is deteriorating so she also has strategies to help her remember things, such as writing notes to herself.

Joyce

Joyce is in her early 80s. She lives alone in a one-bedroom ground floor flat that used to be owned by the council, but has now been transferred to the management of a housing association. The flat is in the centre of a town, so shops and services are within easy walking distance. Joyce has lived in the town nearly all her life. She does not feel very safe in her flat, however, as someone living in the flat upstairs uses drugs and there are 'unsavoury' people visiting. She always keeps her doors locked and bolted.

She was widowed nearly 15 years ago. She had been married for 40 years. She is in regular contact with one daughter, her son-in-law and two granddaughters. Another daughter has no contact with her. She has a number of friends who live nearby and who telephone and visit often. She knows many people in the town and often sees people she knows when she is out. She has a budgie that she feels is good company.

Joyce has a number of health problems including asthma, arthritis in the knees, back and shoulders and osteoporosis of the spine. Her mobility is quite restricted, especially anything involving bending or kneeling. She also has some incontinence problems.

She believes that it is important to make an effort and she struggles to do things herself rather than asking other people. She has a shopping trolley to do her shopping, but at other times uses a stick outside of the house. She manages to do her own cleaning, although her daughter helps her with the jobs she cannot do such as dusting the skirting boards. Her daughter took her to buy a grab stick to help with picking things up. She cooks a meal for herself every day and makes herself do this even when she does not feel like it. Her upstairs neighbours tend the small garden for her.

She attends the local Derby and Joan club once a week and is on the committee, helping to organise raffles and other activities. She sometimes goes on outings with the club. She also enjoys watching television and reading books from the library. She used to like dancing, sewing and knitting, but can no longer do these things because of her arthritis.

Although Joyce is not a churchgoer, she sees herself as having a strong religious faith and she feels this helps to keep her going. She does spiritual healing for people who are sick or in trouble, not for payment but to feel she is using her gift to help people.

Joyce receives Income Support in addition to her retirement pension. She is careful with her money and feels that she can just about manage on her income.

Her original request to social services, at the suggestion of a housing officer, was for a shower as she has difficulty getting in and out of the bath. This request was turned down and eventually her daughter and son-in-law lent her the money to buy a shower. This was fitted inside the bath so it still meant she had to struggle to climb out. The council eventually agreed to fit a shower cubicle but there was a long wait (over two years) before this happened. The district nurse requested a high-seat chair and a toilet seat for her from social services. After many months she did receive the toilet seat but heard no more about the chair. She does not like asking for things and being seen as a 'sponger' so she has not followed this up.

Les

Les lives in a two-bedroom bungalow owned by a housing association (previously the district council) near the town centre. The bungalow is part of a complex of 12 bungalows for disabled or older people. An on-site warden previously supported the accommodation but now it has an alarm system installed. Les has lived there for over 30 years. His wife was disabled for 25 years and used a wheelchair. They tried to buy the bungalow some years ago but were not allowed to because the property had been built especially for disabled people.

Les is in his late 70s. He was widowed six years ago. Les was used to doing things around the house because of his wife being disabled. He has two daughters. One lives in Canada. The other lives about 20 miles away, also in housing association accommodation. This daughter is divorced and has two children, one still living at home. Like Les, she does not own or drive a car. As she lives in a rural area, public transport is quite limited and this makes it difficult for her to make regular visits to Les. She telephones him every morning to check he is all right. She comes over some weekends, but this is difficult as the buses do not run in the evening so she has to stay overnight. It means bringing her daughter, who is in her early teens and has homework and other things she needs to do. Les feels guilty about disrupting her.

The other residents of the bungalows are all widows or widowers and they are all sociable and help each other out. Les is the scheme's representative in meetings with the housing association.

Les has a faulty heart valve and needs frequent hospital outpatient and, sometimes, inpatient treatment. He gets out of breath easily and cannot do any heavy work. He gets dizzy and has blackouts. He has been told that his health will deteriorate over the next few years. An operation could be fatal so his condition is managed with lots of different medications. He also has prostate problems, a leg ulcer and needs to wear a hearing aid. He sees his doctor about every three months and uses the voluntary drivers provided through the local volunteer bureau to take him to hospital appointments. However, he finds this expensive as the hospital is in another town.

Les's daughter has applied to the district council for a transfer to accommodation nearer to Les, but they have been told she does not have enough points for the transfer to be a priority. Les is very upset and angry about this as it would not cost the council anything, but rather would save them money, as his daughter would help him rather than him needing council services. Les feels that if only the transfer could go ahead, 95 per cent of his problems would be solved.

Les likes to keep his bungalow and garden in order. He takes things slowly and manages to do most of his own cleaning, shopping, laundry and gardening. Sometimes it takes him a long time as he has to take lots of rests. A free bus service runs from just outside his house to the local superstore so this is a big help. Someone from the Royal British Legion sometimes helps him with the garden.

After a previous hospital admission, the hospital social worker arranged for him to have one-and-a-half-hours home care per week. He has a small amount of savings, just enough to put him over the threshold for receiving Income Support. This meant he was charged for the home care. He felt it was too expensive for the limited amount the home carer was able to accomplish in the time allotted so he stopped it. Les has to continually draw on his savings to make ends meet and even though he lives quite simply, he worries about being able to pay his bills. By the second visit, he had been granted the lower rate of Attendance Allowance so planned to use this to pay for some help. He had had another hospital admission and believed that social services had arranged for him to have home care again and meals delivered. However, this help did not materialise. Les did not like to make a fuss and, in any case, found using the telephone very difficult because of his breathing problems.

Les died six months after the second interview.

Patricia

Patricia lives with her husband, Malcolm, in a privately owned first floor flat in a large village. Patricia was 74 and her husband 81 at the time the study started. They have lived in the village for over 15 years, but feel this means they are still viewed as 'newcomers'. They have one son, who is married and lives with his family in Jersey. They visit occasionally, but Patricia and Malcolm rarely go there as Patricia does not like flying. They have one daughter who is married and lives locally. Their daughter has three grown-up daughters who all live in the area and visit when they can. Patricia and Malcolm describe themselves as a close family. They do not make demands on their daughter and granddaughters, but know that they are there to help them if they need it.

Patricia has had a number of health problems for most of her life. She had tuberculosis when young and has had continual breathing problems that were later diagnosed as asthma. She has private healthcare and receives regular check-ups. She needs hospital treatment periodically, when she is put on a nebuliser. This is becoming more frequent with time, and she takes longer to recover. She also has osteoarthritis and suffers a lot of pain, particularly in her back. She walks with a stick and can manage the stairs up and down to the flat only with difficulty. She has a wheelchair for when she goes out, but this has limited use as it is too heavy for her husband to push.

At the time the study started, Malcolm had to do everything around the house. This was something that worried Patricia greatly as Malcolm also has health problems. He has high blood pressure and is on beta-blockers. During the study he also had to have some gallstones removed, was found to have an irregular heartbeat and was diagnosed with diabetes. Patricia was concerned about the adverse effect on her husband's health of him having to undertake all of 'her' domestic tasks. She was also aware that despite his best efforts, he did not maintain the same standards as she would have done. Having a less than clean kitchen and bathroom were things that particularly bothered her.

It was the doctor who suggested that Patricia should contact social services for some help around the house. They advised her to apply for Attendance Allowance. She did this and was granted the Allowance. She wanted to use this to buy private help with housework, but she had great difficulty finding someone who would do housework, as opposed to provide personal care. She first tried using a private agency but the helper was both unreliable and inefficient. Patricia eventually found a private cleaner through informal contacts in the village.

They have a small occupational pension as well as their state pension, but they feel their capital is dwindling fast. However, they are frugal and do not spend much; they do not smoke or drink and their main luxury is a short annual break in Devon. Malcolm still drives and this is important for things like getting to the shops and to hospital appointments. They still have access to private healthcare because of Patricia's previous employment with a bank. This enables her to have acupuncture and physiotherapy services.

Patricia and Malcolm describe themselves as quite isolated and fairly reliant on each other. Most of Patricia's hobbies and interests are home-based as she is not able to go out much. She enjoys knitting, sewing, flower arranging and cake decorating. She also likes to read and do crossword puzzles. She and her husband attend church locally, but other than this their main outings are when they have hospital appointments.

Ralph

Ralph lives in a village in a three-bedroom terraced house that he purchased from the district council. The village has a shop, a Post Office and doctor's surgery. It is about 12 miles to the nearest town.

Ralph used to work as an engineer and, later, a greengrocer. His income is made up of his retirement pension and disability pensions. He will soon be celebrating his 90th birthday.

Ralph's wife died six years ago. They had been married for over 60 years. She was ill for several years before her death with Alzheimer's disease. During this time Ralph received help looking after her from the council's home care service. However, this stopped abruptly when she died.

Ralph has arthritis in his hip and trouble with his 'waterworks'. He has had a stroke and has not fully recovered his mobility. He wears a hearing aid. He uses a wheelchair when going out with his daughters and rides a motorised scooter around the village. He does not get on with his neighbours as they park outside his house, across the kerb that was lowered so that he could drive his scooter in and out. He has a ramp from the front door and rails fitted both sides of the stairs. He paid to have a shower fitted as he could not climb out of the bath.

He has two daughters, who are both divorced. They share a house and live nearby. He also has a granddaughter and two great-grandchildren who live 40 miles away. His daughters take him to medical appointments, to do his shopping and on various social outings. He sometimes goes on holiday with them. He telephones them every morning and every night to let them know he is all right. If they do not hear from him, they come to check on him. He has a friend in the village who visits him several times a week and who has said he can call if he needs anything.

His daughters had asked social services for help for him around the house. At that point it was turned down as the help needed was only for cleaning. Following his second stroke, Ralph was offered help before he was discharged from hospital, but he refused this as he likes his privacy and did not want strangers coming into the house.

Ralph likes cooking for himself and he likes making extra so he can give cakes and other produce to other people. He always cooks fresh food, including several different vegetables, for his main meal. He likes reading and gets books every fortnight from the mobile library. He also loves his garden and growing flowers and he has two greenhouses. Even when he does not feel up to doing any gardening, he likes to sit outside and watch the birds. He is hoping to find someone who will mow his lawn for him as the mower is now too heavy for him to push.

He used to go to the local over-50s club but has recently stopped this as he could not hear the conversations. He has also become more worried about going out unless he can be sure there is a toilet nearby.

Following the first interview, Ralph had a second stroke and his speech and mobility became more impaired. At this point, he moved his bed downstairs. He had another stroke a few months after the second interview and moved in with his daughters. I was due to visit him for the third interview at his daughter's house. Just before this, he had a short respite care stay in a residential home. During this stay he had a further stroke and died.

Roger

Roger is in his mid-80s. He lives alone in a privately owned semi-detached house. He and his wife lived in it from the time it was built, about 45 years ago. It was originally a council house but Roger and his wife purchased it from the council 30 years ago. The house is in a small village in a very quiet location at the end of a cul-de-sac.

Roger was widowed 14 months before the start of the study. He and his wife had been married for nearly 50 years. His wife had been ill with cancer for some time and Roger had nursed her at home for three years before her death. During this time he received some help from social services with getting his wife up and putting her to bed, but during the day and night he cared for her on his own. This meant that when his wife died he was already used to cooking and looking after the house, so he did not find these tasks difficult.

When the study started, Roger could not get around very well at all. He was walking on crutches while waiting for a knee replacement operation. He recovered his mobility following the operation. His toilet is upstairs so climbing the stairs does worry him a little. He has had rails fitted up the stairs and a bath seat. He has had heart attacks in the past. He had a number of hospital admissions during the time of the study, including with bronchitis, a fractured rib following a fall and for an adverse reaction to new medication. He is always very determined to get better as quickly as possible and return home.

Roger used to be a farm worker and he likes the outdoors. He loves his garden and continues to grow a wide variety of fruit and vegetables. He freezes these to provide a supply of food throughout the year, as well as giving produce to other people. When he was on crutches, he paid someone to see to the garden for him, as he could not bear to see it untended. Most years, along with other people in the village, he opens his garden for visitors to raise money for charity. He has two dogs, which are a great source of company for him, and he takes them for walks twice a day. He attends a local over-60s club and goes on outings and holidays with them. He also goes to whist drives in nearby villages; a woman in the village gives him a lift. He still drives his car short distances but for longer journeys, such as shopping and hospital appointments, his daughter drives him.

Roger has one daughter, one stepdaughter and a nephew, all of whom he sees regularly. He also has a stepson but they do not get on and see each other only very rarely. Both his daughter and stepdaughter live locally and he is in regular contact with them. His daughter visits several times a week but she runs her own business so Roger is reluctant to bother her. She takes him to hospital appointments, to do his shopping and changes his bed and does his washing. She also looks after his two dogs when he is in hospital.

In addition to his retirement pension, Roger receives a small industrial injuries pension and Attendance Allowance that he uses to pay for private help. He has solid fuel heating and had asked for help from social services with carrying in his coal and emptying the ashes. He was told that the home care service did not provide this type of help so he arranged for a woman who lived locally to call every day and do this and other small jobs for him. He has a lifeline alarm pendant. He cooks a meal for himself every day and often prepares extra portions, which he freezes and can then reheat when he needs them. Much of his food is homegrown produce from his garden. At times when he has been unwell and unable to cook for himself, he has used a frozen meal service that delivers pre-prepared frozen meals to the door.

Roger believes it is very important to keep active, not to give up and to keep a positive attitude. He also thinks it is important not to think too much about your own illnesses and problems but to stay cheerful and to try to help other people.

After the pen picture was written, Roger was told by the heart consultant that he could not operate further on his heart and that he was unlikely to live for more than 18 months. Roger's daughter wrote to me 14 months after the final interview to let me know that he had died.

Winifred

Winifred was unable to speak and had not been able to say more than a few words for some time. The cause of this problem was under medical investigation. She wrote some notes for me and asked for some friends to be present when I went to see her so that they could explain her situation. She also gave permission for me to visit another friend who had known her since her childhood. The information about Winifred is based on these different sources.

Winifred lives in a privately owned flat in a small town. She lives on her own and has never been married. She is aged 79. She has private savings and investments and lives off the income from this. She moved to the flat 18 months ago. Before that, she lived in a large house in an isolated rural location. It was a great wrench for her having to move, but she could no longer manage to look after the big house and garden.

She had been privately adopted as a child but was treated badly by her adoptive family. They did not allow her any freedom and she lived with them until they died. She inherited their property and capital. Because of her early experiences, she is a very private and independent person.

Winifred's only family is a sister-in-law who is in poor health and lives some distance away. She has a number of close friends who live locally. If she needs any help, she telephones her friend who can understand just by the silence that she wants something. However, most of her friends are elderly and have health problems themselves so it is sometimes difficult for them to help her.

She sees a hospital consultant who is investigating the cause of her speech and health problems. She has also been referred to a speech therapist. Her friend thinks the problems began about nine years ago after she suffered a head injury when she was run down by a motorbike when crossing the road. Since then, her health has gradually deteriorated. She started having problems holding her head upright, and then lost her speech. More recently she has had trouble with her vision and has difficulty focusing. Her writing has deteriorated, which is a problem as she relies so much on this form of communication.

Her doctor had contacted social services to ask if she could have some help. Social services wrote to her and asked her to telephone them if she wanted help, saying that they would assess her needs over the telephone. She had to get her friend to telephone for her. When they found out that she could look after herself, but that, because of her anxiety and lack of speech, she wanted someone to check on her every day, they said they could not help. They suggested that she had a lifeline alarm but she wanted someone to call in regularly, not just respond when there was a crisis. She did not want to have to keep relying on her friends.

Winifred was admitted to hospital shortly after the first interview and died a few weeks later.

Further details concerning these older people's lives and experiences and, in particular, how they managed the ageing process, will be presented throughout the remainder of the book.

Origins of the study

The roots of this book lie in interests and concerns generated in my practice as a senior social worker in a local authority adult services team. Although I worked in a generic adult team, most of the work was with older people. I was responsible for supervising staff and managing workloads, including allocating and closing 'cases'. I had worked in the area for some years and, in the mid-1990s, following implementation of the 1990 NHS and Community Care Act in 1993, I was very aware that there were many older people who would previously have received a service from the team who were now deemed not eligible for services. Although the research pre-dated the eligibility framework set out in *Fair access to care services* (FACS) (DH, 2002a), services were already being targeted at those with highest levels of need because of resource constraints. Older people with what were deemed 'lower-level' needs were 'screened out' from receiving services.[1] I was conscious that there was no system for monitoring what happened to these people who were refused services. We did not know whether they soon deteriorated and were referred back to the organisation, perhaps with higher-level needs, whether they managed to purchase care as 'consumers' within the private market or whether extra responsibilities were assumed by families and friends. When I moved into an academic post, I decided to explore for my doctoral research the trajectories of older people who were refused services on the grounds they were 'not eligible'. I wanted to find out about the nature of the need for which they were referred, how they managed this need when it was not met by social services and the short and longer-term consequences for their health and well-being.

In terms of my personal motivation, I was a woman in my early forties, becoming conscious of my own ageing. My mother had been ill for a long time and she died a few months after the research commenced. I had been closely involved in her struggles to manage poor health and I was now very aware of my father's efforts to adapt to changed circumstances. I therefore felt a close personal connection with the question of how older people manage the changes and losses they encounter.

Central to the rationale and methodology of the study was that it was to be grounded in the experiences and perspectives of older people themselves. However, although I felt that I was 'starting from lives' (Older People's Steering Group, 2004), the study was planned and designed from my perspective as a social work practitioner/academic. Listening to the views and experiences of older people during the course of the research took me in different directions to those I had originally envisaged and gave me insights and perspectives that have changed my understanding of older people and the processes by which they manage the experience of ageing. This is discussed further in Chapter Seven.

Rationale for starting from lives

There are a number of reasons why this book roots its analysis in the experiences and perspectives of older people. The first relates to the theoretical standpoint adopted. In the Introduction I indicated that this book is concerned with subjective meanings that older people give to situations and experiences. The theoretical foundations for this approach can be found in the work of Charles Horton Cooley and George Herbert Mead, whose ideas were developed by academics within the Chicago School in the early part of the 20th century. This theoretical perspective, 'symbolic interactionism', embraces a diverse body of theories that share some basic premises. One such premise is that individuals give meaning to situations and behaviour and then use these interpretations as the basis of their own actions (Blumer, 1969; Hewitt, 1994). A second premise of symbolic interactionism is that meanings do not emanate from 'within' individuals but are a product of social interaction: 'symbolic interactionism sees meanings as social product, as creations that are formed in and through the defining activities of people as they interact' (Blumer, 1969, p 306). Meanings are intersubjective in that the 'self' is experienced through perceiving oneself through the eyes of others. My concern is with the meaning of events and processes to older people, how these meanings guide their behaviour with others and what this signifies for social policy and practice.

Although earlier symbolic interactionist theory was criticised for its lack of attention to social structure, later work takes account of the interdependence between individual meanings and the social and cultural context; individual meanings are embedded within a particular social and cultural context but, at the same time, the social and cultural context is shaped by individual meanings (Denzin, 1989). This book explores the relationship between individual and social meanings, considering, for example, the relationship between older people's interpretive processes and prevailing social factors such as ageism, gendered expectations and particular cultural constructions concerning 'independence'.

Within the remit of symbolic interactionism, Erving Goffman was interested in how individuals preserve a moral identity in potentially discrediting situations and environments, such as asylums. He explored the 'impression management strategies' employed by individuals in the negotiation of roles and identities during processes of social interaction (Goffman, 1961). Old age can be seen as bestowing a discredited identity in western society and problems that may be associated with later life, such as declining mobility or memory loss, pose threats to valued self- and social identities as an independent person. Focusing on the perceptions and experiences of older people facilitates greater understanding of how selfhood is supported or undermined during the process of ageing and this, in turn, has important implications for policy and services concerned with the promotion of older people's well-being.

The theoretical perspective of symbolic interactionism therefore provides a rationale for starting from older people's lives in order to understand individual, social and cultural processes. Taking older people's accounts as the starting point for analysis is also legitimated by another theoretical perspective that can be broadly categorised as postmodernism. There is no space here to engage in a detailed exploration of postmodernist theory, but, in very general terms, it can be seen as being concerned with ways of knowing (Fook, 2002). While the term 'postmodernism' is used in diverse ways, a key feature is the focus on the increasing complexity and fragmentation of social life and a questioning of the notion of universal 'truths'. Thus,

> The rejection of the idea that any one theory or system of belief can ever reveal the truth, and the emphasis on the plurality of truth and "the will to truth", captures some of the essential elements associated with post-modern approaches. (Parton and Marshall, 1998, p 243)

In relation to gerontology, postmodernism draws attention to the fluidity of identity in later life. It contrasts with theories such as structured dependency, which understand older people's experiences in relation to broad social and economic factors such as retirement and pension policies, segregation and institutionalisation (see, for example, Townsend, 1981; Walker, 1981). Instead, postmodernism highlights the diversity of lifestyle choices available to older people through consumption (Gilleard, 1996). It holds that, rather than older people's situations being determined by macro social processes, they are free to exercise individual agency in choosing how they wish to construct their identity. However, the construction of identity may be problematic. Phillipson (1998) argues that the demise of previous certainties or, as he terms it, the 'unravelling of institutional identities' (p 106), around, for example, state provision for retirement, has generated new anxieties about personal identity. Later life, in these terms, is a time of risk and uncertainty, as well as freedom and choice. It is also recognised that a visibly ageing body presents an inescapable outward manifestation of ageing, and that this can give rise to contradictions between an individual's self-identity and their social identity, in terms of how they are viewed by others (Estes et al, 2003). Biggs (1999), whose work is considered in more detail later in Chapter Six, argues that these tensions between self-identity and social identity are managed by means of a 'masquerade' through which individuals protect themselves in a hostile social world (Biggs, 1999). Uncovering the individual 'truths' of older people allows exploration of some of these tensions concerning self-identity and social identity that are central to experiences of managing ageing.

Another reason for starting from older people's lives concerns views about the nature and quality of knowledge that will be produced as a result. Postmodernist perspectives highlight the role of language (or discourse) in *creating* meaning, not simply reflecting it:

> Those with power can influence language and discourse and can therefore influence the way in which life is experienced, seen and interpreted. However, because there is a range of different contexts, cultures and discourses available at any one time and place, there is also a plethora of different meanings, knowledges and truths available and many experiences and interpretations of self and identity. (Parton and Marshall, 1998, pp 44-5)

Powerful or dominant discourses may be accepted by those with less power, who are then also involved in purveying that discourse, or alternatively, dominant discourses may be challenged or resisted. Following on from this, it can be argued that because certain knowledges or truths are marginalised and silenced, it becomes more important to uncover them in order to arrive at a less restricted world view. This is based on the premise that, even though some discourses are accorded more social power and influence, all 'truths' have equal validity. Others argue that the perspectives of service users have *greater* validity when we are trying to understand experience because they are based on direct experience rather than on a distant interpretation of it. This view, reflected in the quotation by Beresford (2003) presented at the start of this chapter, holds that the closer the interpretation of experience is to the direct experience itself, the more accurate and reliable the knowledge that is produced is likely to be.

However, it is not universally accepted that closer connections with experience will produce 'better' knowledge. The drive towards 'evidence-based practice' has tended to be associated with traditional approaches that rate 'objective' research, such as systematic reviews and randomised controlled trials, at the top of the research hierarchy and research based on subjective experiences at the bottom (Glasby and Beresford, 2006). The view that those with direct experience should be central to all aspects of the creation of 'knowledge' conflicts head on with these traditional paradigms that require objectivity, distance and neutrality from the researcher. In the Introduction I stated that my objective was to uncover the subjective meanings that events and processes have for older people. The corollary of the subjectivist position is that objectivity and neutrality are not possible since we cannot escape our own particular lenses for making sense of the world. Subjectivity becomes an asset, rather than a problem, as reflexivity on the part of the researcher generates new insights and understandings (Fook, 2001). From this perspective, the 'bias' of older people who are centrally enmeshed in the subject of study enhances 'knowledge' rather than compromising it. The insights of older people who are themselves involved in negotiating the challenges of ageing open up new ways of understanding for the very reason that their perspectives are grounded in direct experience.

The question of who possesses the authority to create and define what is 'known' is at the heart of these issues about objectivity and subjectivity. This brings us to another reason for starting from older people's lives: a concern to facilitate the exercise of power by those who have been marginalised. My professional background is in social work and seeking to increase service users' personal and social power reflects the core principles and values of social work. The International Federation of Social Workers (2002) outlines two key principles underpinning social work: human rights and social justice. Basing social policy and practice on an understanding of the lives of older people potentially upholds both human rights and social justice principles. It respects the rights of individuals to live their lives in the way they choose, acknowledging diversity and valuing difference; it accepts older people's right to be heard and included; it seeks to understand older people in the context of their whole situation and lifecourse; and it recognises the strengths and abilities that older people draw on as they negotiate challenges associated with ageing.

A code of ethics for social work and social care research proposes that the process and outcomes of social work and social care research should 'where possible, seek to empower service users, promote their welfare and improve their access to economic and social capital on equal terms with other citizens' (Butler, 2002, p 245). Historically service users, and perhaps in particular, older people, have had little influence in generating the 'knowledge' that influences social care and social work policy and practice. Their voices were largely silent in literature and research, such that the 'truth' or 'reality' of situations was defined by others with more power from different social backgrounds, who were removed from the experience. There are recent examples of research that give voice to older people and where older people have taken a lead role, including in processes of conducting, managing and interpreting research, such as the Joseph Rowntree Foundation

Older People's Steering Group, mentioned in the Introduction, and the Older People Researching Social Issues (OPRSI) group (see, for example, Clough et al, 2006). There are also publications in which older people's perspectives have made a significant contribution (Reed et al, 2004). Such involvement can bring intrinsic benefits for service users, such as increased confidence and self-esteem and the acquisition of new skills, as well as extrinsic benefits, such as changes in practice and services (Moriarty et al, 2006; Doel et al, 2007). While at a macro level anti-oppressive practice can be seen as being about addressing structural inequalities, such as ageism, it can also be pursued, from a postmodern perspective, at the micro level of challenging dominant discourses and revealing alternative and marginalised ways of thinking and understanding:

> Given that one of the ways in which power is exercised is through some discourses becoming dominant over others, empowerment can be understood as producing alternative power-saturated knowledges rather than as seeking to seize or take power. Political struggle can thus be conceptualised as the struggle between different knowledges. (Pease, 2002, p 138)

Thus, rendering audible the voices of those who are seldom heard can be seen in itself as a route to empowerment.

While the value of listening to older people's experiences is at least now recognised in research, issues remain about the sense that is made of these experiences and the conclusions that are drawn from them. This poses something of a dilemma for researchers and writers trying to narrow the gap between experience and 'knowledge':

> ... on the one hand, we play a critical role in transforming private lives and concerns into public theories and debate and in voicing what might otherwise remain invisible and/or devalued issues.... On the other hand, and in the process of transformation, the private account is changed by, and infused with our identity – and thereby becomes a different story to that originally told by the respondents. (Mauthner and Doucet, 1998, p 141)

The interpretation of older people's experiences is invariably made by others (M. Ray, 2007). Beresford (2001) argues that although social care research draws on the knowledge of service users, for example, by including them as research participants, it also needs to include their meanings, hypotheses and theories. This means facilitating the involvement of those with first-hand experience in processes of analysis and interpretation, as well as in the role of interviewees. I describe in the next chapter how I sought to do this in this study.

There are also policy drivers for connecting more closely with older people's lives. The stated objectives underpinning the community care reforms of the

1990s included increasing the choice and self-determination of 'consumers' of care services and building on their strengths and resources (DH, 1990). New Labour policies have continued this theme, although through the concept of citizenship rather than consumerism, and with an emphasis on individual, family and community responsibilities enshrined in this concept. The theme of promoting independence, choice and control and putting service users at the heart of services is central to the White Paper, *Our health, our care, our say* (DH, 2006a). These aims can only be achieved by engaging with people's understanding of their own situations and by listening and responding to their views about their needs, difficulties, strengths and their preferred strategies for managing their situations.

Conclusion

The stance taken in this book is that older people's stories and experiences make a central and crucial contribution to a more rounded multidimensional understanding of later life. Starting from an understanding of older people's lives will reveal something of their individual meanings and perspectives, but also the social and cultural processes through which their interpretations are shaped. While acknowledging that older people face particular challenges and losses as they age, this book is rooted in a positive view of older people as active agents and survivors, with expertise arising from their experience of negotiating and managing later life. Learning from older people themselves not only produces 'better' knowledge, it also leads to more ethical research and practice and is consistent with current policy themes and objectives.

The next chapter sets the context for learning from older people's experiences of managing ageing by outlining, first, the relevant policy context and, second, the research methods and processes employed in the study.

Note
[1] The policy context of this practice is discussed in Chapter Two.

TWO

Setting the scene

> People who need services are often the experts in their own care, and the system for the future must respect this. People with care and support needs should be treated as citizens with rights, rather than having to fight to get services. Everyone who receives care and support must be treated with dignity and kindness, and their human rights must be respected. (DH, 2009, p 9)

The first part of this chapter outlines the social policy and practice context in which the construction of older people's needs and decisions about whether and how these should be met takes place. It provides the context for discussion in subsequent chapters of how the strategies used by older people to manage difficulties are supported or undermined by policy and provision within the statutory and independent care sectors and by wider political, social and cultural discourses. The discussion focuses on social care policy. The second part of the chapter discusses the research processes and methods used to elicit the needs and perspectives of the older people, introduced in Chapter One, whose views and experiences form the central thread of discussion in subsequent chapters.

Policy and practice context

This section begins with a brief review of the 1990 community care reforms and their impact on social work and social care services for older people.[1] More recent policy developments and initiatives (primarily in England) are then outlined. Moving on from this general context, the chapter reviews policy and practice developments that are significant for older people's management of ageing. The analysis is structured according to three key themes: needs-led assessment and person-centred care; prevention and the promotion of well-being; and care, independence and interdependence.

Community care reforms and the introduction of care management

Economic pressures from the mid-1970s, coupled with an increased demand for care services by older people in particular, led to increasing resource constraints (Walker, 1993). Arguably, it was primarily these economic concerns that gave impetus to the care in the community rhetoric and drove forward the reforms (Lewis and Glennerster, 1996). In 1986 an Audit Commission report, *Making a reality of community care*, identified the increased spending on institutional care for adults as a particular concern. This was attributed, in part, to the perverse incentive for local authorities to place people who were on Income Support in residential and nursing homes, where their care would be funded by central government, rather than to support them living in the community. The fragmentation of organisations involved in providing community care and the lack of coordination of resources were other noted areas of concern.

In response, the government commissioned a review undertaken by Sir Roy Griffiths, delivered in *Community care: An agenda for action* (Griffiths, 1988). The main recommendations relevant to this discussion were that social services should have the lead role in assessing need and planning and coordinating services, including those provided by the independent sector. The proposal was to remove the perverse incentive for institutional care by transferring funding from the social security system to social services and to impose an assessment 'gateway' for those who needed to access state-funded care. This would establish greater control over the finances committed to institutional care and open up greater possibilities for recourse to community-based alternatives (Challis et al, 1994). In 1989, the White Paper, *Caring for people: Community care in the next decade and beyond* (DH, 1989), incorporated the Griffiths Report recommendations that social services should assess individual need, design tailor-made packages of care and ensure appropriate service provision by acting as enablers rather than care providers. The key to achieving this shift was care management, defined as the process of tailoring services to the needs of individuals and described as 'the cornerstone of the community care changes' (SSI/DH, 1991).

As well as the economic objective of containing resources, the *Caring for people* White Paper was also guided by the political objective of stimulating a flourishing independent sector, thereby curtailing rather than increasing the role of local authorities (DH, 1989). Historically, there has been a shifting balance of provision between state, market, voluntary sector and family, and in this respect the 'mixed economy' of welfare was not new. However, the community care reforms signalled a new, more residual, role for the state in welfare provision (Mayo, 1994). In particular, the state's role changed from that of 'provider' to 'enabler' and 'purchaser' (Wistow et al, 1996), mirroring developments occurring in the fields of health, housing and education. Key to achieving this shift in community care provision was the separation of assessment of need from the provision of care services (DH, 1990). The reported rationale for the purchaser/provider split was to free the process of determining appropriate provision to meet need from service considerations and to enable independent sector providers to compete on equal terms with those in-house. In turn, the 'mixed economy of care' was presented as a way of not only improving standards through introducing competition, but also giving service users increased choice and control over services they received (DH, 1990, p 23). Stimulation of the mixed economy was achieved by the stipulation that 85 per cent of monies transferred to local authorities from central government had to be spent in the independent sector in the form of a 'special transitional grant' (DH, 1992).

The NHS and Community Care Act itself was passed in 1990, but not fully implemented until April 1993. As far as social work is concerned, a key duty is set down in Section 47, the duty to assess individual need for community care services. The assessment of the needs of the older people introduced in Chapter One were governed by this legislation. The NHS and Community Care Act was accompanied by policy guidance, *Community care in the next decade and beyond* (DH, 1990). This outlined six objectives for assessment and care management, framed around concepts of independence, prevention, choice, self-determination, partnership and strengths. Similar concepts were subsequently resurrected in New Labour social policy.

Developments under New Labour

The advent of New Labour in 1997 heralded no significant change in that there was a continued, some would argue uncritical, acceptance of the role of the market in meeting social care needs (Drakeford, 2006; Ferguson, 2007; Scourfield, 2007a). This has been accompanied by an emphasis on managerial control and regulation as a way of controlling policy and practice outcomes (Harris and Unwin, 2009). However, a changing emphasis in New Labour's adult social care policy has been observed, from primary concerns with 'the organisation, delivery and efficiency of services' to 'a greater emphasis on enhancing service user control and choice' (Newman et al, 2008, p 535). The state's role has shifted from directly providing for the needs of its citizens to helping people to act in what is seen as their own best interests (Jordan with Jordan, 2000). The Green Paper on adult social care, *Independence, well-being and choice* (DH, 2005), outlined a 'radical vision for the future of adult social care in England', moving from:

> ... a system where people have to take what is offered to one where people have greater control over identifying the type of support or help they want and more choice about and influence over the services on offer.... (DH, 2005, para 4.2)

The subsequent White Paper, *Our health, our care, our say* (DH, 2006a), announced pilot projects to test and develop new approaches in line with this vision. Following on from this, a ministerial concordat Putting People First put forward 'a shared vision and commitment to the transformation of adult social care', stating:

> The time has now come to build on best practice and replace paternalistic, reactive care of variable quality with a mainstream system focused on prevention, early intervention, enablement, and high quality personally tailored services. In future we want people to have maximum choice, control and power over the services they receive. (DH, 2007a, p 2)

The main routes through which the vision for adult social care is to be pursued are the extension of direct payments and the introduction of individual budgets. Direct payments are cash payments made to service users so that they can make their own arrangements to meet needs that have been assessed as eligible for statutory social care provision. Unlike traditional care management, direct payments give service users the freedom and flexibility (within given restrictions) to decide how to meet their eligible care needs and responsibility for making the arrangements and paying for the care using the statutory funds allocated. Individual budgets develop further the model of self-directed support. They bring together different funding streams that encompass social, mobility, housing and work-related needs. There are also plans to extend direct payments to health needs (NHS Confederation, 2009). Key processes within the self-directed support approach are self-assessment and early allocation of resources. With clear information about the resources available, the individual is then assisted to develop a support plan that best meets their needs and achieves the outcomes identified (CSIP, 2007).

The next section presents a more critical consideration of policy developments in terms of their impact on older people with social care needs. The discussion is structured according to three themes: person-centred care; promoting well-being; and care, independence and interdependence.

From needs-led assessment to person-centred care

As already indicated, the growth of the 'mixed economy of care' following the community care reforms was seen as facilitating consumer choice and the provision of 'needs-led' services (DH, 1990). However, a central tension that has reverberated throughout both the 'needs-led' social policy discourse and practice and the subsequent emphasis on 'person-centred' care is that between potentially infinite need on the one hand, and finite resources on the other.

Need is defined in community care policy as 'the requirements of individuals to enable them to achieve, maintain or restore an acceptable level of social independence or quality of life, *as defined by the particular care agency or authority*' (SSI/DH, 1991, para 11, emphasis added). The determination of 'need' by the agency or authority is made by reference to eligibility criteria, which essentially ration services, targeting them on those with the highest level of need. The older people introduced in Chapter One were refused services because their needs did not meet these eligibility criteria. In 2002 a national eligibility framework, fair access to care services (FACS), was introduced (DH, 2002a), now superseded by revised guidance (DH, 2010). This framework identifies four bands of eligibility, according to whether the risks to independence are 'low', 'moderate', 'substantial' or 'critical'. Local authorities are able to decide at which band of risk they will target their services according to their resource availability. In the face of resource shortfalls, many councils raised their threshold of eligibility, restricting further those who receive services. In 2008-09, 72 per cent of councils were limiting their provision only to those with critical or substantial levels of need (CQC, 2010).

Decisions about need are therefore closely bound up with issues of resources (Lewis and Glennerster, 1996). Whereas care management was intended to separate out assessment from decisions about service provision, individuals may be asked about their financial resources even before an assessment commences and this may then be used to screen them out of the process (CSCI, 2008a).

There is considerable evidence that in practice, assessments have been heavily influenced by managerial concerns, in particular, the need to ration resources and complete standard documentation, giving little scope for service users' needs and concerns to be central in the process (Caldock and Nolan, 1994; Caldock, 1996; Ellis et al, 1999; Baldwin, 2000; Richards, 2000; Postle, 2002; Foster et al, 2006). Social work assessment tends to be primarily focused on physical functioning and abilities, creating a disjunction between the concerns of practitioners carrying out assessment and those of the older people. Richards (2000) used a combination of observation and interviews to examine the differing perspectives of professionals carrying out assessment and older people whose needs were being assessed. She describes how the focus on problems and the use of assessment pro formas seduced assessors into becoming 'trapped in a restricted view'. The contributions of older people that did not fit this agenda were relegated to 'background noise', rather than used as the basis for understanding the older person's concerns (Richards, 2000, p 43). Another qualitative study, involving two interviews with 38 older people over the age of 75, compared the language and constructs used by older people when describing their situations to those used by professionals (Baldock and Hadlow, 2002). It was found that the nature of 'self-talk' by the older people, centring around their feelings, family and friends, was significantly different from the professional 'needs-talk' of disabilities and risks that dominated assessment processes and procedures. The researchers conclude, 'The qualitative gulf between the realities that users and service providers inhabit is so profound that it may always be to an extent unbridgeable' (Baldock and Hadlow, 2002, p 48). However, it must be noted that the categories for defining professional talk in this study were devised from written assessment criteria rather than the actual talk of professionals in assessment interviews. This did not, therefore, allow for the 'translation work' of practitioners that one would hope to find in positive assessment practice (Morrison, 2001; Fook, 2002). Nevertheless, research that explored the ideologies underpinning community care practitioners' interactions with older people found that their primary 'frame' of understanding was their organisational role and function. Moreover, they constructed and managed their interactions with older people in ways that affirmed their professional understanding, disempowering the older service users (Sullivan, 2009).

In more recent policy the language of 'needs-led' assessment and services that dominated the community care reforms has changed to a concern with assessment and services that are 'person-centred'. This is potentially a more positive focus since the emphasis is placed on the whole person, including strengths, not just on problems or deficiencies. Standard 2 of the National Service Framework (NSF) for older people concerns person-centred care. The standard clarifies that in practice this means that older people and their carers should: be listened to; have their dignity and privacy respected; have their individual differences and specific needs recognised, including their cultural and religious preferences; be involved in decisions and helped to make informed choices; and receive coordinated and integrated services. In addition, carers should be involved and supported (DH, 2001a, p 23). The requirement for person-centred assessment is developed in the single assessment process guidance (DH, 2002b), which stipulates that when carrying out assessments practitioners should ensure that older people themselves are central to this process: '... of all the experts in the care of older people, the greatest experts are older people themselves' (DH, 2002b, p 1).

From service users' perspectives, a key feature of 'person-centred support' is assistance that puts them in the centre of the process and enables them to have choice and control (Glynn et al, 2008). The inclusion of 'control' as part of service user requirements makes for a stronger definition of 'person-centred' than that conveyed in policy definitions, which rely on weaker concepts such as being listened to and being involved.

There is evidence in general terms that service users experience increased choice and control as a result of receiving a direct payment (Glendinning et al, 2000, 2008; Stainton and Boyce, 2004; Leece, 2010; Glasby and Littlechild, 2009; Leece and Peace, 2009). There has to date been limited research on older people's experiences of direct payments, but that which is available suggests that they experience similar benefits (Clark et al, 2004). The numbers of older people receiving direct payments are still relatively low, however. In 2008-09, of adults receiving community care or carers' services, only 3.6 per cent of older people aged 65 and over were using a direct payment compared with 9.5 per cent of people aged 18 to 64 (CQC, 2010). This may partly reflect the fact that direct payments for older people were not introduced until 2000, as older people were excluded from the original direct payment legislation in 1996. Take-up of direct payments is increasing faster for people aged 65 and over than for younger people, with a 53 per cent increase from 2006-07 to 2007-08 (compared with a 29 per cent increase for younger adults). In terms of the piloting of individual budgets, there was a broadly similar number of younger adults and older people in receipt of an individual budget in 2008, with 52 per cent of individual budget recipients aged 18-64 and 48 per cent aged 65 and over (Information Centre for Health and Social Care, 2009a).

Direct payments and individual budgets enable service users to appoint their own personal assistants (PAs), with potentially greater opportunity for them to recruit people with whom they can enjoy a positive relationship (Leece, 2010). Direct payments and individual budgets may have particular advantages for older people from minority ethnic backgrounds (Clark et al, 2004) and lesbian, gay and bisexual older people (Musingarimi, 2008), enabling them to employ individuals who they feel they can rely on to provide an appropriate and sensitive service. However, there are also some challenges and concerns associated with the implementation of personalization, which are considered later in Chapter Seven.

From prevention to promoting well-being

Another significant theme in social care policy and practice when considering the support available to help older people manage ageing is the balance between meeting 'high-level' or crisis needs and addressing a more preventive agenda. Prevention has been described as 'a slippery concept' in policy (Godfrey, 2001, p 92), with a dual focus on preventing or delaying the need for more expensive services and on promoting quality of life and participation in the community (Wistow and Lewis, 1997). These have been termed respectively the 'cost-effectiveness' and 'consumer' cases for prevention (Fletcher, 1998).

As long ago as 1997 an Audit Commission report drew attention to the 'vicious circle' in which the provision of 'crisis' services was consuming the vast majority of resources, thereby precluding possibilities for more preventive and rehabilitative work (Audit Commission, 1997). The core concern of much care management practice has been not determining need as experienced and expressed by service users, but identifying risk that meets eligibility criteria. Here, the focus is on the meeting of basic physical needs rather than enhancing quality of life (Ellis, 1993; Richardson and Pearson, 1995; Stanley, 1999). National statistics highlight the continuing shift in the pattern of home care support from services directed at promoting quality of life to those concerned with 'survival' needs. There has been a steady decline in the number of households receiving home care alongside an increase in the number of contact hours per household. In other words, more intensive home care services are being provided to fewer households (CSCI, 2008a). Whereas the average number of home care contact hours provided per household was 5.8 per week in 1998, this had increased to 9.1 in 2004 and to 12.4 in 2008. In 2004, 16 per cent of households received one home care visit per week, but this had decreased to 12 per cent in 2008. The number of service users receiving home care during the survey week in 2008 had decreased by two per cent from the estimated figure for 2007, representing an 18 per cent decrease since the figures were first collected in 2000 (Information Centre for Health and Social Care, 2009b). In England, between 2005-06 and 2007-08, there was also a decline in the provision of other community-based support services of which older people were the main recipients – day care and meals (Information Centre for Health and Social Care, 2009a). Older people, when asked about their difficulties or service needs, invariably refer to lack of access to services such as housework, shopping, meals, laundry, gardening and home maintenance (Langan et al, 1996; Bowling et al, 1997; Clark et al, 1998; Bartlett, 1999; Roberts and Chapman, 2001; McCann and Evans, 2002; Clough et al, 2007). These were all areas of difficulty experienced by the older people introduced in Chapter One. Even for frail and vulnerable older people, these services have increasingly come to be seen as relating to personal 'wants' that must be met privately rather than 'needs' to be met by the state.

A review of social care for older people led by Sir Derek Wanless noted in particular the unmet need among older people whose 'dependency level' was 'moderate' or 'medium' (Wanless, 2006). A Commission for Social Care Inspection report (2008a) estimated that, linked with the operation of eligibility criteria, there are a significant number of older people with support needs who experience shortfalls in their care arrangements, either because they receive no care or because the care provided is inadequate to meet their needs. The report (2008a) also expressed concern about people deemed ineligible for council support, who are 'signposted' by councils to other forms of help but who then become 'lost to the system' and experience a poor quality of life. The report notes the conflict between the focus on targeting and containing resources through eligibility criteria and broader preventive agendas:

> The trend towards tightly circumscribed council help with social care needs does not sit well with the personalisation agenda and with wider conceptions of health and well-being. (CSCI, 2008a, para 8.94)

Moreover, implementing more stringent eligibility criteria to restrict access to services only to those with high level needs appears to have little impact in terms of reducing council spending (Audit Commission, 2008, p 15). Indeed, a short-term reduction in the number of people eligible for services may be followed by an increase in the longer term (CSCI, 2008b).

Allied to the concept of prevention are more positive notions of promoting independence and well-being. Standard 8 of the NSF for older people is concerned with the promotion of health and active life in old age more generally (DH, 2001a). It refers to the significance of wider local initiatives 'to reduce poverty and improve housing and local amenities, including transport, also promote good health and support independence' (DH, 2001a, para 8.14). The plans and action include improving access to benefits, addressing fuel poverty, promoting mobility and social contacts, reducing the fear of crime, developing better access to public transport, improving road safety and enhancing access to community services such as libraries and leisure facilities. Research on the effectiveness of low intensity provision generally is limited, perhaps because of the low priority hitherto attached to such services in policy (Quilgars, 2000), but also because of the methodological challenges involved in demonstrating cost-effectiveness (Wanless, 2006). However, a background paper produced as part of the Wanless Review concluded that while there is limited evidence of the cost-effectiveness of preventive initiatives, there is substantial evidence that such interventions have beneficial outcomes for older people in terms of enhancing quality of life (Curry, 2006).

New funding for preventive initiatives was made available through the Partnerships for Older People Projects (POPPs), first announced in 2005. These were pilot projects that aimed to: 'provide person centred and integrated responses for older people; encourage investment in approaches that promote health, well-being and independence for older people; and prevent or delay the need for higher intensity or institutionalised care' (DH, 2007b, p 1). There were two rounds of pilot projects, involving 29 sites and around 245 projects.

All projects had to involve partnership between local authorities, primary care trusts (PCTs) and other health partners, voluntary, community and independent sector organisations and older people themselves. Projects were quite diverse, with approximately one third focusing on older people with high-level needs, for example, averting hospital admission ('hospital facing'), while others were aimed at enhancing the well-being of the older community more broadly, for example, health promotion, improved access to information and community development initiatives ('community facing'). The final evaluation of POPPs concluded that the projects had improved older people's quality of life and well-being, promoted easier access to a wider range of services and proved cost-effective compared to usual forms of care. With regard to services providing practical help with tasks such as gardening, shopping and household repairs, it was found that there was a 98 per cent probability that an additional spend of £96.15 per person per week would be cost-effective compared with usual care (Windle et al, 2009). In terms of older people's own evaluation of their quality of life, 'a small reduction' (Windle et al, 2009, p 182) was noted following the POPPs intervention, although it was pointed out that because of the short-term and low level nature of the services, they could not be expected to have significantly affected perceived quality of life, broadly defined. Various notes of caution were given about the interpretation of this and other findings.

The revised eligibility guidance places considerable emphasis on the significance of prevention, arguing that, '… councils should consider the needs of their wider population and put into place support strategies to reduce the number of people entering the social care system in the first place' (DH, 2010, para 41). It distinguishes three types of services: universal services aimed at promoting the well-being of communities; targeted support, directed at those identified as being at some degree of risk or with low level needs; and care and support, delivered to those with eligible social care needs. Although the eligibility framework remains in place, with councils still able to set their criteria in line with their resources, it is more clearly located within the broader remit of both universal services and targeted support for those who do not meet eligibility criteria.

The policy and practice focus on promoting the independence of older people has, of course, to be understood within the context of concerns about the economic and social implications of an ageing population (DH, 2007a). Means (2007) argues that, despite the rhetoric concerning prevention and independence, the dominant concern of government policies is with long-term healthcare conditions and the role of health services. He sees this as constituting a 're-medicalisation' of later life, maintaining, 'this new interest in the healthcare of older people is being pursued within a very narrow medical paradigm that marginalises quality of life issues for older people' (Means, 2007, p 53). Undoubtedly there are abiding tensions between political priorities to manage high-cost health and social care resources and the more holistic well-being agenda.

From being 'cared for' to interdependence

A third relevant theme in policy and practice concerns the nature and dynamics of caring relationships. This section focuses, in particular, on older people's experience of 'care', their wish to be 'independent' and the interdependence that has been shown to characterise their lives.

Supporting informal carers was one of the objectives underpinning the community care reforms of the 1990s, with official recognition given to the contribution that informal carers made to supporting people in the community (DH, 1989). 'Carers' became a recognised social group in policy and, increasingly in practice, even though many people who undertake 'caring' still do not perceive their roles and relationships in these terms (Carers UK, 2006). The carers movement, through national organisations such as Carers UK and local groups and support networks, has been successful in campaigning for increased recognition and support for carers. There have been several pieces of legislation concerned with the rights of carers to assessment and support (see Clements, 2009) as well as *A national strategy for carers* (DH, 1999), which has been subsequently updated (DH, 2008a).

However, while the carers movement has been instrumental in developing and strengthening a collective identity for carers, it has also contributed to the polarisation of the identities of carers as somehow different and distinct from other identities, including those of people who are 'cared for' (Barnes, 2006). There have been arguments, particularly by some disabled activists, that the whole concept of 'care' is oppressive towards 'recipients' of care, representing them as dependent, passive and subordinate. Disabled people should, it is argued, have their needs met on the basis of their rights and entitlements, not on the basis of their need for 'care' from others. For example, if the factors that disable them, such as inaccessible buildings and spaces, are addressed, they would not need to be passive recipients of 'care' (Morris, 1993). On the other hand, organisations representing carers' interests, such as Carers UK, have argued strongly for the needs of carers to be recognised, for example, in terms of improved welfare benefits, support for employment and better services (see, for example, Carers UK, 2008). These seemingly divergent discourses stand to construct the needs and interests of disabled people (including older people) and carers (including older people) as oppositional, rather than shared. For example, 'caring' has been increasingly recognised as a way of exercising citizenship, yet it may enhance the citizenship status of care givers at the expense of that of care recipients, who may not be able to exercise their civic responsibilities in ways that are recognised socially or politically (Harris, 2002).

In much of the literature on care and caring, the emphasis is on caring as a problem (Barnes, 2006), and earlier literature stressed, in particular, gender inequalities in caring and the disproportionate 'burden' borne by women (Graham, 1983). However, this one-dimensional and negative view of caring as a burden has been challenged by subsequent research that shows that for some people there are rewards and satisfactions to be derived from caring (Nolan et al, 1996; Nocon and Pearson, 2000). In addition, attention has been drawn to the impact of other social divisions for caring, including that of age itself. While older people have commonly been presented as recipients of care or 'the cared-for', with concerns highlighted about the demands of caring placed on younger relatives, friends or neighbours, it has been shown that older people are themselves significant providers of unpaid care (Yeandle and Buckner, 2005; Maynard et al, 2008). Very often this is perceived in terms of relationships rather than 'care'. Ray's (2000) research with couples who had been married for 35 years or more highlighted the dynamic and changing nature of their relationships which were often perceived in terms of mutual support, rather than one party 'caring for' the other. Of the older people introduced in Chapter One, Roger, Harriet, Ralph, Les and Barbara had all cared for their partners until their deaths; Patricia was disabled and being cared for by her partner, although neither of them saw the relationship in these terms; and Elsie had, for several years, acted in the role of parent for her granddaughters.

Research has thus highlighted the reciprocal nature of many caring relationships (Bytheway and Johnson, 1998). As far as older people are concerned, there is evidence that they strive to avoid perceptions of 'dependence' and protect their 'reputations' of independence (Seale, 1996). Receiving care from others can threaten their sense of themselves as independent (Cox and Dooley, 1996). Older people prefer to talk about needing 'a little bit of help' rather than 'care' (Clark et al, 1998). Retaining independence is a consistent theme from research with older people on what gives their life quality, as explored further in Chapters Three and Four.

The next part of this chapter discusses the research processes and methods used to elicit and analyse the experiences and perspectives of the older people whose pen pictures are presented in Chapter One. The aim is to provide a transparent and reflexive account that illustrates some of the complexities involved in research of this nature, not least those concerning ethics.

The study

Much of the discussion in Chapters Three, Four and Five draws on a small-scale qualitative study carried out between 2000 and 2003. The study comprised in-depth interviews with the 12 older people whose pen pictures are presented in Chapter One. They had all either referred themselves, or been referred by someone else, for help from a social services department in one local authority area. In all cases no services had been offered because the need presented at referral fell outside the eligibility criteria used by the agency to determine whether services should be provided.

Aim

The focus of the study was to explore the meanings and consequences for the participants of help not being provided and to examine their experiences and perceptions regarding alternative strategies used to manage difficulties. More specifically, the objectives were as follows:

- to explore the nature of need as experienced by older people refused a service by social services;
- to uncover the immediate consequences and meanings for older people of requests for help not being met;
- to follow up the longer-term consequences and meanings of 'unmet need' and of strategies attempting to address these difficulties;
- to use and develop research approaches which enable and promote the active involvement of older people as research participants.

The study utilised a qualitative methodology to uncover subjective meanings. The main features of qualitative research are: its focus on the 'real' world of lived experience; a concern with meanings and evolving perspectives; an interest in processes of meaning formation and change; and an inductive approach to analysis (Woods, 1999). Qualitative research is understood to have three dimensions: description, which addresses the question 'What is going on here?'; analysis, concerned with the question 'What can be learned from this experience?'; and interpretation, which seeks to find broader application or meaning by asking 'What is to be made of it all?' or 'So what?' (Wolcott, 1994). Of these, Wolcott (1994) argues that description should be the largest component. Chapters Three, Four and Five of this book present descriptive data revealing 'what is going on' for the study participants but this is at the same time 'theorised' in that it is organised and presented according to themes derived from analysis of the data. The intention is to do this in such a way that the descriptive component is clearly discernible in its own right while at the same time being transparently linked with the analytic dimension, 'What can be learned from it'. Chapters Six and Seven address the 'So what?' question of interpretation, seeking to give wider significance to the discussion in the previous chapters by means of an integrative theme, 'sustaining the self'.

Recruiting the participants

The study was carried out in an area of the West Midlands comprising both a main town and outlying rural areas. A multiple case study approach was used in that each older person was seen as a separate 'case' with his or her own individual and developing story to tell over the time period of the study. While each older person was in a unique situation with different life experiences, perceptions and meanings given to events, each 'case' in the study also shared the following features:

- the older person was referred to and lived within the area covered by the social services team participating in the study;
- the older person was over the age of 65 at the time of the referral being made. This age criterion was chosen as it marked the point at which the organisation defined someone as an 'older person' for the purposes of accessing particular services;
- the older person either made the referral herself or himself or had agreed to the referral being made. This criterion was to ensure that the older person acknowledged the referred need and wanted help to address it;
- a decision had been made by social services that the need identified at the point of referral fell outside of the agency's eligibility criteria;
- the referral had been made within a particular time period. This was designed to keep the time period between the referral decision being made and the first interview as short as possible.

Once clear about the boundaries of the 'case', potential participants who met these requirements were identified from social services computer records. Ascertaining the first three case criteria – age, referral location and the older person's agreement with the referral – was straightforward in that this information was all recorded on the computerised client referral and assessment information system. However, identifying the reasons for 'closure' of the case was less clear-cut. Attesting to the 'messiness' of research in practice, it transpired that identifying potential study participants was not just part of the research process, but itself uncovered significant issues in terms of social work assessment practices. There was a lack of clarity in some cases about the reason for no service being provided. The computer system gave a range of possible responses from which the worker could select the most appropriate. In practice there appeared to be a lack of distinction made between the different response options available to social workers, those relevant to this study being 'service not required', 'not eligible for service' and 'duty social worker resolved'. In some instances, a worker might discuss with a person requesting help with bathing or cleaning, for example, the reasons why the authority did not supply this, and then arrange to send out information about how the help requested could be purchased privately. Some workers would record this situation as 'service not required', while other workers would record it as 'not eligible for service' and still others as 'duty social worker resolved'. While this may have little significance for the older people themselves, it has implications for local authority monitoring of eligibility criteria and unmet need and, of course, was an important distinction when selecting participants for the study.

The other issue that became apparent when trying to identify older people who met the 'case' requirements was the lack of consistency as to whether a formal assessment of need was carried out before a decision was made about service provision. Given the clear-cut legal duty of local authorities to carry out an assessment of need for services where it appears that someone may be in need of services they provide (Mandelstam, 2009), it might be expected that all of the older people referred received an assessment prior to the decision about eligibility. However, this was not the case. Referrals could be 'screened' out at the initial contact stage, recorded only as a 'contact', without an initial assessment being recorded. This could be seen as a breach of the authority's statutory duty to assess and as applying the notion of eligibility to assessment, rather than reserving it for decisions about service provision.

The other issue was that assessments were being made on the basis of what appeared to be scant information, and these were then providing the basis for important decisions about eligibility for service provision. In most situations, even where initial assessment was deemed to have occurred, the information obtained and recorded appeared very sparse and selective. In effect, a one-step process was in operation with the distinct assessment stages of screening, information gathering, analysis and decision making happening in the same interaction. While this may be appropriate in some circumstances, it highlights the lack of legal clarity about what in practice constitutes an assessment and whether such brief telephone encounters, sometimes with no direct contact with the person being referred for help, suffice.

The following are examples of recorded information for each type of 'closure', all dealt with by telephone (as were the majority of referrals closed at the point of contact):

> Mrs A wants help with a bath. Informed her that she does not meet the criteria for this service. Offered information re mobile bath nurses. She declined offer. (initial assessment outcome: *closed – not eligible*)

> Mrs B recently in hospital for three days. Had brain scan. Is disorientated and dizzy. Told not to be alone but lives on own. Can't bend or reach. Needs housework and lifeline. Advised could not help with housework only (can manage her own personal care, meals and laundry). Mrs J happy to contact private agencies. Sent list with lifeline details. (initial assessment outcome: *closed – duty social worker resolved*)

> Mrs C has anaemia and currently has urinary tract infection. Feels tired and would like some help in the home with ironing and cleaning. Is able to manage all personal care, shopping, cooking etc. Explained that she does not meet criteria. She feels she can manage and has our telephone number for further advice if necessary. (initial assessment outcome: *closed – service not required*)

These examples support a key finding from other research on assessment, that is, the predominant emphasis on self-care and physical abilities (Caldock and Nolan, 1994; Caldock, 1996; Stanley, 1999). The key factor in terms of determining eligibility was personal care capacity and assessment and recording practice was clearly oriented in this direction.

Bearing in mind, then, the complexities that arose when identifying potential participants from social services records, older people who appeared to meet the study requirements were sent a covering letter, an information leaflet about the study and a letter inviting their participation. The information made clear that no identifying information about them had been disclosed to me and that this would only happen if they chose to respond to my request for their involvement. The information leaflet outlined the purpose of the study, highlighting the fact that participation in the study would not change the outcome of decisions that had been made about service provision, but that it might lead to future improvement in older people's services.

The letter inviting participation was sent to all of those who appeared to meet the case requirements, and from this target population, the sample was to a large extent self-selected. The study aimed to recruit 12 older people. One specific month, two months prior to the start of the study, was initially selected as the sampling time frame. However, as this failed to yield sufficient positive responses from older people, the same procedure was followed for subsequent months until the target of 12 participants was reached. In total, 53 letters were sent out before the 12 participants were recruited. Three potential participants who returned positive responses were either telephoned or interviewed, but not included in the study as they were found not to meet the case requirements. In one instance, the referral had concerned help for someone's mother who was intending to move into the household but at that time was still resident in another area. In the two other cases, it emerged that the potential participants had responded to the letter as they did not know there had been a referral to social services and they wanted to find out the circumstances of this. In neither of these two cases did the person feel that they had an 'unmet need', so they were not included in the study.

As the sample was both small and partially self-selected, there are of course no claims that it is representative of all older people refused a service. A positive response to the invitation to participate may have been prompted by a range of factors such as a desire to voice dissatisfaction, a general enjoyment of talking to someone or a desire to engage in an activity perceived as of social value. The factors influencing participation may, in turn, have inclined the data and analysis in particular directions, as will be discussed in more detail in Chapter Seven.

Seven of the participants were female and five were male. One woman lived with her husband; the other participants lived alone. The age profile of the participants is shown in Figure 2.1. Over two thirds of the participants were aged over 80 when the study commenced. All participants were of white UK ethnic origin, reflecting the composition of the geographical area.

Process and methods of the study

The aim was to interview each participant on five occasions during the three-year period of the study to reveal their evolving strategies for dealing with difficulties over time. In retrospect, insufficient account was taken of likely attrition when

Figure 2.1: Age group of study participants

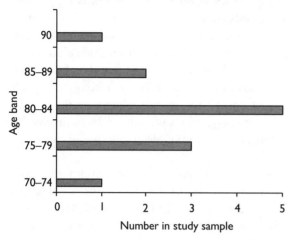

deciding on the sample size. My initial assumption was that because the study focus was on older people with 'low level' needs, the participants who were non-eligible for services might be at the younger and healthier end of the continuum. In practice, all participants had significant health difficulties, including two with serious heart conditions. Of the 12 participants in the first round of interviews, three died during the course of the study. Another moved away from the area and the fifth 'non-completer' had to postpone the final interview indefinitely because of health problems. Half of the participants who began the study completed all five of the interview phases. In addition, interruptions occurred in the scheduling of interviews for three participants due to factors that reflect the realities of older people's lives, such as hospital admission, a move to alternative accommodation and bereavement.

At the start of the first interview, a social network diagram was completed showing potential and actual sources of help. I saw this as a more participatory mechanism for recording information (Hughes, 1993), a tool to facilitate communication and a visible record that could be used as a basis of comparison in later interviews (Hill, 2002). The value of social network diagrams in both social work assessment and research is well documented (Wenger, 1984, 1994, 1997; Hill, 2002). However, my own aim in using network diagrams was not to diagnose problems or to predict vulnerability. Rather, I used them as a visible and shared way of mapping significant relationships and changes in these over time. The purpose was to help me as researcher to understand participants' significant relationships in terms of: who was involved (distinguishing between family, friend, professional helper, volunteer helper and private helper); the quality of the relationship as perceived by the older person; and their perception of its help-giving and receiving potential. Frequency of contact was less significant than how important the relationship was felt to be by the older person. After explaining the different symbols, I drew the diagram in front of the older person, adding the relevant shapes, lines and arrows and checking that this was accurate when the diagram was complete. This provided an easily visible summary of the person's relationships and seemed to trigger thoughts of other relationships they felt should be included ("oh, and there's my nephew"; "I go to the chiropodist once a month so perhaps she should be on there?"). In subsequent interviews, the diagram was a useful starting point from which to review changes. For example, comparing the first and final network diagram for Alice illustrated clearly that professionals had now taken over from family and friends as the predominant source of help.

While social network diagrams provided a record of relationships, self-completed diaries were used as a tool for participants to record their contemporaneous experiences and perceptions related to dealing with difficulties. Self-completion diaries have a number of advantages over other methods of data collection – they can aid recall of events and feelings, facilitate the expression of sensitive information and provide a useful daily record of behaviour and perceptions (Elliot, 1997). Diary material is seen as particularly useful when followed up by interview discussion (Dickinson, 2003), as was possible in this study. At the first interview, participants were left a diary that they were invited to complete between the interviews, although it was made clear that this was entirely optional and continued involvement in the interviews did not depend on completion of the diary. The format and intended use was explained and written guidance was given in the diary itself. Participants were asked to write down difficulties they experienced between interviews, ways they sought to tackle the difficulties and their thoughts or feelings about how useful these strategies were. There was no expectation about the frequency with which entries were to be recorded; rather it was left to participants to decide when they had something of relevance to record.

On a general level, there is evidence that older people enjoy and reap satisfaction from involvement in 'story telling'. One research archive, the Mass-Observation Archive, which relies on diaries and autobiographical writing of self-selected members of the population, reports that a third of its respondents are over the age of 70 (Sheridan and Holland, 2003). However, confidence, skills and enjoyment in writing are likely to be influenced by factors such as social class, education and ethnicity, so reliance on this method alone is likely to exclude certain participants. Five participants in my study returned a completed diary. Reasons given for non-completion included forgetting to fill it in, writing being physically difficult, for example, because of arthritis, and individual preferences, such as 'not being much of a one for writing'. However, the diaries can be seen as offering an optional additional tool for participants to contribute their experiences and perspectives and the diaries that were completed provided useful information that was included in the analysis.

Approximately five months after the first interview participants were contacted again, to ask if they would consent to another interview. At this visit, the themes and issues raised at the first interview were revisited and checked and any changes discussed. A particular focus was exploring whether and how any needs identified at the first interview had been met; the effectiveness of and satisfaction with strategies used to deal with difficulties; and any new difficulties that had arisen and their implications. The social network diagram was reviewed and any changes and additions noted. The diary was collected at the end of this interview and a new one issued for those who wished to complete it. In between the second and third interviews, all participants were sent a copy of a report based on analysis arising from the first two interviews and the diaries. In addition to following up themes and issues from the second phase interviews, the third interviews also aimed to verify and seek feedback from participants on the findings contained in the interim research report. The third interview took place approximately nine months after the second, with participants again being contacted first by letter and then telephone for permission to arrange a third interview. The same processes were followed for the fourth and fifth interviews, with diaries being collected at the end of the fourth interview and another draft report sent to participants between the fourth and fifth interviews. The process of data gathering is illustrated in Figure 2.2.

I endeavoured to maintain some contact with participants in between the

Figure 2.2: The process of data construction

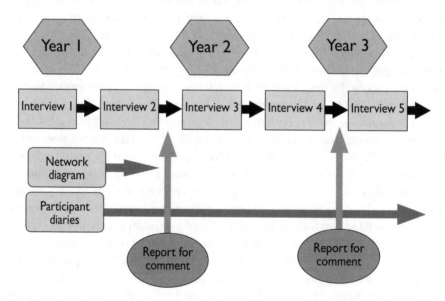

interview phases to provide a sense of continuity and to preserve the relationship established. Sending the report for comment was one way of doing this. Consent was renegotiated before each interview, so about a month before each interview was due, I contacted the older people to check they were willing to participate in the next interview. In addition, I sent thank-you letters after the interviews and cards at Christmas.

The interviews were loosely structured. This allowed more scope for older people's own meanings and perspectives to be conveyed, and also facilitated an egalitarian research relationship by more closely resembling 'ordinary' conversation between two people (Holland and Ramazanoglu, 1994; Moustakas, 1994). For me as a researcher, the use of loosely structured interviews, with no fixed or required agenda, felt liberating as I was free to concentrate solely on what the older person wished to tell me rather than my vision being restricted by my perception of what I needed to know. I also had no time limits as I scheduled interviews so that I could give as much time as was required. This and the open agenda created an encounter markedly different from my experience of social work interviews, a reflection noted several times in my research diary entries in the early phase of the study. As noted in another interview-based study, the skill lay in listening to people rather than in 'assessing' them (Dant and Gully, 1994).

Interview and diary data, like all data, are socially constructed; the accounts given by older people are shaped by the particular form and context in which they are delivered. An understanding of the processes involved is vital to understanding the 'data' itself (Radley and Billig, 1996). Participants were asked to talk about difficulties they encountered and their strategies for managing them, in other words, to give a public account of private experiences. The thoughts and experiences of participants do not just 'pour out' in an interview but are processed, according to a range of factors:

> The interviewee works with a memory that remembers some aspects and not others; which orders memory in the light of what happened subsequently and in the light of the interview situation; which tends to neaten things up; and which tends to put the interviewee in a socially acceptable light. (Arksey and Knight, 1999, p 16)

Interviews can be seen as social encounters in which identities are constructed (Aronson, 2002). As will be discussed later in this book, notions of independence and coping were central to the interview accounts. These concepts are imbued with moral worth and related to claims for legitimacy in the eyes of others (Seale, 1996). There may be gender differences in the reporting of coping strategies (Lee and Brennan, 2002), creating a different dynamic in female to female than in male to female interviews. There are also issues related to my status as a middle-aged woman interviewing older women. One study compared the self-disclosure of older women to younger women on first acquaintance with their self-disclosure to age peers. Interaction with a younger person was found to elicit negative aspects of old age, while positive features were emphasised in conversation with an age peer (Coupland et al, 1991). As will be shown in later chapters, participants in my study presented a predominantly positive rather than negative view of later life. I became increasingly aware of the subtle pressures on participants to offer me, and the study's wider audience, a 'coping' self-presentation. Acknowledging that the accounts we give of ourselves and our lives are contextually constructed, my challenge as researcher was to create a facilitative interview space so that what was reflected was more than the 'contours of the masquerade' that the participant felt obliged to present (Biggs, 1999, p 172). Again, there are parallels with social work practice here in terms of the need for sensitivity to the constraints and influences on the 'story' presented by service users during social work assessments (Fook, 2002). The longitudinal aspect of the study and the opportunity it gave to develop greater trust and rapport with participants, together with the use of diaries, helped to cross, at least at some junctures, the divide between 'private' and 'public' accounts. Revisiting participants and topics on a number of occasions and through different media allowed stories to be retold in different ways, with new memories and perceptions added in the retelling, perhaps resulting in a more rounded self-presentation.

Transcription

I fully transcribed all of the audiotapes from the interviews myself, thereby becoming immersed in the data and heightening my sensitivity to participants' experiences (Fisher, 2002). All but one participant agreed to the interviews being taped, and the presence of the tape did not appear to worry or restrict participants in any way. The most significant problem was that in some of the early interviews the tape failed to record the voices of the participants, even though my voice, despite being further away, was loud and clear. I had not fully allowed for the frail voices of some participants: Les had breathing difficulties and spoke very faintly, Gerald had sustained injury to his voice box during the war and Elsie was plagued by a chesty cough. All of these factors meant that transcription was difficult and time-consuming, with some sections of the recording being inaudible. Transcribing soon after the interviews meant that I could at least recall details and record full notes which would not have been possible even a few days later.

The process of transcribing the taped interviews presented other issues. In particular, it was soon apparent that, as with the interviews themselves, it was not objective or value-free but an interpretive exercise. As Arksey and Knight (1999) note, 'What passes from tape to paper is the result of decisions about what ought to go on to paper' (p 141). For example, I had decided to fully transcribe the interviews since I wanted to examine the meanings of experiences and this required attention to the detail of participants' accounts. Consequently I aimed to transcribe all verbal data, even if I could not at that point see it as having any direct relevance to the study. This still left decisions about whether and to what extent to 'tidy up' the actual recording, with all its 'uhs', 'umms', disjointed and unfinished sentences. I tried to transcribe what I heard as faithfully as possible but there are issues here, too, since when one participant read the transcript of her interview, she questioned why I needed to record this level of detail as she felt it portrayed her as incoherent.

Meaning is conveyed not just by the spoken word but also bodily and facial expression, requiring sensitivity to the visual and sensory as well as auditory content of interviews (Denzin, 1997). Yet audiotape does not capture non-verbal behaviour or the emotional content of interviews (Poland, 1995). Another issue was therefore deciding to what extent transcription should reflect non-verbal cues, such as sighs, laughter, facial expressions, tense body posture and so on. There is also the issue of the significance of silences. Rogers et al (1999) note,

> To preserve the integrity of the interview as a whole, we must be willing to hear silence as a presence rather than an absence and to attend to silence as systematically in our analysis as we attend to the words that have been said. What is said helps us define the landscape of the interview and supplies an interpretive ground for considering what may be missing or unsaid. (Rogers et al, 1999, p 80)

A specific example occurred when drawing the network diagram of Joyce, who told me that one of her daughters had not spoken to her for several years. She said she had got used to it and quickly passed over the subject, but her non-verbal behaviour and later references to her daughter contradicted this. The difficulty here is that I am in danger of imposing certain meanings on non-verbal behaviour, but to check out my tentative interpretations with participants could feel intrusive. While there is ample scope for distorting meanings in interpretation of the spoken word (Wolcott 1994), this is perhaps even more the case for the non-spoken.

Analysis

Grounded theory is a general methodology that reflects a particular way of thinking about and conceptualising data as well as a specific method of data analysis (Strauss and Corbin, 1998). Grounded theory was compatible with the study objectives in that it enabled the theory emanating from the study to be 'grounded' in the accounts of the study participants. It enabled me to 'stay close to the data' in order to 'tell the story' (Janesick, 1998, p 47), thus giving voice to the historically marginalised accounts of older people (Hey, 1999). As the study was carried out over a three-year period, there was a recurrent interweaving of data collection with analysis and the incremental building of theory throughout this time. This also facilitated analysis of change in terms of evolving processes of meaning construction and negotiation of difficulties. In line with a grounded theory approach, contextualising the study in relation to existing literature was an ongoing process, as the analysis yielded new insights and understanding. Finally, the data was analysed following particular methods of coding and categorising that owe much to grounded theory (see, for example, Strauss and Corbin, 1990, 1997; Glaser, 1993). This combined an attention to the detail embedded in the accounts with the facility to move beyond it to address the 'What can be learned?' question of analysis and then on to the 'So what?' question of interpretation.

However, there were some points of tension between a grounded theory and the orientation of the study. Denzin and Lincoln (1994) see grounded theory as residing in the 'modernist' phase of qualitative research and this points to a disjunction in relation to some aspects of this study. Grounded theory is conceived as a systematic, disciplined and detached research approach (as seen, for example, in the work of Miles and Huberman, 1994). While grounded theory sees theory as generated in 'pure' fashion from the data, an alternative view, and one taken in this study, is that researcher theorising, in the form of preconceptions, biases and taken-for-granted understandings and assumptions, will inevitably influence both data collection and analysis (Silverman, 1993; Wolcott, 1994). The conception of research, whether rooted in quantitative or qualitative methodology, as orderly, coherent and devoid of problems and emotions is challenged by feminist researchers who argue strongly for recognition of the central influence of the researcher's 'self' (Stanley and Wise, 1993). Similarly, reflexive social work practice requires practitioners to examine the role of their 'self' in creating knowledge and constructing social work assessments (Fook, 2002; Milner and O'Byrne, 2009). As outlined in the Introduction, this more closely reflects my own orientation, that of a critical, reflexive and active participant in an interpretive and creative research process. While grounded theory, as its name implies, is aimed at producing theory that will explain phenomena, my own position is more tentative. Although I suggest a way of understanding older people's strategies for managing the ageing experience, I offer this as a selective and partial account. It has emerged from the interaction of my 'self' carrying out research in certain ways and situations with particular other 'selves' and I do not present the resultant 'theory' as reflecting the single nor the 'whole picture' of what is going on.

I followed a grounded theory *approach* when analysing both the interview transcripts and participant diary records. This was based on the stages of analysis described by Strauss and Corbin (1990) in which data is broken down, conceptualised and then reformed in new ways. Strauss and Corbin note three important points about analysis that proceeds in this way: the analysis is an interpretive process; the procedures and techniques should be used flexibly; and the process of analysis should be accompanied by the posing of continuous and diverse questions.

My own process of data analysis proceeded as follows. First, an interview transcript was read line by line and a list of open or descriptive codes was compiled. This line-by-line reading can be seen as 'the guts of the approach' (Orona, 1997 p 179). Second, the development of axial codes involved conceptualising the open codes, making connections and distinctions between them. I refer to this stage as devising categories. I found it useful to ask of each open code, 'What is this an example of?', taking account as I did so of the whole context of the recorded utterance. By doing this for each open code, a range of categories gradually developed. On completion of analysis of that transcript, I had a list of categories, each subsuming varying numbers of open codes. It was important to write a simple definition for each category in order to clarify the decision making about where each open code belonged. Categories should be mutually exclusive (Woods, 1999). If some open codes appeared to belong potentially to more than one category, I made a note of this and returned to the code later in the analysis when the category definitions were more clearly defined. A key element of the process was asking questions about relationships: how did the open codes grouped together relate to each other and what defined the relationship? The same process was applied for the second interview, with categories being developed independently of those arrived at from the first interview to reduce the likelihood of data being made to 'fit' preformed categories. This tendency was not removed, just reduced, since clearly I had some recall of the first interview categories that influenced development of categories from the second interview. The categories arrived at were then compared directly with those from the first interview; where there were clear overlaps and similarities, a shared category was developed, with category definitions sometimes needing to be adjusted. If an open code did not fit any existing categories, a new category and definition were created. Earlier open codes then had to be revisited to check this new category was not more appropriate.

These same procedures were followed for each of the interviews, with initial analysis followed by direct comparison with previous categories. As the study progressed, the process became increasingly complicated, as the analysis had to be compared not only with that from other interviews in that stage, but also with the analysis from all of the previous stages. The categories and their definitions had to be reviewed continually to ensure that codes were being allocated consistently. It was also necessary to examine closely open codes that did not appear to fit any of the categories and also contradictions between different open codes within categories. Rather than seeking to confirm categories, it was important to look for areas of confrontation (Dey, 1993). Over time I saw new patterns and possibilities for interpretation arising from the categories. Sometimes analysis indicated the need to 'split' categories, so that a category was divided into sub-categories. For example, a category of 'keeping active' was sub-divided into four different sub-categories: keeping busy, pushing yourself, finding solutions and adjusting. Further analysis could also suggest that one category actually represented another dimension of another category and the two categories could be 'spliced' (Dey, 1993) or combined.

On completion of analysis of all interviews in that stage of the study, all of the transcripts were revisited and adjustments made to the categories in the light of the 'whole picture'. Whereas at the end of the first round of interviews there was a long list of categories, continual refinement of categories through splitting and splicing led to a smaller number of eventual categories at the final stage of analysis. The categorising process was therefore fluid throughout analysis of the transcripts with new categories created, existing categories combined, sub-categories identified and open codes moved between categories. To aid data retrieval, the final phase of analysis included producing summary sheets cross-referencing 'case' (participant), interview number (1-5), category and open code.

Despite the rigorous processes for analysing the transcripts, at no stage did it feel like a 'scientific', that is, detached or objective, process; rather it was a creative one, allowing for 'interpretation, intuition (and) ruminating' (Orona, 1997, p 179). While I do not claim to have followed faithfully all aspects of grounded theory analysis as outlined in any one text, a grounded theory approach to analysis provided a framework for the development of concepts and themes and helped to degenerate a 'theory' of how older people manage the experience of ageing.

However, when one of the participants, Elsie, read the interim report after the first round of analysis, her comments led me to rethink my approach to the analysis. She commented that although quotations were used in the report to illustrate themes, there was 'no sense of the person behind the words'. On reflecting on this observation, I could see that the fragmentation and decontextualising of participant accounts required by the grounded theory approach was not fully conducive to exploration of participants' understanding of their experiences. While coding and categorisng of transcripts enabled relationships to be identified between different segments of 'data', it lost a sense of the 'whole person', both in terms of current social context and life history (Butler, 1963; Bornat, 1999).

In contrast, looking at interview transcripts and reflective diary entries as integrated narratives allows more scope for understanding the 'whole' person. Since attention is directed beyond the verbal utterance in its present context to consideration of wider context and meaning, interpretation is less 'grounded' in the text and more focused on how the self of the narrator is constructed and revealed in the telling of the story (Kelly and Dickinson, 1997). This approach is therefore of particular value when examining the cognitive strategies used by participants to deal with their difficulties. These may be unacknowledged or unconscious aspects of experience that are less likely to be uncovered in analysis of discrete segments of the transcript of the spoken word. For example, looking in depth at narratives as represented in transcripts across five separate interviews allowed for interpretation of the significance of silences, laughter and things that remained unsaid. In this sense, grounded theory can be seen as an example of what R. Ray (2007) refers to as 'paradigmatic knowing', as distinct from 'narrative knowing': 'The paradigmatic mode of knowledge making relies on observation, description and reason, deriving empirical "truths", while the narrative mode emphasises people, feelings and relationships, deriving personal or emotional "truths"' (R. Ray, 2007, p 61).

Narrative knowing respects the integrity and context of interview accounts; unlike grounded theory, it is not primarily concerned with comparison between accounts or theory derived from analysis of multiple accounts. In effect, I combined the two approaches, first arriving at tentative themes from coding and categorising the data and then reading the data as narrative wholes. I see this second stage as having supplemented and enhanced the understanding derived from the grounded theory analysis rather than as constituting an alternative approach.

Three themes were identified from the analysis and, embracing all of them, an overarching or core theme was selected through which the three subsidiary themes can be understood. The themes and core theme are used to structure Chapters Three to Six.

Ethics and research relationships

The study participants were potentially vulnerable by reason of age, disability and ill health. A suggested code of ethics for social work and social care research confirms that particular care must be taken by social work researchers to protect participants from harm, discomfort, disruption of their daily lives and invasion of privacy (Butler, 2002). I invited participants to talk about their difficulties and this in itself can create the potential for distress and demoralisation. However, the emphasis in the study and in the talk with participants was on ways of managing, and this constructs them as active and coping, rather than as passive and oppressed. The loosely structured nature of the interviews enabled participants to control the agenda of topics discussed; the process was not seen as one in which 'the researcher' asked certain questions and 'the subjects' answered them, but rather as one in which meanings were jointly created together through the encounter (Holstein and Gubrium, 1997). Participants could avoid issues they preferred not to talk about.

Another aspect of preventing discomfort to participants, all of whom had some form of illness or disability, was being alert and responding to cues that they were becoming tired or experiencing strain during the interview. Disruption to participants' lives was minimised by giving them the choice of precisely when interviews took place. Participants selected interview days that accommodated their weekly routine and preferences. For example, Gerald, who lived in sheltered accommodation, liked me to visit on a particular morning of the week when the residents' meetings were held as he welcomed an excuse not to attend them! The format of the interviews followed a path laid down by participants, for example, whether and when there was a refreshment break, the extent of general social talk and whether or not the location of the interview was confined to one room or spread to other areas of the home and garden. These were all aspects of recognising that the research was intruding into participants' lives and private spaces and that they should therefore have as much control as possible over the terms on which it proceeded.

Ethically, social care researchers 'must retain a primary concern for subjects' welfare' (Butler, 2002, p 245), and my concern for participants' welfare extended beyond the research process itself. At the outset of the study, I was careful to make clear to participants that involvement in the study would not change anything for them personally; in particular, it would not alter the decision that social services had made about their entitlement to services. Any benefits would be of a more general, long-term and indirect nature and arise from changes in policy and practice that might result from the study. It was also important to be clear in my own mind that my role was that of researcher, not social worker, despite the latter role being more familiar to me. Maintaining 'a primary concern for subjects' welfare' presented something of a dilemma in that it could imply that if I was in a position to enhance the welfare of participants, then ethically I should do this. Dilemmas and compromises are invariably part of the research experience, and here the dilemma was between detached inquiry versus helping (Miles and Huberman, 1994; Sword, 1999). Given my professional social work background, there were a number of situations when participants were talking about their difficulties where I could see possible ways in which I might be able to help them, for example, contacting agencies on their behalf or giving them information. On the other hand, the study was concerned to explore their strategies for managing difficulties and intervention from me could distort study of their own coping mechanisms. This was an irresolvable tension. My approach was to acknowledge the conflicting interests and weigh them in the balance in each situation. I clearly had no authority or remit to attempt to offer any sort of professional social work service, but one question I found useful to ask was whether the help or information was something that could potentially be provided by 'ordinary' members of a social network. Taking this as a guide, I did intervene in small ways that could have tainted the study 'results' but which maintained the ethical standard of promoting participants' welfare. For example, Joyce (see Chapter One) was keen to obtain gadgets to improve her mobility and dexterity within the home, but knew that social services did not supply these; I told her where they could be purchased and her daughter subsequently helped her to arrange this. On a visit to Gerald, I found he had experienced a fall and could walk only with great difficulty. He was concerned about how he would do his shopping so I offered to buy basic provisions for him.

A more serious concern arose in the second interview phase when I could see that Les's health had deteriorated significantly since the first interview. He had recently been discharged from hospital and had expected to receive home care support, but no one had visited him. He had no immediately available informal sources of support and his frail physical condition made it difficult for him to take the action necessary to trigger help, for example, telephoning the hospital social work team. I felt very concerned for his welfare following my visit (these concerns are noted in my research diary) and, after some deliberation, I telephoned to ask him if he would like me to refer him to an organisation that might be able to assist him. He assented and I contacted an advocacy service that agreed to visit him. In this sense I contaminated the findings in that this was a strategy I contributed rather than one that came from within his own network of resources. However, my decision was that the moral and ethical concerns were of prime importance in this situation, a perspective corroborated when I found that by the time of the third interview he had died.

The conflict between ethical considerations and research interests becomes less significant if the research endeavour is not viewed as a quest to reveal the unadulterated 'truth' of what is going on in situations but rather as a process in which participant and researcher are together creating one particular version. Therefore, if I have in some situations contributed strategies rather than dispassionately studied them, this itself becomes part of the 'data' that is explored. The most important factor is not that it has happened but that it is laid open to critical reflection.

Establishing a genuine concern for participants' welfare makes problematic the ending of research relationships:

> We need to be aware of the power we hold as interested strangers who, having established trust and encouraged disclosure, can then move on. Leaving "the field" may well mean consigning elderly people back to heightened awareness of their social isolation. (Hey, 1999, p 107)

I was aware in my research that participants looked forward to and enjoyed my visits; most were explicit about this, commenting in particular on the value of talking to someone who showed an interest in what they had to say. However, there is a danger that where positive relationships have been developed, participants will feel used and let down when the research ends. The participant 'has welcomed you into his or her life; you've learned there and come to care yourself; and then, when the research is over, typically you break it off and go about your business' (Harper, 1992, p 152). This issue is perhaps a greater concern for longitudinal studies and those involving in-depth interviewing where relationships are closer and involve higher levels of trust (Shaw and Gould, 2001).

Whatever the impression given during the process, research relationships are not governed by the same rules and expectations as ordinary social relationships. I was clear with participants throughout the study about its planned process, and each interview was located for them in terms of its place in this sequence. The ending was therefore clearly signposted from the beginning and throughout the course of the study. Even so, I had developed warm relationships with the participants and I was sorry to be ending these when we reached the final interviews. I was conscious that this ending of the relationship might be difficult for them also. We dealt with this by leaving 'openings' on both sides; for example, I was invited to visit if I was in the area, and I left it open for the participants to contact me if they wanted to. As with other ethical concerns discussed here, these are not perfect solutions, but represent efforts to grapple with the tensions and complexities inherent in research relationships. This reflects a more flexible 'ethics-as-process' approach that involves the ongoing balancing of risks against benefits as issues emerge (Cutcliffe and Ramcharan, 2002).

It is suggested that the emotional demands on interviewers are increased with both the degree of sensitivity of the topic area and in inverse proportion to the level of structure of interviews (Arksey and Knight, 1999). In these terms, my research carried potentially high emotional demands in that the interviews were loosely structured and topic areas included discussion of experiences such as increasing disabilities, problematic health difficulties such as incontinence, bereavements and other types of loss. Hey (1999) discusses similar issues in respect of interviews with frail older people. In addition to the frustration and helplessness I sometimes felt at not being in a position to assist with difficulties, the most significant area of emotional demand was dealing with the deaths of some participants, particularly when I knew that their last months or years were characterised by avoidable 'struggle'. The relationships formed with participants and my ability to connect at an emotional as well as intellectual level with their experiences was central to the research. While to an extent my professional social work education and experience provided some element of preparation and protection in managing distressing situations, dealing with the deaths of three participants during the study was nevertheless upsetting, not least because my own mother died just as the empirical work commenced. In line with the reflexive approach to the research, I found it helpful to record my thoughts and emotions in my research diary and to allow these reflections to inform the analysis, for example, concerning issues of loss, change and coping. As Howe (2008) argues in relation to social work, 'If we can be intelligent *about* emotions – what they are, why we have them, how they affect us – we can be more intelligent *with* them' (p 195).

Conclusion

This chapter has set the context for subsequent chapters by outlining relevant policy and describing the research processes and methodology used to explore how older people managed difficulties they encountered as they aged. The next three chapters discuss different dimensions of older people's experiences of negotiating and managing difficulties in later life. They feature the experiences and perspectives of the older people introduced in Chapter One, but also refer to other relevant research and literature. Chapter Three discusses practical strategies, Chapter Four explores cognitive ways of coping and Chapter Five considers the threats and resources that support or undermine older people's efforts in managing ageing.

Note
[1] A longer-term historical analysis of policy development can be found in Means and Smith (1998a) and Means et al (2002).

THREE

'Keeping going'

> To maintain one's aspirations in the face of grave adversity, to work hard to contend successfully with the daily assault of an impaired body on a robust spirit, to be victorious over the long course of losses and threats that constitute disability – these are lessons for us all, examples of what is best in our shared humanity. (Kleinman, 1988, p 137)

This chapter focuses on the practical or 'doing' strategies used by older people to manage the ageing experience. This theme is called 'keeping going' and three dimensions of older people's efforts to keep going are discussed. These are efforts to: maintain social roles and activities ('keeping active'); maintain standards and routines ('keeping stable'); and preserve relationship boundaries ('keeping balance').

Keeping active

Keeping active refers to older people's efforts to be proactive, accepting responsibility and taking action to manage everyday living and address difficulties. Keeping active contains four interrelated sub-categories: keeping busy, pushing yourself, finding solutions and adjusting.

Keeping busy

'Keeping busy' encompasses three related strands: older people's organisation of their lives in such a way that they are busy; their perceptions of themselves and presentation to others as busy; and their beliefs about the physical and psychological benefits of keeping active that sustain busyness.

Participants' accounts of their daily lives were replete with references to various activities that occupied their time. These included social and leisure pursuits as well as tasks with functional value. During the interviews, I frequently observed the processes and outcomes of busyness. For example, I overheard telephone calls from friends or family planning to visit, I saw jam being made, homegrown vegetables prepared for freezing, gardens attended to, and the finished products from needlework, art and craft activities. Other studies corroborate the importance older people attach to living active lives (see, for example, Langan et al, 1996; Bowling et al, 1997; Bernard et al, 2004). Concurring with other research, the lives of most participants in my study could be described as 'characterised by variety, diversity, activity, energy (and) interest' (Thompson et al, 1990, p 121).

In addition to being busy, participants perceived and presented themselves as busy, belying stereotypes of older people as having lots of time on their hands:

> "I always make a list of things I want to do and I never get them all done, partly because it takes me such a long time to do things but I've always got things I'd like to do and haven't got time to do.... There's lots of things I'd love to do but I haven't got time to do them all."
> (Alice, interview 3)

Self and social perceptions of busyness appear to be associated with the construction of independence and, perhaps, moral connotations of being active and responsible:

> "I'm so used to doing things, I never sit idle. I'm always doing what I refer to as my hobbies. There's never enough time for me to do the things that I want to do.... But if you're sat all day all round the wall like you see them sat in those homes, just staring into space or staring at each other, it's soul destroying isn't it?" (Harriet, interview 2)

Some participants had been obliged to relinquish some of their activities. For example, Ralph had stopped attending his local over-60s club as his increasing deafness meant he could not join in conversations; Elsie could no longer go on her daily long walks and relied more on people visiting her rather than her seeing them out and about in the village. However, as the next chapter explores further, even in situations where participants had given up some of their activities, they invariably still managed to experience their lives as busy and fulfilling.

Older care receivers in one study who were asked what advice they would give to others cited the importance of retaining personally fulfilling interests (Cox and Dooley, 1996). Busyness is seen as intrinsically beneficial in sustaining well-being and warding off illness and disability:

> "[My daughter] says, 'You shouldn't be so damned independent, mother'. And I say, 'It's not being independent, it's keeping my bones moving', if you know what I mean. Yes, I could sit down here and I could sit in this chair all day or stay in bed all day and have somebody to do my jobs for me if I'd got the money to pay them but what good would that do me? It wouldn't do me any good because I would just be there rusting up and my joints wouldn't move at all then." (Joyce, interview 4)

Involvement in activities is important psychologically as well as physically; it serves as a distraction, reducing the time and opportunity to dwell on problems. My research diary notes the difference between Barbara's demeanour in the first and second interviews. Whereas in the first interview she had appeared depressed and tearful, in the second she was much more cheerful and talkative.

She attributed this change to the fact she had started weekly craft classes and was now spending several hours a day engaged in this activity at home. She said that she lost track of time when involved in the craft and that it took her mind off her worries. It also gave her a goal to work towards as she was making craft items for her granddaughter's wedding later in the year. Her activities were therefore also contributing to her sense of value and usefulness within the family. Similar issues were observable with another participant:

> "When I'm doing a sketch or a painting, I'm lost to the world and nothing bothers me. I can easily go for a day without eating because I just don't notice I'm hungry." (David, interview 2)

David gave his sketches and paintings to friends and acquaintances, again enabling him to have a sense of value in informal relationships.

Older people have been found to equate 'health' with carrying on with normal living, believing this will hold in abeyance or minimise illness (Sidell, 1995). There appears to be empirical support for the view that keeping busy has physical and psychological benefits. A strong relationship has been found between social and physical activity in later life and both longevity (Glass et al, 1999) and life satisfaction (Fernandez-Ballesteros et al, 2001). Older people living in a retirement village who participated in village activities were found to have improved self-esteem and self-confidence (Bernard et al, 2004). A research study conducted as part of the Economic and Social Research Council's (ESRC's) Growing Older Programme identifies keeping busy as an important means of coping for older people who are widowed (Bennett et al, 2004). However, the emphasis on activity in this and other studies does not imply that keeping busy is unproblematic for older people, as illustrated in the next sub-category, 'pushing yourself'.

Pushing yourself

A related category to 'keeping busy' is 'pushing yourself' and this is defined in terms of activity involving effort, a sense of 'struggling against the odds' or 'soldiering on'. In the same way that 'keeping busy' is associated with perceived physical and psychological benefits, some degree of struggle is linked with perceptions of coping and independence:

> "You've got to push yourself through some days. Some days I feel, oh, I'd love to stop in bed all day and then I get up and I start my jobs and when I've done what I want to do I think, I'm glad I didn't stop in bed, you know ... you have got to push yourself; you must force yourself to do things, even if you don't like doing things, you must do it because it wants doing. You can't keep relying on other people to wait on you hand and foot. You just can't. And if you've got the energy and the effort, you've got to do it. That's my advice to people.

Otherwise you must sit in your chair or lie in your bed and you
deteriorate don't you? And I don't want to do that, I'm not ready for
that yet. No, I might be getting old, well, getting, I reckon I am old!
But I'm not ready to give up, not yet. No way." (Joyce, interview 3)

The importance of pushing yourself for maintaining mental and physical well-
being has been identified as a theme in other research involving older people
(Langan et al, 1996; Cox and Dooley, 1996; Godfrey et al, 2004). Minichiello et
al (2000) report that older people in their study endeavoured to be perceived as
'still trying' and sought to distance themselves from its ill-favoured alternative,
'no longer trying'. Participants relayed stories about other people that illustrated
the dangers of 'not trying' or 'giving in':

"My sister used to sit in her chair … she just sat there and let people
run round her and do things. She used to ask people, 'Will you come
and do so and so?'.…The health visitor came and talked to her and told
her she should get out of her chair and walk. 'I can't', she said.… But it's
no good giving in, it really is no good giving in." (Elsie, interview 3)

"You must keep active, you must keep going, even if it's just walking
round with the duster or something like that. But you mustn't give
up. Forget about your illness. Although at times I've felt ever so ill, you
know, but I've thought well, I'll go into the garden and I go in the
garden for half an hour or so and I've forgotten about it. But I know
one or two people who've had an illness and they've just sort of sat
in the chair and done nothing and then you've just passed away like
that. Well, that's no life. No, I want to keep going till the day I die."
(Roger, interview 4)

The association of 'pushing yourself' with independence is explicit within Harriet's
account of her struggle to maintain her garden:

"I realise now that those sorts of jobs [in the garden] are very difficult
for me … if I'm feeling OK I shall still [do them] because … if you
give up doing these things then you lose independence entirely."
(Harriet, interview 2)

In a later interview, she again talked of her continuing struggle to maintain her
garden, but now acknowledged that there were tasks she could no longer do:

"I am still doing it [the garden] but I'm only doing things I can do.
There are things I can't do but Brian [daughter's partner] will come.
He's been very busy so I haven't troubled him … but I'll see if Brian
can do it." (Harriet, interview 4)

In this way, careful judgement is exercised to decide the extent and limits of 'pushing yourself':

> "I say [to my daughter], 'While I can do it, even if I'm in pain, I will do it. When I can't do it, then I'll appreciate you doing if for me but as long as I've got the strength to do it, I will do it'…. You've just got to keep yourself going. Like I say, when I can't, I'll appreciate anybody helping me but as long as I can I'll do it myself. I mean, that cabinet's got to be turned out, it looks a damn mess. But you see I can't get down to do it so I'll get my daughter to do it for me." (Joyce, interview 4)

For some people, pushing themselves was more out of necessity than choice. This was evident in the diary entries of Les, who had a serious heart condition. The diary entries are recorded on different days over a period of several months. Although brief, they convey his repeated efforts to tackle daily tasks:

> Tried moving furniture; only managed easy chairs. Left the rest for another day.
> Tried doing a little weeding. Went dizzy bending over. Left it alone for another time. Cleaned cooker and kitchen. Very slowly.
> Was very short of breath; cleaning and general housework very difficult. Very slow, takes a lot of time.
> Looks like I shall have to get help with the bushes. (Les, diary)

Alice, who had arthritis and incontinence problems, was finding that managing her personal care in the mornings was involving increasing time and struggle. At the time of the fourth interview, she had reached the point where pushing herself was no longer viable, but equally there seemed to be no acceptable alternative:

> "I manage to do all the things I did, in a fashion, but it takes me so long to get round to do things. I got up at a quarter past eight this morning…. It's often 10 o'clock or after before I've got my breakfast. By then I've washed, strip-washed, and dressed, made the bed and washed my pants but it's a long time…. I'm tired, you know, by the time I've done all that. I have to sit down a bit." (Alice, interview 4)

Alice's comments illustrate that while pushing yourself is valued, carefully balanced decisions are made about its limits, in this case in relation to personal care tasks. Relevant factors involved in such decision making are the perceived necessity of the tasks, weighing up personal costs and benefits, the availability of alternative sources of help, its perceived quality or effectiveness and likely costs to the helper, such as being worried or inconvenienced. Similarly, it may be that while keeping active is valued and a goal that older people strive to retain, as discussed in the previous section there are limits here, too, in terms of how far it is reasonable to continue striving to stay busy, or at least, busy in the same way. Thus, research on the 'oldest old' suggests that there comes a point at which it is no longer possible or desirable to continue to push yourself, and there is a process of withdrawal from activities (Johnson and Barer, 1997; Lee and Brennan, 2002). There would therefore appear to be preventive value in making it as easy as possible for older people to continue to engage in valued activities and roles even when, or perhaps especially when, their health or mobility decline. As 'Bea' is quoted as saying in a study of older people living in a retirement village,

> "If I'd to get a bus to town to go to aerobics, I wouldn't dream of it. I come down here and quite enjoy it. Some days you think, 'Oh, I don't think I can cope today. I'm not feeling too good', you come down and you feel so much better for it." (quoted in Bernard et al, 2004, p 14)

Finding solutions

The determination to make an effort and the process of weighing up when this is no longer a viable strategy for 'keeping going' are related to a sense of personal responsibility for managing one's situation. This sub-category, 'finding solutions', is characterised by agency, as older people adopt an active role in the attempt to address difficulties.

There were numerous illustrations of participants taking the initiative in an attempt to manage or improve their situation. Sometimes this was about making creative use of their own resources. Gerald was awaiting an operation on his Achilles tendons and in the meantime he was having considerable difficulty walking. He explained how he tried to build up the support in his shoes to make walking more comfortable:

> "As I say, I've got some what they call saddles, they're in the bottom there [of shoes]. They go underneath the instep.... I bought a pair and they were so good I bought two or three pairs. I pack them underneath with stuff you put around the door, draught-proofing; that's a cheap way of doing it. You can adjust it and it works very well. That again is helping, it's trial and error." (Gerald, interview 4)

Some participants used their financial resources to purchase particular services that they identified as potentially helpful in addressing difficulties. Roger was determined to continue tending his garden for as long as possible and had purchased special equipment to help him:

> "I've got a spade, an automatic spade, which I bought some years ago, you just push it into the ground, just pull the handle down and it clicks over itself. And that's very useful; I'm managing quite well, yes." (Roger, interview 3)

Alice supplemented NHS treatment by arranging private hydrotherapy and chiropody. This was not straightforward as it was too far for her to drive, which meant that she also needed to arrange transport to and from the appointments using a local voluntary driver service. In these different ways, participants demonstrated their resourcefulness in trying to find solutions to difficulties they experienced. This is reminiscent of Richards' (2000) study that contrasts the professional construction of older people as helpless and passive in referral documents with the accounts given by the older people themselves:

> Many were waging a determined struggle to manage increasing disabilities and demonstrated an internal resourcefulness – the ability to perceive and analyse problems and to identify solutions – that is essential for coping. (Richards, 2000, p 40)

Another aspect of finding solutions was making decisions about risk taking. For example, Barbara enjoyed attending a craft-making club but this entailed her driving several miles. She had lost confidence in driving and explained how she made a decision each week on whether to attend based on her assessment of the weather; if it was foggy or icy, then she would not attend. The same assessment of driving conditions determined her decision about whether to drive to the supermarket or to walk to the local store. Participants were aware of threats to their physical well-being and part of finding solutions was seeking to manage these risks by making carefully calculated decisions, weighing up the dangers and potential consequences of actions to both themselves and others. Finding solutions involved participants making their own decisions about acceptable risks, these decisions sometimes being at variance with the views of others:

> "We have a harvest festival coming up and they're having a barn dance … and my daughter says, 'You are not to dance', she said, 'You must slow up'…. But I said to my daughter yesterday, 'Supposing I do dance and I drop dead when I'm dancing, I shall die happy won't I, I'll be doing something I like doing'." (Elsie, interview 4)

Elsie gave another example of her decision to act according to her own assessment of risk rather than her daughter's:

> "I don't mind standing on stools but it's my daughter, she won't let me. She'll stop me. But I get up there [points to the top of the dresser] to clean things, she doesn't know." (Elsie, interview 4)

When deploying their own resources to deal with difficulties proved insufficient and there were perceived to be unacceptable risks to well-being, finding solutions involved decision making about when help was needed:

I find housework and gardening very exhausting since I collapsed last
August. I go dizzy if I look up or bend down. Changing bed linen is
a problem and bending over is extremely painful. I have to keep my
back straight at all times so most of my gardening is done on my hands
and knees.... Have risked cutting the lawn myself, it took me over
an hour and I feel exhausted. Shall have to find a long-term solution.
(Harriet, diary)

Sometimes participants addressed risks by seeking or accepting help from family
or friends. Joyce had been awaiting a shower installation in her housing association
(previously district council) flat for two years:

"The thing that worries me, it's bad enough getting into the bath to
have my shower but it's getting out. I have to hang on to the wash
basin and get this leg out first while that leg is still in the bath and if
that leg gives way, then the wash basin comes down with me and it
will be on top of me so now my daughter and son-in-law have bought
me the phone so I can lift the phone off and take it in the bathroom
with me. So that's what I do." (Joyce, interview 4)

As will be shown in more detail in Chapter Five, some participants sought to
address problems they had identified by seeking help from within the formal sector:

Owing to angina attacks felt I needed help with housework. Saw
advert in local paper for housekeepers. They came to have a chat and
I decided to try them fortnightly. (Barbara, diary)

"I've got solid fuel central heating and ... I told them [social services],
it [carrying in coal] is the only essential thing I want the help with....
I'm not worried about cleaning, it's keeping the fire going because
if that's not going, I've got no heating and no hot water or anything.
And that's, you know, the only thing." (Roger, interview 1)

This section has shown that participants were active in a number of ways in
trying to manage their situations. This included seeking to manage difficulties
by creatively deploying their own resources, identifying when external help was
required and for what specific tasks and taking the initiative to try to secure
this help. Participants assumed responsibility for managing difficulties and took
proactive steps within the confines of the resources available to them to address
these defined problem areas.

A process of adjustment

Participants often had to adapt their usual ways of doing things in response to changes brought about by illness or disability. These efforts to adjust to changing circumstances were an essential component of 'keeping going'. One frequently mentioned method of adjusting was 'slowing up':

> "I've found now that I am slower, much much slower. I'm still getting things done but much more slowly.... I do so much and then I sit down and when I've had a little rest, I get up and start again ... and that's how I get through my work, by doing a bit and resting." (Harriet, interview 4)

> "I like to keep myself fit. I do my exercises every morning and I sometimes walk to my daughter's house though I'm much slower now and have to take my sticks." (David, interview 2)

> "I've always been active and I still am but I have had to slow up a bit." (Elsie, interview 1)

> "I do try to go out every day to keep my joints ... and I mean I do all my own jobs and everything so that keeps me active. But where it used to take me say an hour to do something, it takes me two or three now, you know.... You know, it all takes time because you have to be careful how you move because of the pain. If you move awkward or do something awkward, then you're in a hell of a lot of pain and I try to avoid that, that's why it takes me so long." (Joyce, interview 3)

As well as doing the same things but at a slower pace, adjusting also involved finding different ways to undertake tasks and routines:

> "One of the things I find extremely difficult is changing the bed because I can't bend over so I do it all on my hands and knees.... I've had this rheumatoid arthritis since I was in my forties so everything that requires bending I do on my hands and knees, so I change the bed like that. There are things like that that I do find very difficult but I do cope.... I am so used to doing things on my hands and knees, like dusting or anything at floor level, that I just do it. It only leaves me with one hand free because with the other hand I have to support myself, so it means doing things one-handed. Quite often I've cut round the edges of the lawn with a pair of scissors because I can't cope with shears you see." (Harriet, interview 1)

"[When carrying hot pans] I make myself do that, very slowly, very carefully. I do it but instead of carrying it I just lift it out and put it on top of the stove so that I don't trip or lose my balance." (Joyce, interview 3)

Alice described how she did not let her incontinence problems stop her from going on social outings or holidays. She endeavoured both to prevent problems by adjusting her diet and to deal with problems by making necessary preparations:

"[When I go away] I have to take all sorts of things, to put on the bed and pads and dozens of pants. But they supply sort of net pants which wash easily and dry quickly.... I take a lot so I'm always all right ... the family always say, 'Why the heck do you always carry that bag around with you all the time', and I never say." (Alice, interview 3)

In this way, by detailed attention to specific difficulties experienced in particular situations, participants negotiated their way around everyday difficulties so that they could maintain their usual lifestyles as far as possible. These examples illustrate participants' resourcefulness in finding strategies to address difficulties as well as their attempts to take charge of their situations, discussed earlier.

Adjusting sometimes meant giving up a particular activity when it became impossible to persevere with it and instead substituting a different, perhaps related activity. For example, David described how he tended plants in his window box now that he was living in a sheltered flat and had no garden. Patricia explained that the arthritis in her hands meant she could no longer sew or do embroidery but she could manage to knit as it did not strain her fingers or eyes in the same way. Similarly, she found it strained her eyes too much to read a book, so instead she had started doing crossword puzzles:

"It's been a process of adjustment, I've started doing other things....
I mean when I was at work for instance or after I'd finished work
I wouldn't bother with crosswords, I didn't have time because I was
doing other things but now I've adjusted to it ... I can't read a great
deal now, I do read but only a little at a time.... No, it's just a case of
adapting isn't it?" (Patricia, interview 4)

When Roger could not get out in the garden because of poor weather or when he was ill he busied himself with other activities:

"I sit here, if I'm not working, I sit here and do jigsaw puzzles or something like that to keep myself occupied. And now my daughter's going to get me, I've asked her to get me a couple of rug-making outfits, you know, to make mats and rugs. I used to do that and I said I'd like to do some of that again, it occupies the time ... I should only do a little bit at a time but I do them pretty quickly. I've done several in the past, you know, and given them all away. I just like doing something like that. And of course, I used to do a lot of wood carving but now you see I've got arthritis in my hands and I can't do it any more." (Roger, interview 3)

This picture of the resourcefulness of older people in finding new ways of carrying out tasks or routines or in substituting goals has been found in other studies. Thus Wenger notes from her research how older people manage their day-to-day lives:

> ... for the most part the elderly and their families respond to the challenges of ageing through adaptive and coping strategies and the majority make creative changes in life-style to accommodate the inevitable losses which are part of the ageing process. (Wenger, 1984, p 179)

Baltes and Carstensen (1996) equate successful ageing with the minimisation of losses and the maximisation of gains, and they propose a metamodel of the processes involved, 'selective optimisation with compensation'. These processes can be illustrated using the examples of the study participants presented here. *Selection* involves the older person selecting goals that allow the desired gains to be achieved. For example, when David moved from a house to a sheltered flat, he changed his goal from maintaining a garden to tending a window box. Roger, as shown in the earlier quotation, could no longer do wood carving so spent more time making rugs instead. *Compensation* concerns finding alternative ways of meeting the same goal. The process of 'slowing up' described in the extracts from interviews with Harriet, Joyce and Elsie, illustrates efforts to achieve the same goals by working more slowly and taking frequent rests. Harriet retained the goal of walking to the High Street to do her shopping but found new routes to find safe crossing places and to minimise the number of steps she had to negotiate. She still did jobs around the house and garden but now accomplished these on hands and knees as she could not bend. *Optimisation* refers to efforts to boost the resources and abilities necessary to achieve goals. It was shown earlier that keeping busy is itself seen as a form of optimisation by study participants, enabling them to keep physically and mentally active. Alice's changes in diet and use of incontinence aids are other examples of optimisation to enable her to maintain her social life. Clearly the processes can and do frequently operate in conjunction with each other, with some new goals being selected in favour of those no longer achievable, new strategies being devised for meeting existing goals and efforts being made to enhance the ability to attain goals. The study findings therefore provide empirical support for Baltes and Carstensen's model that enhances understanding of participants' processes for adapting to loss and change. The model's focus on individually defined goals allows for the different priorities and concerns of participants, and it also highlights the significance of resources in supporting the three components of selection, compensation and optimisation.

Keeping active: summary

The three categories within the theme of keeping active – keeping busy, pushing yourself, finding solutions and adjusting – are all concerned with older people's endeavours to remain active in a physical sense, but also to retain a sense of agency and control in relation to their lives. This is consistent with research on the outcomes valued by older people which identifies that having control over daily life and the processes through which services are received is an important factor in maintaining or preventing deterioration in health, well-being and quality of life (Glendinning et al, 2006).

In relation to activity more specifically, the 'activity theory' of ageing maintains that well-being in later life is enhanced by older people retaining involvement in social activities, roles and relationships (Havighurst and Albrecht, 1953). Research evidence seems to support activity theory, with numerous studies attesting to older people's efforts to remain active and engaged. However, as illustrated by the quotations cited in this section, older people do not want or benefit from just *any* activity, but from activity that is meaningful to them personally. It may be the relational dimension of activities that is significant for well-being rather than the activity in itself (Litwin and Shiovitz-Ezra, 2006). A key point is that experiences of 'meaningful activity' are very diverse and how older people define 'activity' may be very different from how activity is understood in professional or policy discourses. For example, meaningful activity for older people may include everyday activities such as reading or completing a crossword puzzle (Clarke and Warren, 2007), having a nap, watching television, drinking, gambling or having sex (Katz, 2000). It may also encompass the 'inner world' activity of thinking and reflection (Katz, 2000). Katz (2000) argues that the promotion of activity has become 'a panacea for the political woes of the declining welfare state' (p 147) and 'a disciplinary strategy of the greatest value' (p 148). Acquiring a detailed understanding of what activity means to older people is therefore an important mechanism for challenging prevailing discourses that restrict and homogenise policies and practices concerned with promoting older people's well-being.

Keeping stable

The second category within the 'keeping going' theme is 'keeping stable'. This refers to efforts to keep some stability in life, often in the face of threats brought about by illness, disability and other forms of loss. The two sub-categories of keeping stable are maintaining routines and maintaining standards.

Having routines

Other research with older people has observed that,

> Across all of the interviews – from those who spent most of their time "out and about" to those who were restricted to home and neighbourhood – lives were structured in patterns that had a daily and weekly rhythm. (Godfrey et al, 2004, p 128)

During the course of my interviews with participants, a clear sense of routine in the ways they lived their lives emerged. This applied to both daily and weekly routines, with tasks and activities performed in regular orders and according to certain patterns. Accommodated in daily routines were prescribed times for eating meals, carrying out household chores and engaging in leisure activities, while the weekly pattern included regular days for visits to clubs, shopping trips or visits from or to family or friends. This is shown in various excerpts from two interviews with Ralph:

> "They [daughters] don't do my shopping but they take me every Friday."
> "I always have a roast on Sundays, potatoes and goodness knows what."
> "I've got a friend who comes in once a fortnight."
> "I always make myself a drink about half past 10, I make it different from some people, mine's all milk.... I have six drinks during the day.... You get used to certain things, like the coffee, I make it my own way."
> "I go round to the [mobile] library, it only comes on a Tuesday once a fortnight."
> "I'll have my lunch in quarter of an hour, I have fish on Thursdays."
> "They've got a club here I go to on a Monday." (Ralph, excerpts from interviews 1 and 2)

Following established routines seemed to give a sense of structure, purpose and achievement to daily life:

> "I have my routines. Like yesterday, I went to fetch my pension and did some shopping. I came back, hoovered everywhere, did my ironing, cooked myself a lunch and then I sat here with a cup of tea." (Joyce, interview 3)

Routines such as shopping have a practical value in helping older people to keep both physically and socially active (Sidenvall et al, 2001), but also a symbolic significance, acting as a mechanism for preserving reputations for independence and continuing ability (Wenger, 1984; Seale, 1996; Sidenvall et al, 2001). At the same time, maintaining established routines is counter-balanced with the need to adapt, discussed previously. Participants worked out for themselves the necessary adaptations to their usual ways of doing things to accommodate their changing abilities and situations These new ways were learned by trial and error and the outcomes of these experiences then became incorporated into new routines for managing what needed to be done:

> "When I go to bed, I prepare my breakfast as that's when I can move better. In the morning, I just come and sit here for an hour, then by that time my joints are more relaxed and I can go upstairs and wash and dress and tidy round ... at seven o'clock I come down for an hour. I go back upstairs to get ready, tidy the bathroom, do the bed, which takes an hour and a half or more so by that time it's a quarter to nine. Then I do my chores which takes up most of the morning. I might have another cup of coffee about 11 o'clock if I've done something that's tiring like hoovering or something like that. Then I normally do some dusting. I have my lunch at 12 o'clock because I'm hungry by then. Then I have a nap for a few minutes, or a rest anyway. Sometimes I do have a nap after lunch, between one and half past. I'll do some more jobs, then have another rest between three and half past probably. At about five I sit down and I watch the headlines on the six o'clock news, then I go and get my supper. I work to a routine, I always have done.... Then in the evening, I'm always sat down, or nearly always, that's when I do my quilling or something. I keep myself busy. I go to bed between 12 and one o'clock because I know I'm not going to sleep. I find what I do works for me and I get as much done because I'm not in bed so long." (Harriet, interview 2)

The maintenance of routines is therefore important in a number of respects. It encourages physical and social activity, it facilitates processes of adaptation and it reinforces a sense of stability and continuity. Johnson and Barer's (1997) longitudinal study of the 'oldest old' found that daily routines were significant for perceptions of 'coping' and for conveying a sense of being in control. The older people adjusted their physical environments to make routines more manageable and regulated their time, creating rituals to give daily life predictability and meaning:

> Time has discrete segments that establish a rhythm to the days and a pacing of their activities. With methodical care and planning, the mundane activities can become a productive busyness that gives daily activities greater significance. (Johnson and Barer, 1997, p 156)

Keeping up standards

The second sub-category of 'keeping stable' is efforts made to maintain certain standards. This is closely related to maintaining routines since many of the routines followed by the participants are centred on keeping up standards of maintenance of the body, home or garden:

> "I can't understand people neglecting themselves, I can't, because soap and water's cheap enough isn't it?... There's no need to neglect yourself, no need at all. I shower every day, sometimes twice a day, it's all according to how I feel, if I feel like a shower, I'll go in and have a shower. But I don't understand people neglecting themselves because they're old, I just don't." (Joyce, interview 4)

Bathing was not regarded by the social services team who had assessed the study participants as 'necessary' unless there were specific hygiene or medical reasons that required bathing. This was at variance with the perspective of the older people who had been referred or referred themselves for help with getting in or out of the bath. Elsie, for example, expressed her incomprehension and dismay at being refused help with the installation of a shower:

> "I do not understand it.... Normally I like to bath every morning, now I can't and I feel dirty." (Elsie, interview 1)

Efforts to maintain standards of personal care reflect social and cultural statements about normality, coping and successful ageing (Stanley and Wise, 1993; Tulle-Winton, 1999) as well as individual meanings concerning personhood, dignity and control (Hockey and James, 1993; Twigg, 1997; Williams, 2000). Social services' restrictions on help with bathing threatened Elsie's 'coping' at personal and social levels and undermined her sense of dignity and control.

Similar points can be made about the emotional and symbolic significance of other seemingly 'functional' tasks related to maintenance of the body, such as eating 'proper meals', shopping and cooking:

> "And I do cook meals for myself. I mean a lot of people say, 'Oh, I can't be bothered to cook', oh, so many people, they get on my nerves. You can cook for yourself, it's just that they're too damn lazy to do it. I cook for myself, I cook lamb, pork, beef, chicken, you name it, I do it, and my fish, yes, I do all my cooking." (Joyce, interview 3)

The cultural significance of 'a proper meal' and its importance in both maintaining structure in the day and preserving continuity with earlier lifestyles was highlighted in a study based on older people's completion of food diaries (Dickinson, 2003). Food preparation and consumption have been linked with preserving continuity of the feminine role for women (Howarth, 1993). The purchase, planning and preparation of food has been shown to be a significant area for the preservation of self-esteem to older women in Sweden, with a loss of function in these areas linked to a loss of personhood (Sidenvall et al, 2001). However, it should not be assumed that preserving continuity in patterns of food consumption is only significant to women. The importance of cooking 'proper' meals was emphasised not just by the female participants, but also by two of the male participants for whom preparing and eating food was linked with their passion for gardening:

> "You can't beat it, your own, when you can go in the garden and pick something fresh, it's a different taste altogether." (Roger, interview 3)

Gerald also referred to the importance of having a daily cooked meal but, as he no longer cooked, this was achieved by eating out at local cafes and pubs. Whereas for Roger a 'proper meal' was associated with his lifelong interest in gardening, for Gerald it was closely connected with his social life and his need to 'get out and about'.

Maintaining standards of cleanliness within the home was another area important to some participants. This was perhaps partly influenced by generational expectations about the role of women as well as concerns about demonstrating 'coping' to others. Elsie took pride in her clean home, as shown in her diary entry:

> I have no difficulty looking after my home which I keep clean and shining. I do about half an hour's housework every day. (Elsie, diary)

She feared letting her standards slip since she saw this as having negative associations with old age:

> "I do my own housework, I like to keep a place clean. I've got a friend, she's younger than me, she's in her 70s, she's got a similar bungalow to this and it's dirty, there's cobwebs on the ceiling, there's dust over everything. It smells old and I can't bear it. I'm always frightened, I say to my daughter, does my bungalow smell old?" (Elsie, interview 4)

Different tasks were important for different individuals and it was when there was a sense of 'letting things slip' that the significance of these standards became apparent. For Harriet, seeing daily evidence of household tasks she could no longer complete was a source of reproach to her that she was not discharging her responsibilities, as well as a constant reminder of her deteriorating health and abilities. It left her feeling helpless and hopeless:

> "When you're young you don't really understand about trivial little things older people can't cope with, like dusting the tops of the doors and things like that and there are pictures on the landing, every time I

walk downstairs I look at the layer of dust on the top and I just can't reach them.... You can live with it for a certain time but there are things that need doing. I mean all my cupboards need doing, they need cleaning and I just can't do it. It's not hygienic. Like moving out the fridge and the spin dryer and things like that and cleaning underneath them; things do drop on the floor, if you spill milk or something, it runs underneath and turns sour. These jobs need doing and they're jobs I can't do. I have done them up until now but I daren't do them now." (Harriet, interview 1)

She expressed her disagreement with social services' policy of only providing help with personal care rather than domestic help. She argued that poor standards of cleanliness could create physical risks and could also lead to older people, in their concern to maintain standards, putting their own welfare in jeopardy:

" ... how many elderly people have fallen trying to do things to keep things clean, and fallen off chairs and stools and steps and all sorts of things?... It would worry me to death. I would have to keep on trying to do them and would probably have another fall and end up in hospital. I mean there must be thousands of elderly people who've died trying to look after themselves and do jobs that they know they shouldn't do." (Harriet, interview 3)

This indicates that not maintaining certain standards may be associated not just with the psychological risk of lowered morale and diminished perceptions of 'coping', but also at a practical level with specific physical risks.

'Keeping things clean' and 'keeping things like you used to' were noted to be important for older people who were receiving home care (Raynes et al, 2001, p 28), and this was corroborated by the concerns expressed by participants in my study. One of Patricia's biggest worries was that she could no longer maintain her standards of cleanliness in her flat:

"It was terrible, and of course everything, the kitchen especially, you know the walls and everything, you've got to keep the kitchen tidy, and that worried me because I love a clean kitchen. It's the most essential part, and the bathroom I think." (Patricia, interview 3)

In the first interview, she became tearful when talking about no longer being able to keep her kitchen clean. As she pointed out, the importance of these issues is magnified when increasing disability means that a greater proportion of time is spent within the confines of the house. In these circumstances, objects and spaces can acquire increased significance (Peace, 1998).

The ability to maintain standards in terms of upkeep of the garden was another area holding both practical and symbolic significance for some participants. As already mentioned, this was partly associated with the role of the garden in producing nutritious food but, like maintenance of the body and home, the garden served as an important signal of continued coping for some participants:

> "[Keeping up with the garden] means everything to me. Yes, if I couldn't get out in my garden, well, I mean I know, I had nearly 18 months. I used to get out on my crutches but it only used to depress me more to see it all grown over." (Roger, interview 4)

These extracts demonstrate that being able to fulfil personal and social expectations in terms of standards of care of the body, home and garden, in accordance with individual priorities, has a wider resonance than the mere practical and functional performance of the task. This is confirmed in other research (Bury and Holme, 1991). From qualitative interviews with older people, Percival (2002) noted the connection between the upkeep of domestic spaces and the maintenance of self-esteem and self-determination. These cognitive dimensions of coping are considered further in the next chapter.

Keeping stable: summary

Having routines and keeping up standards are related to older people's need to preserve self and social perceptions of 'managing' and 'independence'. Maintaining normal routines and standards is an indicator to self and others that you are 'keeping going'. As Raynes et al's (2001) study of older people receiving home care observed,

> It appears as if the older people wish to control their immediate environment and ensure that it is kept the way it was. The care of their home is a reflection of them and their pride in who they are; it is also what they see each day. (p 29)

Maintaining standards and routines helps to preserve continuity with previous lifestyles and identities. Continuity is compatible with some degree of change, as older people make adjustments and compromises in ways that enable them to retain links with past practices and values. Again, this is consistent with psychological models of ageing based on the view that when individuals are not able to change the situation, they are resourceful in adapting their goals and values to be compatible with the situation (Brandtstädter and Greve, 1994). If maintaining routines and standards has such significance for psychological as well as physical dimensions of coping, this also makes sense of older people's determination in respect of 'pushing yourself', discussed previously. However, this section has also shown that routines and standards are not static, but evolve in response to changing needs and circumstances in such a way that both coping and continuity are felt and seen to be maintained.

Keeping balance

The third category within the theme of "keeping going" is 'keeping balance'. This is defined by efforts to maintain an acceptable balance between giving and receiving within relationships. The two related sub-categories are concerned with maintaining boundaries in relationships and maintaining reciprocity.

Not putting on others

As noted in Chapter Two, many older people are concerned about being a 'burden' on their families. Without exception, the participants who received support from family and friends in this study perceived that there were boundaries to the seeking and receiving of help from others, and they expressed concern about transgressing these. There were a number of relevant factors. First, participants were aware that some potential helpers were contending with their own problems and they were wary of adding to this 'load'. For example, Joyce judged the help it was acceptable to receive from her daughter in terms of her understanding of the difficulties inherent in her daughter's own situation:

> "Then you see my daughter and son-in-law, they both work and he gets called out at night … then he still has to be at work at the same time as if he hadn't been up all night, you know. He gets very tired, he works very hard…. And then you see they live about a mile and a half out of town…. Jane [daughter] … has to walk into work. And when you've been stood in a shop all day and then you've got to turn round and walk all the way back home and cook a meal and what have you, it's hard going. So I don't put on either of them, you know, I think they've got enough to do." (Joyce, interview 4)

Extracts from interviews with Joyce, discussed earlier in relation to 'pushing yourself', show that she was willing to accept help from her daughter, but only with tasks that she saw as essential and was unable to complete herself. The further qualification about when help is seen to be acceptable, illustrated here, is that the help giving must not place undue demands on the helper. Thus concerns about maintaining boundaries are not just about preserving equity in relationships, but also prompted by anxieties about the welfare of others in the caring network. One study found that married care receivers were particularly likely to worry about the health of their carer (McCann and Evans, 2002). This was illustrated in this study by Patricia, who became tearful when voicing her concern about the implications for her husband's health of his assuming what she perceived to be her domestic responsibilities.

There was a clear sense among participants of not wanting to transgress their perceptions of acceptable boundaries in relationships as this would be interpreted as indicating dependence. Where these boundaries were located varied according to participants' individual perceptions of what was acceptable, and this in turn was influenced by how they perceived the relationship. It was also mediated by their own self-perceptions of independence, as illustrated in Barbara's diary entries. She sustained a wrist fracture following a fall while shopping and she recorded in her diary how she negotiated the difficulties this presented for her. This conveyed the conflict she experienced between her need for help from her daughter, her awareness of her daughter's difficulties (her daughter had recently experienced a period of depression) and her desire to maintain a sense of independence:

> Marion [daughter] came to help me at the weekend. It helped very much but I felt I was asking too much although she said she didn't mind and would do it willingly. It helped enormously but I am trying to be independent. (Barbara, diary)

Similarly, Roger saw asking for help as encroaching on his sense of independence:

> "I mean, I've had lots of people say, if you want anything, give me a ring but I don't like ringing people, I like to cope as long as I can." (Roger, interview 3)

On the other hand, some help from certain individuals was perceived as acceptable and Roger spoke in matter-of-fact terms about his daughter taking him shopping, to the doctor's and to hospital appointments. However, even here there were boundaries in terms of types of help he would not accept:

> "She [daughter] knows I won't go to stay with her. I wouldn't put on anybody. If I go at Christmas, I only just stay the one night and come back Boxing Day. But she has the dogs when I go on holiday." (Roger, interview 5)

Phillipson et al (2001) found that although children formed the 'emotional core' within the networks of older people, the older people retained a sense of limits in terms of the amount and type of help perceived as acceptable. Thus, the giving and receiving of help is underpinned by normative expectations (Qureshi, 1996) and gender differences may play a part here. One study reported that men were more likely to rely on support from their immediate families while women were more likely to access support outside the family (Lee and Brennan, 2002).

Concern about overstepping helping boundaries was not confined to family members. Harriet expressed her reluctance to ask any of her neighbours for help because of her sensitivity to the demands of their own situations:

> "My neighbours next door are my age so I would hesitate to call on them if anything happened to me because they are about my age, in fact the husband and I are exactly the same age.… If there was an

emergency in the night or anything like that, I would be very reluctant. And the young couple next door are new neighbours…. In any case, they have a young family so I would hesitate to call on them, although I'm sure they'd be very helpful." (Harriet, interview 1)

She saw being independent as 'not needing to call on anyone, other than paid help', and she described her difficulty in asking for help:

" … it's very hard for me, very hard. I feel a nuisance. I feel like I'm eternally apologising for being a nuisance, for saying can you do this for me, will you do that." (Harriet, interview 1)

There was a sense of not wanting to impose psychological as well as practical burdens on others, in particular, not causing other people worry or anxiety. Here, too, there were boundaries to be preserved. Joyce described her efforts to conceal from her friends the extent of her physical pain and discomfort:

"Well, they've got their own worries and troubles, you know. They know my situation, and they're there if I want them, but they've got their own families, worries and troubles, so why should I put it onto them?" (Joyce, interview 1)

Concern about the psychological burden placed on other people could act as a restraint on risk taking, influencing participants to act contrary to their own more risk-oriented inclinations:

"There are certain jobs I just wouldn't attempt. I mean all my cupboards need doing, they need cleaning and I can't do it…. I have done them up until now but I daren't do them now. If it [blackout] happens again, it isn't fair to other people who have to, it isn't fair to my son and daughter, who feel responsible for me but can't do anything really to help me, it isn't fair to other people." (Harriet, interview 1)

In some instances there was clearly some tension between the 'keeping active' strands of 'pushing yourself' and finding solutions and the 'maintaining balance' concern with not imposing practically or psychologically on others. Harriet went on to say:

"I feel it isn't fair to the family to take risks. I try to be very very careful but things need to be done that I've always done. The first thing they [hospital staff] said, 'Don't ever attempt to stand on a stool or steps or a chair or anything like that'. I mean, I'm used to standing on steps to do things, I'm not very tall … so it's cut out so many things I've always done." (Harriet, interview 1)

Putting a little bit back

Contrary to popular and policy conceptions of older people as primarily recipients of services, discussed in Chapter Two, the interview and diary data highlighted the extent of activity that can be categorised as 'giving' among the participants. This included their contributions within the context of relationships with their family, friends and wider communities.

Giving to others sometimes took place in the context of directly reciprocal relationships. Elsie had an agreement with a neighbour that he would tend her vegetable plot and mow her lawn in return for keeping most of the produce from the garden. She and her daughter had a similar directly reciprocal agreement about washing and ironing:

> "Well, ever since I moved, let's see, 31 years ago, I left my home and went into a flat and I had trouble with the washer.... So I said to Mary [daughter], 'Well, I can't have the washing machine and that's that'. And she said, 'Well I'll tell you what, I'll make a bargain with you, you do my ironing and I'll do your big washing'. So she does my sheets, pillowcases, towels, duvet covers, tea towels and that's it. And I do all my own underwear and small things. And that's the bargain. She does my washing and I do her ironing." (Elsie, interview 5)

Thus, 31 years later and at the age of 94 (at the time of the final research interview), Elsie still maintained her side of the bargain. In this way, established reciprocal relationships support 'keeping stable' as well as 'keeping balance'. 'Keeping busy' is also relevant to maintaining reciprocity in that the products of keeping busy are often given to others. Elsie, for example, gave people pots of jam, Ralph gave cakes or plant cuttings, Roger gave away fruit and vegetables from his garden and David gave sketches and paintings.

Other giving was less directly reciprocal but based on more general feelings of wanting to help out family and friends who either gave now, or had given previously, different forms of help to participants. Elsie, for example, received various forms of practical help from her daughter and grandchildren and she regularly babysat her many great-grandchildren. Patricia's daughter visited weekly and performed various 'odd jobs' while Patricia and her husband 'dog-sat' for their daughter, staying at her house and looking after the house and pets while she was on holiday. Roger had purchased a wheelchair from the Red Cross when his wife (now deceased) was ill and he now loaned this out to people in the village:

> "I think I told you before about the wheelchair I bought, well, that's been out twice before, now I've just loaned it out to another person down the village who's wife's got ulcerated legs and so it's come to good use.... It's surprising how people want these things and I know I had the trouble with my wife, I couldn't get one for her you see,

when she was ill, and I couldn't get one for myself till the Red Cross helped out … it's wonderful to be able to help people to get about because I know what I went through." (Roger, interview 3)

The husband of the person who borrowed the wheelchair gave Roger lifts to the over-60s club meetings once a fortnight. Patricia and her husband collected an elderly widowed friend once a week and took her shopping with them. This was done in the spirit of 'helping out a friend' who was now widowed and without transport and seen as less fortunate than them. Barbara and another woman who lived in the same sheltered housing complex took turns at entertaining each other with morning coffee every day. Barbara, who still drove, also gave this friend a lift to the shops once a week. These examples support the view that much help giving and receiving is negotiated within the context of relationships over time rather than arising from a sense of duty or obligation to ensure they are directly reciprocal (Nocon and Pearson, 2000). As Burnette (1994) concludes from her study of older people's management of long-term illness, 'Informal supports in late life often represent invested ties between people who have nurtured a sense of mutuality in their shared lives' (p 22).

As well as giving to particular individuals, participants were also involved in more general help giving within their communities. Roger, along with others in his village, opened his garden to the public every year to raise money for different charities. Patricia knitted clothes for a special care baby unit while both Alice and Harriet donated their craft work to local charitable sales and coffee mornings:

> "They're all for good causes, the coffee mornings, you know. I take some of the work I've been doing for the bring-and-buy so, you know, I try and put a little bit back into the community. Well, now that I can't actively help anyone physically, you know." (Harriet, interview 2)

For some participants, namely, Elsie and Alice, giving was associated with religious activity. As part of this, Alice volunteered her services as church treasurer while Elsie had until recently helped to deliver church magazines and give guided talks to visitors to her village church. In these examples, giving was associated with a sense of contributing to the wider community.

Even when older people are not in a position to give practical assistance to others, they may be able to offer emotional or psychological support. Alice experienced a number of different illnesses and increasing restrictions on her mobility, but her comments illustrate that reciprocity may take expressive rather than instrumental forms (see also Wenger, 1984; Phillips et al, 2000; Phillipson et al, 2001), and that perceptions of giving can be sustained even in objectively adverse circumstances (Burnette, 1994; Nolan et al, 1996). Alice's diary referred to telephone calls with ill relatives and an elderly friend:

I have rung as often as possible and tried to give advice and let Cheryl [niece who cares for her 99-year-old mother who has dementia] talk as long as she wanted – which seems to help her. I also ring an old lady near to me and listen to all her health and other troubles and that relieves the tension. Talking to others seems to help both them and me. (Alice, diary)

In this way, even older people with low levels of mobility or who are physically frail can experience being of value to others. For example, older volunteers who staff a telephone help line for isolated older people report benefits from their involvement, feeling that they are using their skills and helping others (O'Shea, 2006).

Many studies confirm the significance of perceptions of equity and reciprocity and being able to support others for feelings of self-esteem and independence (Bury and Holme, 1991; Finch and Mason, 1993; Pratt and Norris, 1994; Langan et al, 1996), and it is suggested that this may be as significant for positive experiences of old age as keeping active (Nilsson et al, 1998). Conversely, self-perceptions of dependency appear to be related to feelings of having nothing of value to exchange in relationships (Wilkin, 1990). The significance of being able to see oneself as a giver, rather than, or as well as, a receiver, becomes particularly apparent when this is lost or threatened. At the time of my first interview with Harriet, she had just had to relinquish driving because of blackouts and had sold her car. She experienced this as a major threat to her independence, not least because she was now suddenly recast in the role of recipient of help and favours:

"I do feel that I have lost my independence to a great extent. Although as I've said, friends have been very kind and if I ask anybody, they'll take me but I feel a nuisance because I'm the one that's always done the running about and always given other people lifts and taken people everywhere, and now it's not like that and it was very sudden." (Harriet, interview 1)

However, it is possible for notions of reciprocity to be renegotiated and reinterpreted in the light of changing abilities and circumstances, as considered in the next chapter.

The perception of reciprocity would seem to be more important than the 'facts' of helping, and there was evidence in this study that reciprocity has to be carefully managed to preserve the self-esteem of all parties. Les referred to the help he gave to some of his older neighbours living within the housing complex, where helping relationships appeared to feature 'covert' reciprocity:

"Some of the widows here ask me if they need anything doing, like if they want a light bulb changed or the sink is blocked....There is one lady who can't read English well and she asks me to come over if she has any correspondence she can't understand and I explain it to her. Then, a day or two later, she will phone and ask me to go over and she will say 'I was cooking and had some left over, here you are', and I say 'right, thank you'. She always has some left over! Another one, I helped her when the water was overflowing and she was flooded. She came round the next day with something she had bought too many of and would I like one." (Les, interview 1)

This illustrates the interconnection of the material and moral dimensions of help giving and receiving highlighted by Finch and Mason (1993), and the significance of the way these aspects of relationships are worked out between parties:

> … through negotiations about giving and receiving assistance, people are being constructed and reconstructed as moral beings.… A person's identity or reputation gets confirmed or modified as a result of the way in which they conduct themselves on each occasion. (Finch and Mason, 1993, p 170)

This has been affirmed in research with older people in New Zealand, for example. Discourses of reciprocity were seen as reconciling tensions between older people's desire to be independent on the one hand, but socially connected on the other:

> The notion of reciprocity allowed them to describe social connections that were without dependency.… Reciprocity understood as an equivalence of giving and receiving offers older people a clear rejection of the position of dependency through the maintenance of equal relationships. (Breheny and Stephens, 2009, p 1308)

However, Johnson and Barer's research on the 'oldest old' found that few among this group of older people were able to sustain reciprocal social relationships, expressing views such as, 'How can I help others when I can barely take care of myself?' (Johnson and Barer, 1997, p 40). This suggests that what is expected of oneself in terms of reciprocity is mediated by judgements about what is reasonable in terms of individual abilities and situations.

Giving up

These aspects of "keeping going" – keeping busy, keeping stable and keeping balance in relationships – seem to be fundamental to perceptions of managing. Not managing, on the other hand, is seen as 'giving up', and this is what participants were working hard to avoid. Roger had experienced several heart attacks and was waiting for a heart valve operation. He expressed his determination to keep on with his normal daily life and routines:

"I'm not going to give up, I'm not going to give up. When my time comes that's different but until then, I'm not going to give up." (Roger, interview 4)

Where interview and diary data appeared to be discrepant with the categories within "keeping going", I looked carefully at the nature of the discrepancies. From this it seemed that those individuals who were not "keeping going" in terms of the categories outlined did not perceive themselves as managing. 'Giving up' represents the opposite dimensions of "keeping going", that is, not keeping busy, disruption of previous habits and routines and infringement of perceptions of acceptability in terms of boundaries and balance in relationships. This was shown by Roger's reflections in the third interview on his situation at the time I first visited him. He was then awaiting a knee replacement operation, could only hobble on crutches and was unable to tend his beloved garden. By the third interview, his operation had been successfully completed and he was mobile again:

"Do you know, this time last year, I sat here and I thought, well, I'm never going to get out again, I'm never going to do my garden, and I felt so down, and I was just giving up, you know, and then I thought to myself, well it's only another couple of months before I have my operation, you know, and that's what kept me going, but I never thought I'd come back like this.... I used to sit and watch the garden get overgrown, you know, it was terrible.... When you sit here for hours on end and can't do anything, it's terrible. But that's behind me now." (Roger, interview 3)

This illustrates that where the situation is perceived as temporary and there is still hope for "keeping going" in the future, the effects can be mitigated, as discussed later in relation to psychological strategies. For another participant, Winifred, her loss of speech, for which no medical explanation had been found, and general physical deterioration signified failure of all three dimensions of "keeping going". She had to relinquish her large house and garden for a small flat with no garden, thus undermining her primary sources of both activity and stability. Equally, her inability to communicate and physical frailty meant that she became increasingly reliant on friends (she had no family) to do things for her. In this way, the 'theory' about the crucial importance of the dimensions of 'keeping going' to managing in later life is corroborated through the significance of their absence in not managing. These and other aspects of 'giving up' are considered further in Chapter Six.

Conclusion

This chapter has presented both descriptive and analytical data, addressing the questions of 'what is going on here' and 'what can be learned from this experience' in relation to the category of "keeping going". This is an appropriate term not only because participants frequently used it, but also because it reflects their resourcefulness, resilience and high levels of activity. It embodies the dynamic between preserving continuity ('keeping') and pressures to change ('going'); it implies movement as well as stasis. Whether concerning strategies for preserving stability or strategies to manage change, what the sub-categories subsumed within the category of "keeping going" have in common is that they are 'doing' strategies, involving some form of physical activity on the part of participants. They reflect the effort involved in 'managing', as also highlighted in other research:

> One of the facets of ageing described by older people was increasing awareness of mind and body. They "worked at" keeping well. Moreover, the language used – "pushing yourself", "not letting yourself go", "not giving up" – expressed the hard work involved. (Godfrey et al, 2004, p 102)

The next chapter, structured around the 'staying me' theme, discusses other primarily cognitive or existential strategies revealed in the accounts of participants. These also convey the dynamic between continuity and change. The distinction between physical ('doing') and cognitive psychological ('being') strategies is for the purposes of clarification and explanation and not a suggestion that the two function as separate entities. It will be apparent that even the "keeping going" strategies discussed so far reflect dimensions of both 'doing' and 'being'. For example, I have discussed how busyness is sustained by beliefs about the value of activity and its perceived relationship to maintaining a status as independent. Similarly, it has already been shown that participants' efforts to preserve boundaries in their relationships are governed by their beliefs about what it is acceptable to give and receive in different relationships and in particular circumstances, all of this again being closely related to beliefs about independence. This interrelationship between 'doing' and 'being' is highlighted in research by Maynard et al on quality of life with older women from different minority ethnic groups in the north of England. The authors note:

> Through physical activity these women resist aches and pains and changes to the physical capability of their bodies as they age. Physical activity also provides women with opportunities to move and exert their bodies and act out social identities. In this respect the women ... are not simply resisting changes to the physicality of their bodies. They are also constructing and renewing identities that generate feelings of agency. In this body and self are closely entwined so that the acts of "doing" and "being" become inseparable. (Maynard et al, 2008, pp 111-12)

While acknowledging the inseparability of action and identity, in the next chapter I explore ways of managing the ageing experience that primarily concern 'self' and 'being'.

FOUR

'Staying me'

> ... if the intention is to understand the causes, connections and consequences of power processes, we have to look very closely at the everyday lives of the actors, explore the small, ordinary issues that take place within different contexts and show how compliance, adaptation but also resistance and open struggle are generated. In this endeavour, we shall find no strong visible manifestations of power. Rather we have to look for small flashes of command that may peek out from behind the screens. (Villarreal, 1992, p 258)

While the previous chapter addressed the 'doing' strategies employed by older people, this chapter focuses on their cognitive ways of coping. The chapter title, 'staying me', refers to older people's efforts to retain a sense of continuity between their past, present and anticipated future lives, and to sustain a sense of self, often in the face of situations that threaten to disrupt continuity and undermine a positive self-concept. The 'staying me' theme encompasses two categories, continuity and self-affirmation. Given the concern with cognitive rather than practical ways of managing, there is more scope for researcher interpretation of meaning, as discussed further in Chapter Seven. The title of the 'staying me' theme and some sub-themes in this chapter reflect my interpretations, rather than necessarily the words of participants. While this chapter is informed by and structured in line with the grounded theory approach outlined in Chapter One, the analysis is further developed and enriched by reading the transcripts and diaries as narrative 'wholes'. As in the previous chapter, findings from the study are interwoven with other research findings and theoretical material.

Continuity

The previous chapter explored ways in which participants strove to maintain a sense of continuity through 'doing', for example, by keeping up their usual routines and by maintaining standards of care of the body, home and garden. According to Atchley's (1989) 'continuity theory', older people attempt to preserve continuity both in terms of circumstances and behaviour (external continuity) and also in ways of thinking and perceiving (internal continuity). Although Atchley sees identity as relatively fixed across social situations, he also allows for processes of reinterpretation as new information and experiences are incorporated within an individual's identity:

> Reinterpretation is an important adaptive process through which individuals create coherent pictures of the past and link the past to a purposeful, integrated present. Identity evolution is thus an active, cumulative and life-long process of restructuring ideas to fit current realities. (Atchley, 1989, p 187)

In contrast, postmodern theories of ageing emphasise the fluidity and multiplicity of identity as individuals are free to choose and construct their identities through consumerism (Gilleard, 1996). Discussion of how these different theoretical perspectives inform understanding of how older people manage the experience of ageing is developed in Chapter Six. In relation to this part of the chapter, a key point is that as well as seeking to maintain continuity through practical activities, it seemed that participants also preserved a sense of continuity by making connections between their past and present situations and experiences. This was not so much about things they did, but about ways of thinking and perceiving that helped to maintain a sense of coherence between the past and present. Different dimensions of continuity are depicted in the four sub-categories of life themes, attitudes and values ('not going against the grain'), relationships and home.

Life themes

A lifecourse approach to ageing draws attention to the connections in experience across an individual's lifetime (Arber and Evandrou, 1993). Life themes act as building blocks for identity and are used by individuals to attribute meaning and purpose to their lives (Atchley, 1989). Some of these connections were explicit within the participants' accounts and identified in coding of the text; others were implicit and highlighted by detecting patterns and themes across the transcripts read as integrated narratives.

A life theme of privacy, encompassing concepts of self-reliance and independence, can be seen within Winifred's life story. Winifred could not speak (this was subject to medical investigation) so she communicated with me by written notes and by asking a close friend to talk on her behalf. What follows is therefore largely the friend's interpretation of Winifred's life history, rather than her own first-hand account. Themes of privacy and independence emerged strongly from this, both as a lifelong pattern and a factor relevant in understanding her response to her current situation. Winifred's mother had died when she was a baby and her father made an unofficial arrangement for her to be brought up by a couple she called aunt and uncle. However, these people were abusive toward her, dominating her life and allowing her no freedom. She lived with them until they died, at which point she inherited their house. As a result of these experiences, she was fiercely protective of her own independence and privacy:

> "She was always very independent, very very independent. She has a privacy about her that stems from childhood, she didn't have a very

good childhood and I think that has all tended to make her like she is, that independence. She never really, up to the last 25 years, had anything to call her own, she'd always been dominated by other people, so when she got her independence, she treasured it.... She would really fight, really fight, if she was going to lose her independence or if she thought she might have to go into warden-controlled, somebody else is controlling her life, because she's fought that over the last 25 years and she doesn't want her life controlled." (friend of Winifred, interview 1)

Winifred was now losing her vision and unable to speak. She had no family, only a few friends, and had reached the point where she felt she needed formal help. Her written notes stated that she wanted someone to call in on her once or twice a day to check she was all right. Social services had told her this was not possible unless she needed specific help, such as personal care. Winifred's desire to maintain her privacy and sense of control over her situation made her averse to any help that felt intrusive, including assessment processes that invaded her privacy and home carers giving help she did not want or feel she needed. Equally, she was loath to ask her friends for help unless she was desperate and there was no alternative.

"She just needed to know there was somebody looking after her, and that she wasn't really relying on her friends, when she knows we're all, not busy, but we've all got our own lives to lead." (friend of Winifred, interview 1)

These views and behaviours make sense when set within the context of Winifred's life history and the strategies for living that she had developed in response. When contacting social services, she was seeking support to maintain her privacy and sense of control over her life. It is possible that in the light of her early family experiences, she perceived professional help as posing less risk to her privacy and independence than help from friends. However, the help she sought was not forthcoming as it did not fit with social services' interpretation of 'need'.

A life theme for Alice was being part of an active social network. She had been brought up in a village community where her family had lived for many years and had many friends and acquaintances. In her married life, the theme of engaging in many and varied relationships continued with her involvement in her husband's activities as a headteacher:

"It's marvellous because my husband was retired nine years and, as I say, it's 19 years since he died and I still hear from all his staff and some of the pupils." (Alice, interview 3)

She saw wider connections between the way she lived her life now and the shape of her married life with her husband:

"I still miss him, it seems strange really because life is quite different, it's never the same, but you just have to make the best of what you've got and sort of make a new life for yourself. But the influence is still there, you know. I mean I lead a disciplined life, even though I'm slow, as long as I get plenty of notice I'm never late and that's him, he used to go mad if he was late. Yes, yes, it's surprising really, the influence doesn't die at all, it's still there after all those years." (Alice, interview 3)

Alice's social activities included involvement in the Women's Institute, attending meetings related to her role as treasurer for the local church and helping to run a weekly 'shop' at a local nursing home. All of these activities helped her to create and sustain social relationships. Although her disability and illnesses restricted the amount she was able to go out socially, she managed to maintain her social life by letter and telephone. This ability to maintain longstanding and multiple relationships provided an historical link, not only with her husband, but also with her biological family. She saw the commitment to sustaining friendships as a family trait, shared with her mother and brother. Her mother had been to Canada in her teens and met a friend with whom she corresponded regularly until she died at the age of 90, and Alice commented, "I'm just the same". Similarly, holidays away were a significant part of her life with her husband and, despite the difficulties imposed by her severe arthritis and incontinence, she showed considerable determination in continuing to arrange holidays for herself. She had been on the same holiday every year for 30 years and derived particular satisfaction from the fact she was 'still able to keep it up'.

One of the major concerns about being refused home care expressed by Alice in the first interview was that she was finding it difficult to maintain her social life. Because she had to do things very slowly, she could not be ready in time to go out for certain activities, such as attending church. Equally, she was reluctant to invite people back to her house when this would expose her inability to keep the house clean. By the final interview, Alice was receiving home care. The greatest value of this for her seemed to be not so much the practical help as the way this served to extend her social relationships at a time when her ability to go out was declining:

"At first I was a bit, well, I kept getting different ones [home carers].... It was a bit difficult to get used to them, you know, they're getting used to you and you're getting used to them. I think I've had 21 different ones up to now and I can quite honestly say there's not one of them that I've thought, I don't like you, I don't want you. They are all ages, all kind to you; all different but they are all so kind.... And it isn't that they just do the job. They take a real interest in you and nearly always ask, 'What are you doing today? Got anything on this week?' and they remember and ask how you've got on. And that's lovely because that's what you miss when you haven't got anybody to talk to regularly, you know. Yes, they're great." (Alice, interview 5)

By providing help with personal care, the home carers not only enabled Alice to get out to her social activities but also, at the same time, became part of her social network. They showed an interest in her life, while also involving her in their lives, by talking to her about their families, interests and activities. In this way, the service they provided supported an ongoing life theme of social activity and relationships.

As well as examples of continuity of life themes, there were also examples of discontinuity, defined by Atchley (1989) as involving 'change seen by the individual as sharply diminishing her or his capacity for coherence in some aspect of his or her identity' (p 187). A life theme for Gerald, perhaps associated with key components of a masculine identity, was success and being in control, not just of his own life, as with Winifred, but also exerting control or influence over others. He had been self-employed all of his working life and took pride in the fact that he had never worked for anyone except himself, building his profitable businesses up from scratch:

"I've been retired 33 years. Never had a job [working for others] in my life. I've only ever worked for me. The idea of me working for somebody else and making them profit makes me shudder. When I managed to I bought a couple of motors and started from there and I never had any trouble at all.... I retired with 11 businesses. I was chairman and managing director seven times if I remember correctly." (Gerald, interview 3)

He spoke of the success of his businesses, also of his own business acumen in knowing when to buy and when to sell. His success had given him financial power, and also the means of directing others. In dealing with difficulties in later life, he sought to employ these skills and resources. For example, when seeking to address his hearing impairment, he contacted various companies to supply him with information about their products and he then used his private resources to buy what he decided would be the most appropriate equipment. When he sold his bungalow and moved into a sheltered flat and, later, when he exchanged his car for a smaller model, Gerald proceeded in a planned and orderly way, researching the options, considering costs and benefits and then making his decision. Gerald came to be included in the study because he had approached social services to find out what help would be available to him if in the future he needed it. He applied his managerial experience to his attempts to deal with personal difficulties, seeking to take control of the situation by anticipating problems, weighing up the options and then taking action. This theme of being in charge featured throughout his interview accounts. When these tactics did not yield the results he wanted in terms of enabling him to discover the information he needed or obtain the services he required, Gerald's sense of 'coping' was undermined. There was a stark contrast between the language of being in charge and successful when he spoke of his life up to that point and the language of being powerless and vulnerable when he sustained a leg injury:

> "I had no trouble at all. I was perfectly all right until I was 82 and then everything fell apart.... I don't quite know what to do. I'm just sitting here working it out. I don't know what to do.... I don't know quite what to do, to be honest because in a minute I'm going to need help and I don't know which way round to go.... My leg had got bad and I'm in real trouble, I can't even do any shopping, although it's only over the road.... The point is, what do people do who can't get out?" (Gerald, interview 3)

David's situation provides another example of discontinuity in life themes. He had moved from Scotland to a privately rented sheltered flat in the West Midlands to be near his daughter. The move had been instigated and arranged by his family, who were concerned about his increasing frailty, and his son was paying half of the rent on the property. The flat was in the town centre so it was convenient for David to do his own shopping and access public transport. His daughter visited often to help with domestic tasks and the on-site warden provided ongoing monitoring and support. However, attention to the detail of David's narrative highlighted the theme of loss of freedom. He used to be a postman and was used to "being out and about". He said he felt "cooped up" in his flat and bothered by the roar of the traffic outside the window; he felt "hemmed in" by the tall buildings that meant he could not see any expanse of sky from his window. He found the pre-set heating in the flat too warm, making him feel "stifled"; the secure entry system and "concierge at the door" made him feel "watched" every time he went in and out. Equally, he felt "cosseted" by his daughter. He was aware of not wanting to cause her anxiety but at the same time this meant thwarting his own inclination to get out of the flat as much as possible, go for long walks and, above all, to be geographically mobile, moving house frequently, as he had in earlier stages in his life:

> "Sometimes I'm full of energy for things but then I sink down and can't seem to finish anything. I get like this. Perhaps it's because I'm not happy in the flat.... I always want to move on after I've been in a place for three or four years. My daughter, she thinks I'm too old to be moving, she thinks I'm not capable and shouldn't be moving. But I like to dream." (David, interview 2)

These examples illustrate the significance of attending to lifelong themes. Experiences of ageing have to be understood in the context of the whole lifecourse since 'the life lived gives meaning to old age' (Ruth and Oberg, 1996, p 186).

Giddens (1999) locates the source of individual identity in, 'the capaci[ty] a particular narrative going'. He goes on to argue, 'The individual's ... must continually integrate events which occur in the external worl[d] them into the ongoing "story" about the self' (Giddens, 1999, p 54). to prevailing 'stories' is important for understanding an individual's bi~~ography~~ a general level, but also specifically for understanding the significance of certain difficulties and preferred strategies for managing them. Where key life themes are substantially disrupted, there are implications for how participants perceive themselves and their ability to manage everyday life. At the same time, these life themes also reveal particular social and cultural discourses, perhaps linked with gender. For example, in the examples described here, beliefs about the virtues of independence, the significance of family and social relationships, particularly perhaps for women, and the association of a masculine identity with assertion and control are indicated. I return to these issues in Chapter Six when discussing wider meanings of participant narratives and mechanisms for 'sustaining the self'.

'Not going against the grain'

This sub-category refers to persistent attitudes and values that appear significant to understanding ways participants sought to manage difficulties and their approach to seeking and receiving help. Baldock and Ungerson (1994) used the term 'habits of the heart' in their study of how people recovering from stroke reacted to the prospect of becoming consumers of community care. They found that the likelihood of participation on the basis of consumerism was influenced by deeply embedded values and assumptions underpinning how people lived their daily lives. 'Not going against the grain' refers to similar entrenched attitudes and values demonstrated by participants.

While independence might be taken as a general life theme for Roger, he revealed particular beliefs and attitudes towards financial independence that had direct implications for his behaviour in respect of receiving help. His perception of financial self-reliance as an indicator of independence is demonstrated throughout his interview accounts:

> "I can cope. I mean I haven't got any savings or things like that but I can keep going. I've got enough to keep going and I've always paid my bills as they come in. I've never owed anybody a penny in my life. I've never had anything on hire purchase, I wouldn't have it. I wouldn't have a credit card for love nor money. No, everything's straight; if I can't pay for anything, I won't have it." (Roger, interview 3)

This sense of paying what was owed and not being beholden underpinned his behaviour when seeking and receiving help. He was reluctant to accept help unless he perceived it as essential and even then, he liked to feel he was 'paying his way'. On his discharge from hospital, he sought to repay the care he had received:

"Every time I go in hospital, you know, I always give them a good donation for the nurses because they have a nurses' fund and they appreciate that." (Roger, interview 4)

He sought to maintain a sense of equity through financial reimbursement in his interactions with people who provided a service for him:

"If I've got any little jobs in the garden, I say to Dee's lad [neighbour], I say, 'Do you want to come and do a little job for me?' and he comes and does it and I give him a pound or two and he's thrilled to bits you see. And that's the way to get on. The same with the postman and the dustman and everybody like that. I always give them a tip at Christmas." (Roger, interview 4)

His approach was based on only asking for help from others when essential and, even then, ensuring that he reimbursed the person concerned, usually financially:

"I don't cry out for help, you know. All my life I've been the same. Even nursing my wife for three years before she died, I didn't call out for help until the last, it was only the last few weeks, well, two or three months that I had a bit of help.... Oh yes, I like to be independent. My daughter says, 'You're too independent', and I say, 'No, that's the way I like it'. I don't want to put on anybody at all, and anybody who comes and does anything for me, I pay them something." (Roger, interview 2)

Alice's sense of independence was rooted in managing without help from family. Her sister lived in the adjoining property but they liked to keep independent of each other as much as they could. Alice had one daughter whose husband was very ill so she was careful never to make demands on her daughter. Her sister next door had three sons who were frequent visitors but she was loath to ask them to do anything, believing, "it's better to deal with things outside the family". Harriet shared this preference for not asking family or friends for help:

Harriet: "I find it very difficult to ask anyone to do anything actually, unless it's on a paying basis.... I do want to be independent."

Interviewer: "What does being independent mean to you?"

Harriet: "Well, not needing to call on anyone, other than paid help." (interview 1)

Like Alice, she had the financial resources to enable her to pay for private help, although this could not always be found, as shown in the next chapter. As well as retaining a sense of independence through paying for help, Harriet also highlighted the importance of not being in the position of having to ask for it:

> "I still don't like asking [for help]. I wait until someone volunteers. I don't like asking. It goes very much against the grain. Always having been so independent, you know, always helping other people, you know, I hate to be on the other end of the stick, sort of thing.... I would rather pay for the help than have to ask friends." (Harriet, interview 4)

Joyce also referred to the difficulty of asking for help and for her this was associated with a fear of being seen as 'a sponger':

> "The nurse from the surgery ... she put it all in for me [request for raised chair and toilet seat], I never asked for them. She said it's what I needed and she told them [social services] on the phone it was what I needed.... I'm not a person that will say, 'Oh, I'll have this, I'll have that'. I can't, I'm too independent probably. But I couldn't phone up and ask them for it. No, no, I couldn't. How can I put it? I've never been a sponger. Never. And I never will.... I've always been one that's been very independent. I won't ask anybody for anything, never have and I hope I never will." (Joyce, interview 3)

Similarly, Ralph emphasised his independence. His account reflects the themes already discussed – not wanting to burden others and the equation of independence with 'doing things for oneself' – but it places a different interpretation on the power dynamic between help giver and help receiver:

> "I'm independent. I do lots of things myself. Although I'm a bit slow getting up to the door, I'm independent and I don't want to bother people.... My daughters, they only live up the road, but my daughters are not my slaves. I don't want them to be, let me do this, let me do that ... no, I don't want it." (Ralph, interview 1)

Ralph refers to the potential givers of help, his daughters, as slaves, portraying himself, the receiver of help, as in the more powerful position. Other parts of his interview convey his construction of himself as in the more dominant role, for example:

> "[My daughters] don't do my shopping, but they take me. I do the shopping.... Most times when we go shopping, one [daughter] will come in the house and they will do what I want." (Ralph, interview 1)

At the time of the second interview, Ralph had recently been discharged from hospital following a stroke. He explained his reasons for refusing help when this was offered:

> Interviewer: "Were you offered any help for when you came home?"
>
> Ralph: "Well, they asked me in there and I told them, I'm on my own, I do most things myself. I don't really want anybody in here, you know what I mean?" (interview 2)

As well as not wanting to impose on other people, independence for Ralph was also associated with maintaining control and he did not want 'strangers' infringing on this within his home:

> "I didn't actually say I didn't want anyone coming in but I suppose they got the idea. My friend once said to me, 'Would you like anyone in with your housework?', and I said 'No'. I've got used to being on my own. I do what I like.... I've got lots of bits and pieces around and it's all in a certain place. I like that. TV times, it's there, I pick it up, see? I know where everything is. They [other people] come in, tidy it away." (Ralph, interview 2)

'Not going against the grain' for Ralph related to doing things for himself, being in control and retaining privacy. It is noteworthy that he still managed to retain a sense of being in control, despite his increasing need for help from his daughters following a further stroke. After this stroke, he moved in with his daughters. When I telephoned to arrange the next interview, his daughter said, "He's fine, he's got us all running round after him!". Despite the 'objective' view that Ralph was now more 'dependent' on his daughters for his care needs, both they and he continued to construct the situation in terms of his powerfulness and their subservience. This provides further illustration not only of the significance of 'not going against the grain' for help seeking and receiving, but also of the need to understand the dynamics of caring relationships within their current and historical interpersonal context.

The examples of 'not going against the grain' that have been described in this section all relate to attitudes and values developed and sustained across the lifecourse that formed part of participants' coping repertoires. As shown by Baldock and Ungerson (1994), these attitudes and values have implications for whether and when people seek help, who they prefer to provide it and the terms on which they find it acceptable. Although 'not going against the grain' is discussed here as a coping mechanism, the next chapter argues that it can also act as a barrier to managing, preventing participants from accessing help.

Relationships

The significance of family and social relationships for some participants has been discussed in the earlier section on life themes. There is evidence that the quality and continuity of social relationships, and the various forms of support that derive from them, affect all aspects of well-being – physical, psychological and emotional (Stevens, 2001; McMunn et al, 2006). This section is concerned primarily with psychological well-being. Other individuals 'are the necessary foils against which we come to know ourselves' (Jenkins, 1996, pp 49-50), and ongoing relationships are one way in which continuity of the self is experienced. Family and social relationships help to maintain a sense of continuity between past and present lives and contribute to coherence in the sense of self. If identity is constructed through social processes of interaction (Jenkins, 1996), it follows that continuity and disruption of relationships has implications for selfhood. This was demonstrated in a number of ways during the course of interviews with study participants.

Although the prime source of significant relationships for most participants was family, the ability to maintain friendships may have added significance in terms of what it conveys about continuity of social roles and identity (Nocon and Pearson, 2000; Phillipson et al, 2001). Friendships represent 'the active expression of interdependence experienced throughout the life course; of valuing and being valued' (Bury and Holme, 1991, p 138). It became clear that 'staying me' was not just about having close and continuous relationships, but implicated specific features of the nature of these relationships. Alice illustrated this when talking about the 'old lady' she talked to regularly on the telephone:

Interviewer: "Are you the only person she's got to talk to?"

Alice: "She's got her children but I think it's different with your children, you know, they're still your children. I remember my grandma saying she was lonely. She'd only got the children, and she'd got umpteen, I don't know how many there were, there were about four or five at home, but they were all 70ish. And I thought it was screamingly funny when I was young, but I realise now what she meant. They're still your children and they're a different generation. They think differently."

Interviewer: "So you feel loneliness isn't just about not having people around you?"

Alice: "No, that's right. I mean they're company but it's a different sort of company." (Alice, interview 3)

Alice proceeded to talk about the friendship she had formed with a woman who had come to live in the village, how much pleasure they had each derived from their conversations and shared interests and how much she missed this friend when she died.

Continuity of friendships conveyed self-worth. Elsie had lived in her village for many years and had many friends and acquaintances. Some had moved away over the years, but she kept in touch with several of them. At regular times each year she went to stay with friends who had moved south, and at another point in the year, they made a return visit to her. At the time of our first interview, she had recently celebrated her 91st birthday and she told me about the number of cards she had received on her birthday and when she was in hospital:

> "When I was in hospital I had over a hundred cards and 12 visitors on one day. When I came out, I had meals brought to me and I stayed with friends so I'm very lucky." (Elsie, interview 1)

Friendships played a key role in enabling Elsie to fulfil her desire to live a busy, active life and also in reflecting her own social worth as someone with lots of friends and social invitations. Research on women and depression has consistently demonstrated that the ability to create and sustain relationships supports a positive self-evaluation (Brown and Harris, 1978; O'Connor and Brown, 1984). Given older people's particular vulnerability to depression (Banerjee and Macdonald, 1996), enduring relationships appear to have a significant role in maintaining social and psychological well-being (Murphy, 1982; Wenger, 1997).

It was also possible to detect underlying themes that participants sought to sustain or resurrect in the nature of their relationships. Gerald's only family was a niece with whom he had little contact. Most of his other relationships had been formed relatively recently since he moved from a bungalow in a village to a sheltered flat in a town. His new acquaintances were primarily with other older people in the accommodation, many of whom were in poor health, and this clearly carried implications for his own identity:

> "They think I'm like them, an old fuddy duddy." (Gerald, interview 2)

> "This is how the place is. They are all, I won't say ga-ga, but this is the last, I've always said, they're waiting here to die, which is what they are, which is what I didn't want, to start getting into that position myself." (Gerald, interview 3)

In this context, his longstanding friendship with Bill, an ex-employee with whom he used to go sailing, seemed to have particular significance, enabling him to recapture preferred components of his identity. Talking about his relationship with Bill allowed him to reminisce about his experiences as managing director of a business, the boats he had owned and the friends he used to take sailing. His role in the relationship with Bill was portrayed as that of benefactor, both as employer and host on the sailing trips. Despite his changed circumstances, his relatively strong financial position allowed him to continue to perform a benefactor role in relationships. This was particularly the case with one woman, Ann, but also with others within the accommodation complex he would take out to lunch:

> "I've got enough money you see. Ann hasn't. It's just one of those things, like some of the others. If they stretch out a little bit, they have to cut back on something else.... They have to be a bit careful, they don't say so but I know they have to. I mean I sometimes take them out. Sometimes she [Ann] has got somebody with her and I include them – 'Oh, thank you very much, I'd like that', sort of thing.... I'm not being big headed but I'm quite wealthy. I've got enough, let's put it like that." (Gerald, interview 4)

Through maintaining particular types of relationships, Gerald was able to preserve continuity with past narratives of financial power and beneficence in the face of perceived threats of vulnerability and dependency.

Another example of the significance of continuity in relationships was Barbara's efforts to establish a new relationship following the death of her husband. Her husband had died three years previously and prior to that she had cared for him for 10 years when he had dementia. She commented that during her husband's illness and since his death, she had missed male companionship since this had always been part of her life. During the course of the study, she registered with a dating agency and formed a close relationship with John, a man who lived locally. She often cooked meals for John, and when he had a leg ulcer, she delivered meals to him and did his shopping. In return, he provided the transport for their outings; he organised a holiday for them both and did odd jobs around the flat. As mentioned in the previous chapter, Barbara appeared tearful and depressed in the first interview, but she became more cheerful and outgoing as the study progressed, despite the emergence of new health problems. She felt her life had "turned around" and she accounted for this in terms of making new friends and taking up new activities. She felt that her relationship with John had given her "a new lease of life". Although the relationship itself was newly formed, its nature and gender balance represented aspects of continuity with her previous long-term marital relationship. Her relationship with John enabled her to fulfil her (female) nurturing role and legitimised her feelings of vulnerability while at the same time reducing the threat they implied because of John's (male) role as protector.

For all of these participants, particular relationships were important not just for their intrinsic value, but also for what they represented more widely in terms of supporting life themes, role expectations and positive self-perceptions. When considering the role of social networks, it is not therefore simply the proximity, number and intensity of relationships that is important (Wenger, 1994), but also people's subjective experience of these relationships and what they signify for individual and social identity (Nilsson et al, 1998).

Home

Feelings of attachment and belonging to town, village and home constitute another dimension of identity and continuity for many older people (Phillipson et al, 2001; Godfrey et al, 2004; Kellaher et al, 2004). Continuity of place of residence was important to Joyce in terms of signifying 'belonging':

> "I know a lot of people because I went to school with them, grew up with them, you know ... it's everywhere around me, people I've worked with, people I've been brought up with in the same street and that, you know....There's quite a few of us from South Street still living which is nice to know." (Joyce, interview 3)

Joyce spent some time in one interview expressing her anger and disappointment at how the town had "gone downhill" over the years, with new buildings replacing old, and newcomers moving into the area so that it no longer felt like the same town. However, when asked whether she ever thought about moving somewhere else, she replied,

> "Oh no, no, no, no. I wouldn't live anywhere else ... no I wouldn't. No it's my, well, I was born here and it's my home town and I shall die here I expect." (Joyce, interview 3)

Alice had moved away from the area she regarded as her family home town, but the continued residence of other family members in that area helped her to preserve biographical connections with significant people and places. She referred to the death of her sister-in-law as representing the loss of a connection with the place where she grew up:

> "Both my sister-in-laws have died this year.... It seems funny not to have anybody there. I've just got my niece there now, whether she'll stay there or not I don't know. She's lived in that house all her life and whether she'll want to leave it ... but that's the last link, and we lived next door and opposite to one [sister-in-law], next door to the other so it's a big miss really." (Alice, interview 3)

In addition to locations, particular aspects of the home environment were also significant, described as 'parts of lives':

> "I love the garden, if I can just get in the garden.... I know it seems not a necessity but to me it is, really and truly, it's part of my life and

it helps keep me contented and keeps me active as well you see."
(Harriet, interview 1)

Roger also described his home and garden as 'his life':

"She [daughter] keeps saying, 'Well, have you thought of having a
bungalow?'. I said, 'Well, I think I'd like to have one before it gets too
bad but, I don't know, I wouldn't like to leave this place. I've lived in
it ever since it was built." (Roger, interview 4)

Roger's home embodied his past as well as his present life. He saw his home and
village as representing continuity in his relationship with his wife, now deceased.
They were married for 50 years and had lived in the house for all of that time:

"And the vicar came up one night and he said, 'Do you miss your
wife very much?'. I said, 'Of course I miss her but not in the way you
think'. As far as I'm concerned, she's still in the house. I can still feel her
presence in the house. And I haven't been lonely right from when she
died.... If I go out to the whist drive or anywhere, you know, I walk
in the house and I quite expect her to be here. I'm not upset because
she's not there because I just feel that presence." (Roger, interview 4)

One way of dealing with loss in relationships is to preserve a sense of closeness
by keeping others alive in memories (Johnson and Barer, 1997), and continuity
of place would seem to facilitate this process. For Roger, maintaining his garden
also represented continuity with his previous occupational identity as a labourer:

"I've always been an outside worker, and I've always done my garden
and everything and it keeps me going, it keeps me fit.... I mean I'm
out in the garden no matter what the weather is you see. If I've got
any jobs to do, I go out there and I walk my dogs every morning,
things like that." (Roger, interview 4)

These representations of continuity made Roger reluctant to consider moving,
even though he could see that a move might be advisable for practical reasons.
He explained that the only thing that would induce him to move would be if he
could not maintain the garden:

"I wouldn't want to sit here and watch it go. I've watched it once when
I nursed my wife and it nearly broke my heart then. No, I wouldn't
want that. My daughter said, oh, you can always stay with us but I said,
no, I'm not going to impose on you or anybody else. I said if I can't
do it I'd rather die. This is my home." (Roger, interview 4)

For Roger, there is evidence that home and garden are significant for preserving continuity in a number of areas: his relationship with his wife; his lifetime occupation and interests; and 'habits of the heart', about not imposing on others. In their research with older people on the relationship between environment and identity, Kellaher et al (2004) observe the different ways in which objects within the home represent the self. They represent self to self, self to others and others to self (p 73). From Roger's narrative, it appears that this also applies to other aspects of the home environment, in this case the garden. Not being able to maintain the garden would have implications for his own view of self ('I can no longer cope'), for how he imagined himself viewed by others ('he can no longer cope') and for what this communicated about his connection with others (for example, feeling he had let his wife down by letting her favourite plants die).

Gerald moved both home and area between the first and second interviews. As mentioned earlier, he moved from a large bungalow in a rural village to a one-bedroom warden–controlled flat in a town 15 miles away. This move necessitated disposing of many pieces of furniture and other items. In my first visit, when he was still living in the bungalow, he had shown me his display of old china plates, taking up an entire room. He was only able to retain a few of these when he moved. When I asked him after the move how he had felt about disposing of so many of his things, he appeared unconcerned. Instead, he gave a detailed account of his negotiations with the house purchaser and the deals he made with various people who bought the household effects. For Gerald, therefore, continuity was represented not through place, but primarily through the life themes of 'doing good business', being in control and managing others, discussed earlier.

Kellaher et al's (2004) research highlights older people's strategic actions in creating or maintaining the type and level of connections with their environment that they need and can manage in order to experience quality of life. These adaptive processes are described as follows:

> ... individuals judge which features of environment are significant at any given moment, mapping their needs and aspirations onto what is available and attainable in their physical and social environments.... It is clear that subtle and strategic assessment in the context of a particular setting and circumstances is a constant requirement.... These individual, constantly reflexive and flexible calculations represent a level of engagement with the physical and social world which many have not associated with older people. The physical and material environment is acted upon and brought into play so that the person becomes as centrally placed as feasible in relation to their social network, however thin this may be. It is the fit between the nature and intensity of the connections a person has, and the level they want and can manage, that generates a life of more or less quality. (Kellaher et al, 2004, p 78)

This sense of older people as agents, taking a proactive role in relation to their environment, whether by the 'letting go' of certain aspects or the strengthening of connections in other areas, is borne out in my study. For example, Roger lamented the loss of village life that had resulted from native villagers moving away and property being sold as second homes. However, compensating for the loss of belonging to a community were strong feelings of connection to his house and garden and, through them, his deceased wife. Gerald had relinquished former connections to his home and objects in his move to sheltered accommodation, but he dealt with this by minimising the significance of these losses and imposing his personality and 'style' on his new environment.

Continuity: summary

This section has discussed participants' efforts to preserve continuity, using the examples of life themes, 'not going against the grain', relationships and home. In these examples, following Atchley (1989), continuity is not interpreted as everything remaining the same, but rather as conveying the sense of a basic structure persisting over time, with diverse changes occurring within that structure. Thus, Atchley (1989) writes:

> ... continuity is not sameness, but rather is characterised by very gradual evolution in which new directions are closely linked to and elaborate upon already existing identity. Change occurs constantly, but in each of the components of identity new information usually can be absorbed fairly easily. (Atchley, 1989, p 187)

Departing from Atchley, however, I am not proposing a distinction between normal and pathological ageing or seeing an older person's inability to retain continuity as 'pathological ageing' (Atchley, 1989, p 184). Atchley sees continuity as maladaptive when an individual lacks the physical or mental capacities necessary to retain continuity, citing the example of someone who insists on living independently when he or she lacks self-care abilities. This appears to reflect an individual or medical model of disability that perceives individual functioning as pathological or maladaptive, rather than the environment as disabling in the barriers it presents to the retention of continuity (see, for example, Oliver and Sapey, 2006; Swain and French, 2008). Rather, participants' experiences suggest that being able to perceive threads of continuity between past, present and perceived future lives is one dimension of 'coping' for older people and something they strive to retain, facilitating a coherent sense of self (Heikkinen, 1996). Resources in the external environment may support or obstruct the preservation of continuity.

Continuity theory is also criticised for making ageing itself and the 'existential doubt' that may be linked with it irrelevant (Estes et al, 2003, p 32). It is important, therefore, to consider the dynamics of continuity specifically in relation to older people and ageing processes. Older people's immense capacity to adapt, accommodate change and reconstitute their identities has been illustrated in the previous chapter and in other studies (see, for example, Thompson et al, 1990; Johnson and Barer, 1997). In the latter study of people over the age of 85, discontinuity of the self, rather than continuity, was highlighted:

> To adapt, the oldest old must reconstitute a self-concept that is consistent with the realities of late life. Consequently, discontinuities rather than continuities in self may be necessary or even desirable. (Johnson and Barer, 1997, p 220)

Other research (for example, Coleman et al, 1999) reports continuity rather than discontinuity in older people's life themes. Part of adapting is embracing inevitable change. While older people are engaged in continuous processes of adaptation, both physical and psychological, the argument here is that they seek to do this in ways that are compatible as far as possible with themes of continuity. Thus, Ray (2000), for example, found that long-married couples sought to manage the transitions triggered by disability within the context of long-standing continuities in their relationships. Similarly, Chambers (2000) noted that when older women were adjusting to widowhood, continuities were more evident than discontinuities. In my study, participants sometimes interpreted the significance of changes in ways that were compatible with themes of continuity, and at other times shifted their focus and sought continuity in other areas of life, as illustrated in the example of Gerald, considered previously. Andrews (1999) argues that the realities of ageing in terms of the changes it brings should not be denied, but that these need to be understood within the context of lives as lived up to that point (p 313). In this way, elements of continuity and postmodern theories that see ageing as a fluid and dynamic process can be reconciled. Discontinuities are managed within an overall framework of continuity, with individuals as active agents, reflexively interpreting this continuity (Giddens, 1999).

It is also important to note the different ways in which central themes such as continuity play out in the context of older people's lives. The sub-categories of life themes, 'not going against the grain' relationships and home reflect dimensions of continuity that were significant to the particular (all white UK) sample of older people who participated in the study. The sub-categories are presented here as examples, not as representative of all types of continuity. The threads of continuity that are significant and meaningful to individuals are infinitely variable, shaped by particular social and cultural backgrounds, life histories and personalities. For example, while the white UK participants in this study who had lived in rural areas for many years of their lives demonstrated the importance of geographical connections based on community and home, continuity may be important in entirely different ways for older people from minority ethnic communities who have migrated to the UK. However, while experiences of migration disrupt the physical continuity of 'home' for some people from minority ethnic groups, it seems that they nevertheless find ways both to preserve connections with 'home' and also to re-establish identities that incorporate new bases for belonging, such as social networks (Maynard et al, 2008). The experiences of the migrant women are described as follows:

> They had moved across state boundaries and by doing so had become constructed as "different" and "ethnic minorities". The move had challenged many of their understandings about social life and their sense of who they were ... Nevertheless, the women whom we interviewed had a clear sense of their own identities and had their own specific forms of hyphenating their earlier nationality or faith with their current citizenship, without feeling uncertain about either. What was important was the social support offered to them by other migrants of the same family, faith, language or culture, which provided them with an anchor and a sense of belonging. (Maynard et al, 2008, pp 71-2)

It is possible that psychological strategies intervene, and where certain aspects of continuity (such as geography or 'home') are disrupted, the significance of lost elements is minimised, while retained aspects (such as faith and culture) are accentuated. There seemed to be some suggestion of this in the example of Gerald, cited previously, in which he dismissed questions about the possible loss signified by his move to sheltered accommodation, instead pursing a narrative that emphasised alternative dimensions of continuity.

Self-affirmation

The second category of 'staying me', self-affirmation, refers to participants' self-evaluations and social presentation. It has been noted that individuals construct themselves 'morally' in their public accounts of 'coping', and this includes in research interviews (Seale, 1996; Aronson, 2002). The category of self-affirmation highlights mechanisms through which the presentation of a positive self is attained, sometimes despite objective deterioration of health, abilities and circumstances.

Doing well

Within participants' interview accounts it was possible to discern different ways in which the self was affirmed. Participants invoked a range of strategies to support the view that they were 'doing well'. These included: making positive comparisons between their current situation and how it used to be, how it compared with that of others and how it compared to negative stereotypes of old age; modifying their attitudes and what they expected of themselves; tempering 'problem talk'; and perceiving themselves as lucky.

Participants used their own situations as the basis of positive comparisons, conveying a message that they were 'doing well'. One type of comparison was temporal, involving a comparison between their situation now and how it was previously. Patricia highlighted how well she was doing by comparing her survival with the serious health problems she endured in her earlier life:

> "I consider myself very lucky because at 25 I didn't know whether I was going to exist for a year because I'd got chronic TB [tuberculosis]. The cavity in one lung was as big as a half crown, you know, it was a fifty chance, sort of thing. But to have reached 76, I shall be 76 in January, is pretty good." (Patricia, interview 4)

Similarly, Harriet compared her current situation to the years she spent caring for her husband, and then at the time of his death:

> "Actually when I lost my husband, I thought my life was over, that was it, you know. I didn't think I would be going out and doing things again because of course I'd been, I hadn't done anything for 10 years while I nursed him. I was confined to the house with him all the time. It's just amazed me that I've picked up life again. I'm more outgoing today than I was when I was younger actually, more leisure time, of course, so I go out more." (Harriet, interview 3)

Roger made favourable comparisons between his current level of mobility and that in previous years:

> "Do you know, this time last year I sat here and I thought, 'Well, I'm never going to get out again, I'm never going to do my garden', and I felt so down and I was just giving up, you know, and then I thought to myself, 'Well, it's only another couple of months before I have my operation', you know, and that's what kept me going. But I never thought I'd come back like this … all that's behind me now, I can start a new life again." (Roger, interview 3)

Participants also made positive comparisons on the basis of their expectations of what old age would be like:

> "People say old age is awful but it isn't you know.… I think I've been happier the last four or five years than I've been for a very long time." (Elsie, interview 3)

Sometimes this involved comparing how they saw themselves with how they saw other older people. Elsie described attending her grandson's wedding and chatting to a man in the garden:

> "I heard all about his angina, his aneurysm, his heart, he'd got all sorts of things wrong with him. I said, 'You have been through the mill',

and he said, 'I've had everything, how about you?'. And I said, 'I'm very well thank you'. He said, 'So you should be, you're younger than I am'. I said, 'Oh yes, how old are you?'. And he said, '82'. And I said, 'You can put 10 years on that' [laughs]. I mean it's ridiculous because I don't feel old." (Elsie, interview 4)

Other studies have found that almost unanimously and whatever their situation, older people do not tend to perceive themselves as old, ill or disabled (Thompson et al, 1990; Townsend et al, 2006; Degnen, 2007). Participants tended to be very open in disclosing their age since this highlighted their 'doing well' status, reinforcing their difference from what the term 'old' represented. This was a reflexive process with participants not only considering themselves to be doing well, but finding affirmation in how they saw themselves perceived by others:

"I have good, sensible meals and I do vegetables from the garden, lots of fruit, not heavy fry-ups and things like that, you know. Mr C [hospital consultant] said, 'You're a fit man', he said, 'I wouldn't have dreamed you're 80'." (Roger, interview 2)

Equally, relating stories about others who were perceived as less fortunate enabled them to evaluate positively their own 'coping'. Making favourable comparisons between oneself and others has been found to be one dimension of successful or good ageing (Nilsson et al, 1998), and an adaptive strategy that enhances perceived quality of life (Beaumont and Kenealy, 2004). Bury and Holme (1991) found that people over the age of 90 made positive comparisons between themselves and other people of the same age, believing that they were faring better in terms of their health and abilities. A similar phenomenon has been noted in younger people (ages 43 to 72) recovering from heart attacks (Johnson, 1991) and in women facing the menopause (Granville, 2000). A literature review on older people's experiences of adjusting to a care home environment identifies 'reframing' as one of the ways in which older people dealt with the transition and the feelings it generated. Older residents compared themselves with others in relation to health, social status, family visits and financial circumstances. The cognitive strategy of 'doing well' helped them to retain a more positive perspective and manage feelings of loss and threats to identity (Lee et al, 2002).

Another strategy used by participants to uphold a view that they were 'doing well' was modifying what they expected of themselves to accommodate changing abilities; lowering the standard expected enabled a sense of doing well to be maintained. There were a number of comments by different participants to the effect that 'You've got to expect it at my age'. For example, Roger talked about his difficulty climbing the stairs and the problems this caused in his day-to-day life, particularly as his toilet was upstairs:

> "I have to go upstairs, yes. I have to go up for everything you see. But anyway, I can't expect much more. If I go on for another year or two, that'll do me ... as long as I'm all right, you know, can keep getting about ... that's good enough for me ... I mean at 82 you can't expect much more can you?" (Roger, interview 4)

He contextualised his mobility problems in terms of what could reasonably be expected for someone of his age:

> "I can walk about the same [distance] but I get breathless and tired, you know, and have to keep stopping and having a rest. But still, you can't expect anything else can you? I'll soon be coming up to 83." (Roger, interview 5)

In this way, as well as invoking age stereotypes and expectations to highlight their departure from these and confirm their status as 'doing well', participants also used age expectations to normalise and legitimate difficulties they experienced, thereby diminishing their significance:

> "Sometimes I just can't remember things. But I'm not too bad for 90." (Ralph, interview 2)

The longitudinal nature of the study facilitated some insight into the process of positive reconstruction as attitudes and expectations were modified. In the first two interviews with Harriet, her feelings of loss of independence, triggered by having to give up driving, dominated the interview:

> "That [not driving] is the worst aspect of the whole thing because I do feel that I have lost my independence to a great extent. Although as I've said, friends, they have been very kind and if I ask anybody, they'll take me but I feel a nuisance." (Harriet, interview 2)

Other studies have noted that having to depend on others for lifts can generate concerns for older people about being a burden and not being able to reciprocate (Gilhooly et al, 2004; Davey, 2007). In subsequent interviews, it became apparent that Harriet's friends and her daughter's carer were frequently giving her lifts. However, rather than talking in negative terms about her loss of independence, she now emphasised her continued ability to pursue her activities. The earlier narrative theme of being a nuisance and imposing was replaced by an emphasis on the help she had given to others previously and the current reciprocal nature of her relationship with friends: "We all help each other". Her situation in these latter interviews appeared no different to that at the first interview, but over the period of three years, she had found ways to adapt in practical terms and to adjust psychologically in a way that affirmed her self-perception as 'still doing well'.

Similarly, Bury and Holme (1991) found that older people (aged 90 or above), while still valuing independence, came to accept their increasing dependency by setting it against a lifecourse of hard work and helping others.

The previous chapter discussed adjusting as a sub-category of keeping active as participants sought to do things differently or substitute activities to accommodate increasing health and disabilities. A similar mechanism appears to operate in relation to cognitive processes. Participants modified their expectations and, in some cases, attitudes to accommodate changed circumstances and abilities. A process of 'renormalising', involving a lowering of expectations to accommodate reduced abilities, has been shown to operate in people recovering from heart attacks (Mullen, 1993). In this way adaptation can be highly functional at the individual level of 'coping' (Bury and Holme, 1991). When participants did talk about difficulties, these were often qualified by a positive comment, indicating that really they were doing well. When Ralph was talking about his incontinence problems, he commented,

> "He [the specialist] said he couldn't do any more for me. They did two operations, at first it seemed better but it didn't last. But I'm doing all right. I get by." (Ralph, interview 2)

Other participants made similar comments qualifying or mitigating difficulties:

> "As long as I sit with a cushion there and if I press on it it's all right but if I sit up I can't knit.... Never mind, I'm not too badly off." (Elsie, interview 4)

> Still feel lonely. But I am coping with it much better. (Barbara, diary)

> "The last blood test I had, well, last week he [doctor] only rang up on Tuesday and said you're anaemic again.... But apart from that, I mean, I'm doing very well." (Roger, interview 3)

Langan et al (1996) noted the theme of 'making the best of things' among the 39 older people they interviewed, and this is reflected in my study, for example in the language used by participants to talk about difficulties.

Another way of detracting from the negative impact of 'problem talk' was to temper its impact by following it with a joke or laughter. The positioning of laughter after 'problem talk' was particularly notable in Alice's narrative since it featured after what appeared to be the most difficult and sensitive issues, such as how she managed her incontinence. Jokes and laughter have been noted to play an important protective social role:

> A light-hearted manner, the apparent distancing of the narrator from the disagreeable course of events they experienced, can signify to the

reader that s/he doesn't need to feel upset in sympathy. The element provides a critical cue for practical intersubjectivity and sharing the lifeworld. (Kelly and Dickinson, 1997, p 270)

Through qualifying discussion of difficulties, following it with positive statements and inserting humour and laughter at potentially sensitive junctures in the narrative, participants diluted the impact of 'problem talk'. Thus, too, Aronson (2002, p 415) noted the 'conversational repair work' engaged in by older women receiving home care in Canada following potentially threatening disclosures in research interviews. It is suggested that one way individuals manage the risk and uncertainty inherent in current day-to-day life is to 'bracket out' negative possibilities (Giddens, 1999), and a similar process appears to be at work here as participants acknowledged problems, but then endeavoured to reduce the identity threat that they posed.

Participants also conveyed a sense that they were 'doing well' by making reference to their good luck or good fortune. Perceptions of being lucky embraced having good friends, being physically healthy and generally having had a good life:

> "I have some very good friends, I'm very lucky actually, I do realise that I'm one of the lucky ones." (Harriet, interview 3)

> "I've been very lucky in my declining years. I've got this little bungalow and it's nice and quiet.... I've no complaints, I've had a jolly good innings and if I go tomorrow, I've had a good innings." (Elsie, interview 3)

The sense of luck or good fortune was enhanced by comparison with others who were perceived to be in a worse situation. This included comparison with specific individuals or with generalised others:

> "I've had a hard life but I've no grumbles. No, I think about all the poor people who don't get this far in life." (Roger, interview 5)

Elsie compared her own good health with that of a friend of the same age who had recently died:

> "I miss her, poor J.... She was blind, nearly blind. Oh, she used to make me feel guilty. I'd go along all full of health and there was only two months in between us and there she was, she couldn't see, and the pills, 'Have I got the right ones, dear?' she'd say because she was almost blind and I used to feel guilty because I was so healthy and there was poor old J ... in a wheelchair." (Elsie, interview 5)

For Harriet, it was her good fortune in having hobbies and interests to occupy her that she compared favourably with the predicament of others:

> "It doesn't bother me if I don't go out because I'm always doing something, you know, there's never enough time for me to do the things I want to do so that I'm lucky in that respect. But you hear so many old people saying they're bored and they wish they could die because there's nothing to do and they're bored. It must be dreadful." (Harriet, interview 3)

By these different strategies to show they were doing well – making positive comparisons, modifying expectations, mitigating 'problem talk' and perceptions of being lucky – participants signalled to themselves and to me that they were 'doing well'. Similar cognitive coping mechanisms have been noted in a small-scale study of 20 older people with incontinence problems (Godfrey et al, 2007). Alongside practical strategies, such as being prepared and limiting food and drink intake, the older people also engaged in coping mechanisms such as positive comparisons with others and minimising their own difficulties and the use of humour (Godfrey et al, 2007). Older people may be particularly adept at resisting 'assaults to the self' presented by experiences such as loss of mobility, forgetfulness and incontinence. A study that compared self-descriptive statements by 300 young people and 300 older people found that while the older people acknowledged the negative aspects of their experience, they were more positive towards themselves than the younger respondents. This was achieved by dropping higher aspirations and adopting goals concerned with maintenance, rather than change. Referring to the older people's positive attitudes, Dittmann-Kohli concludes:

> Positive criteria for self-evaluation in social comparison and for personal pride are now focused on being younger or already so old, on being still healthy, active and vital or still feeling well. There is even gratefulness for lack of disaster. These examples show that the self can be protected by such strategies as downward comparison or devaluation of reference standards. (Dittmann-Kohli, 1990, p 290)

These strategies of self-affirmation enable older people to dissociate themselves from negative stereotypes and expectations of old age, thereby resisting the imposition of a damaging social identity (Thompson et al, 1990; Ginn and Arber, 1993; Hockey and James, 1993).

Life is what you make it

Chapter Three discussed the sub-categories 'finding solutions' and 'pushing yourself'. Underpinning these activities are beliefs about the duties and responsibilities of individuals to 'keep themselves going'. This, by implication, holds people responsible for their own physical and psychological well-being. Participants' accounts indicated beliefs about their individual responsibilities to keep going and resist threats to doing so. This encompassed the dimensions of 'putting on a brave face', 'positive thinking' and 'not giving in'.

Mitigating 'problem talk' with laughter, discussed previously, reflects efforts to present a positive social façade despite the acknowledgement of significant personal difficulties. In some interview accounts, this belief in the importance of presenting a positive social face was explicit. Comments by Joyce, discussed in Chapter Three, revealed her belief that she should 'put on a brave face' to mask her pain and difficulties.

In her diary, Elsie referred to the pain in her neck but commented that she tried to 'grin and bear it'. The personal responsibility to 'age well', psychologically as well as physically, was again conveyed through stories told about others:

> "I think a lot of the trouble is that people give up, I really do. My friend, she's much younger than I am. Every time I go there, she's full of misery. Nobody wants to know other people's miseries, nobody loves a misery.... My sister used to sit in her chair and she did nothing but moan. 'Do you see my scar?' Well, she had exactly the same as I did and she used to sit in her chair and say, 'I've broken the most important bone in my body, I couldn't have done anything worse'. And I said, 'Oh yes you could, you could have broken your spine and been paralysed'." (Elsie, interview 3)

While there is substantial support for a disjunction between physical presentation and feelings in later life, there is a difference of view about how this operates. The extracts referred to here suggest not that the ageing body is 'masking' the real youthful inner self, as suggested by some writers (Hepworth, 1991; Conway and Hockey, 1998), but rather that the perceived necessity of presenting a positive and, by implication, more 'youthful', social façade leads older people to conceal pain, distress and negative emotions (Biggs, 1997).

The previous quotation from Elsie illustrates not only the pressure to achieve a positive social presentation, but also the perceived personal benefits of positive thinking. Positive thinking was prevalent throughout participants' accounts:

> "I do take life easy now and I enjoy my life, yes I do. Oh I do, I enjoy my life. I mean if I only go out to the Post Office to get my pension, I enjoy it.... Oh yes, I enjoy my life. Although it's lonely, I enjoy it. I've been on my own what, 11, 12 years now. It does get lonely but you get over it." (Joyce, interview 3)

> "I'm not going to give up ... you see, 81, it's only 18 the other way round isn't it?" (Roger, interview 3)

Roger was able to maintain positive thinking even after receiving news that his life expectancy was about a year. He described his response to the doctor who told him this:

> "And when he left, he said, 'I hope you go on all right'. I said, 'I'll come back when I'm 90 and tell you you were wrong!'. He said, 'I hope you do' [laughter]." (Roger, interview 5)

Alice acknowledged the difficulties she experienced, but explained how she managed to avoid these 'getting her down':

> "The frailties get, you know at times a bit depressing, you sort of have to cope with different things as they come along, you know. But during this cold weather I'm terribly slow, I can hardly walk when I first get out of bed, you know, it takes me such a long time to do things and at times I could get depressed about that but I think, well, I'm still doing it.... I have trouble with my bowels occasionally. It's just the muscle's sort of gone, you know, and I've got to be careful.... I could get depressed about that but ... I don't try to think too much. I can cope with it, I've got quite good at cleaning myself up ... sometimes when I go out I think, gosh, I hope I'm all right, sort of thing, but I usually manage to cope.... I don't think about it too much. If I manage once a fortnight I think, 'Well, that's improving' [laughter]." (Alice, interview 3)

The perceived personal value of having a positive attitude was explicit in some accounts:

> "It's no good just sitting back and saying poor me. I mean that gets you nowhere.... I've always been the same, I've always led a pretty happy life and I mean if people want to be miserable, let them be miserable. You know, I meet a lot of those sort of people, 'Oh, I can't do this and I can't do that' ... if you want to try, then you will do things. I can't understand people with that attitude, sitting down and having people running round after them all the while. That's not my idea of life." (Roger, interview 4)

> "You've got to, I think you've got to adapt to life. It's no good just sitting and whining is it?" (Patricia, interview 4)

> It's no good dwelling on things, you have to look forward and get on with life and what it brings. (Barbara, diary)

Other research based on interviews with older people notes evidence of their 'relentless cheerfulness' and capacity to reconstruct difficult situations as opportunities (Hey, 1999, p 104). It may be that these mechanisms are not consistent throughout the ageing process. Another study of 'old older people' found that they were less inclined to rely on positive thinking and were more stoical about the existence of problems (Lee and Brennan, 2002). It is likely that psychological strategies evolve in response to changing situations, as discussed further in Chapter Six.

Another dimension of 'life is what you make it' was not giving in. While being lucky, discussed earlier, suggests that your situation is a matter of chance, an alternative strand within the category of self-affirmation is taking responsibility for your situation. The discourse of responsibility appeared to confirm the status of participants as people in control of their lives. Chapter Three referred to participants' beliefs about the importance of pushing yourself and this theme also emerged strongly in research by Townsend et al (2006). Pushing yourself implies some measure of control over the situation, that there is a choice to be made whether to 'keep going' or 'give up'. In the same way that finding solutions was presented as a significant component of keeping going in practical day-to-day managing, emphasis on an individual's capacity for agency and resistance appeared significant for managing in cognitive terms. The implication is that coping is a matter of personal will and determination:

> Nobody can help physical disabilities but old age is largely a state of mind and you do not *have* to give in to it. (Elsie, diary)

> "You do the best for yourself and that's how you go on and I mean, you don't have to give in to these things do you? If you do then you've had it, haven't you, that's how I look at it." (Joyce, interview 3)

These statements appear to associate being positive with 'strength of character' or desirable personal qualities and moreover to imply that this is a matter of individual choice:

> "If I was different, I could sit here and just mope all day long. That's no good to you at all. Lots of people say, 'My word, you do make a quick recovery when you come out of hospital, you're soon up and about again'. I say, 'Well, that's the way to do it'.... That's the attitude you've got to take. It's no good just sitting back and saying, 'Poor me'. I mean that gets you nowhere.... I've known one or two people who've had an illness and they've just sort of sat in the chair and done nothing and then you've just passed away like that. Well, that's no life." (Roger, interview 4)

"The other day people said to me, 'How do you do it?'. 'Do what?' 'Keep so young.' I said, 'I don't do anything, I just have young people around me, that is it'. My sister, N ... she says, 'I wish my grandchildren and great-grandchildren wouldn't come. They come and I think, "Oh no, here they are again", and I get tired to death'. And I said, 'N ... aren't you pleased to see them?'. And she said, 'No, they tire me out'. And I thought, 'Oh dear'. She's not a happy sort of person.... She doesn't seem able to pick herself up, some people can't can they? But still, never mind, I'm not going to give up." (Elsie, interview 5)

Research with older people receiving care noted their acceptance of responsibility for maintaining positive attitudes. This was interpreted as a psychological mechanism for coping with a loss of independence or autonomy (Cox and Dooley, 1996).

As well as general coping, there were more specific areas where a discourse of personal responsibility was apparent. Roger believed that you received the treatment you deserved:

"At the hospital they gave me wonderful treatment, there's no getting away from it.... I think if you work with them and you're pleasant to them, then you get on well. You get a lot of them, you know, who moan over nothing and keep calling the nurse when there's no need to, things like that, you know." (Roger, interview 4)

While Harriet commented on her good fortune in having hobbies to occupy her, there was at the same time within these comments an implication of responsibility:

"I know one person and she's been virtually housebound for at least 20 years. Well, what must it be like? And no hobbies! I cannot understand people not having hobbies to pass the time. It must be soul-destroying, to just sit, all day long. I mean the days are not long enough for me." (Harriet, interview 5)

Patricia talked about her supportive family:

"I'm very lucky with my family.... I mean the children visit every week. My daughter comes at least once or twice a week if not more, I mean she's not far, she just pops in and ... [the granddaughters], they're ever so good, as good as gold. It's lucky these days because a lot of people don't bother, especially teenagers, I mean they don't bother.... I think it depends on the family doesn't it? It depends on your family unit, whether you keep a family unit. I mean so many people seem to break the family unit, they never sit down for a meal together, it starts at that stage then it gradually breaks up ... it's the early stage of the family that helps to hold it together." (Patricia, interview 5)

Again, implicit within this was some attribution of personal responsibility for the availability of a supportive family; it was not seen just as a matter of luck.

There are, then, a number of distinct features within participants' beliefs that 'life is what you make it'. There is an inherent assumption of individual responsibility; living a 'positive life' is seen as largely within the control of individuals, an indicator of desirable personal and family characteristics and a signal of moral worth. A study of older people who had become housebound observed their need to be seen as self-defining and their tendency to attribute their coping to 'the sort of person I am' (McKevitt et al, 2005, p 137). Positive evaluations of the 'inner self', that is, emotional and intellectual resources, have been shown to be highly significant for self-esteem (Baldock and Hadlow, 2002). The emphasis in participants' narratives on the strengths of their 'inner selves' can perhaps be interpreted in this light as a way of bolstering self-esteem. Combining a perception of doing well with a belief that they were responsible for that situation appeared to contribute to participants' positive self-evaluation; in other words, if life is what you make it and life is good, then you have done well! Self-affirmation operated in a way that both enabled people to construct their situations positively while at the same time maintaining a sense of agency and personal responsibility. While many other aspects of older people's lives may be changing against their will, maintaining positive attitudes and perceptions is one way in which they can still exercise a sense of control (Johnson, 1991; Coleman et al, 1999). These processes may explain why a reduced sense of control associated with deteriorating health or abilities (Charmaz, 1983) may be matched by an increase in these types of adaptive strategies (Pratt and Norris, 1994; Biggs, 1999).

The view that 'life is what you make it' also highlights the significance of moral judgements to self-evaluation. 'Moral narratives' communicate an individual's self-worth but at the same time create social distance with others deemed less worthy. As Bury (2001) notes: 'By developing a narrative of "successful living" in the face of illness ... the individual may, of course, be self-praising or implying criticism of those that fail' (p 277). By 'not giving in' but discharging their responsibility to keep going physically and psychologically, participants conveyed their moral worth in contrast to others who 'gave up'. Unjustified demands for help and a refusal to make an effort were some of the components illustrated in Joyce's comments about a neighbour:

"That lady there [pointing in direction of adjacent flat], it doesn't matter what she asks for she gets. Everything, yes.... She says she's disabled but really and truly apart from her speech, there's nothing wrong with her. She's just decorated her two rooms out.... And she's round at the doctor's two or three times a week. I couldn't bother a doctor like that when I know there's other people worse off than me that need it. I couldn't do that, no way. I'm not that type of person ... no way could I go bothering them with petty things, sort of thing." (Joyce, interview 3)

In research by Townsend et al (2006), mentioned previously, older people relayed stories that constructed other older people as 'heroes', 'villains' and 'victims'. A status as 'villain' was accorded to those who 'gave up', refused to be helped or who were perceived as selfish or imposing a burden on others. The researchers see these moral narratives as part of a coping strategy through which participants distanced themselves from negative stereotypes of old age. So, too, Granville (2000), in her study of women facing the menopause, notes the judgemental comments passed by the women she interviewed on other women. She sees the women as colluding with ageist attitudes and distancing themselves from negative attributions of age through this process. An ethnographic study by Degnen (2007) also describes ways in which older women in one community distanced and 'othered' other older women who were seen as 'old', in the sense of 'not being all there'.

Managing is, then, not just about exercising agency to keep going but also about exercising resistance to not give in. Efforts to 'put on a brave face' about illness and impairment, to 'think positive' and 'not give in' reflect not just individual attitudes but social representations:

> Health beliefs are ideological in that they are sustained within a wider social discourse that shapes not just how individuals think, but how they feel they ought to think. The sick are encouraged by the healthy to redefine their misfortune in positive ways, thus avoiding embarrassment (for the healthy), while resulting in the sick being accorded attributes such as "strength of character". By being "strong of character" they can be credited with being worthy to be looked after, as if too much weakness should be unsupportable. If this is to be achieved, then the sick must make manifest their difficulty while showing how they either have borne it or have overcome it. (Radley and Billig, 1996, p 227)

The attitudes expressed by participants reflect the influence of social representations of age as well as of health and illness. 'Successful ageing' is a goal esteemed both individually and socially (Nolan et al, 2001); it is associated with retaining characteristics associated with youthfulness, hence participants' efforts to dissociate themselves from negative attributes of 'old age'. Equally, beliefs concerning individual responsibility reflect powerful social and political discourses. These issues are explored further in Chapter Six.

Conclusion

The category 'staying me' reflects two aspects of participants' experiences. First, the 'staying' refers to the theme of continuity discussed in the first part of the chapter. People who experience old age positively have been found to view it as an integrated part of life rather than a distinct phase (Nilsson et al, 1998). This indicates the importance of helping older people to preserve across the lifecourse threads of continuity that are significant to them while recognising the necessity of change and adaptation. The 'me' represents strategies concerned with management of the sense of self. In this way the categories of both 'keeping going' and 'staying me' embody the dynamic between change and continuity in the lives of older people. 'Staying me' encapsulates efforts to preserve a sense of continuity with past 'selves' as well as efforts to preserve a positive sense of self in the face of changing abilities and circumstances.

This section has considered specific strategies employed by older people, sometimes consciously but often unconsciously, to sustain a sense of self. These comprised two main elements. First, by preserving threads of continuity they were able to retain a sense of personal meaning and coherence. Second, in presenting themselves as doing well and as discharging their social responsibilities by displaying a positive social 'face', positive thinking and valued personality characteristics, participants' narratives reflected and supported a positive self-evaluation. This supports the observation by Johnson and Barer (1997) that the 'oldest old' were 'active agents in moderating the effects of negative emotions and enhancing positive emotional states' (p 175). Whereas Chapter Three suggested that adapting was a 'keeping going' strategy, here it is proposed that a similar process of cognitive activity and reconstruction is at work, allowing participants to retain a sense of personal coherence and a positive view of their situations and themselves. Changes tended to be negotiated within a broader framework of continuity. Where difficulties were acknowledged, these were qualified by a focus on strengths or their impact diluted by the use of humour. Negative stereotypes and images of old age were used to highlight their own status as 'ageing well'. Stories of others perceived as doing less well or as less fortunate were relayed in a way that emphasised positive dimensions in their own situations and their own strength of character and moral worth, legitimating any help received or potentially needed.

This chapter and Chapter Three have explored the practical and cognitive mechanisms used by participants to manage ageing. The two categories of 'keeping going' and 'staying me' reflect Bury's (1991) analysis of how individuals manage the experience of illness. He distinguishes between 'strategies', that is, the actions people take to manage illness, and 'coping', that is, 'cognitive processes whereby the individual learns how to tolerate or put up with the effects of illness' (p 460). Radley (1994, pp 148-9) makes a similar distinction between what he terms 'action' or 'problem-based' strategies and 'cognitive' or 'emotion-based' coping in relation to illness. Following this distinction, the actions and behaviours discussed in the 'keeping going' category can be seen as 'strategies' and the cognitive processes subsumed within the 'staying me' category as 'ways of coping'. Both dimensions attest to the 'hard work' involved in constructing a positive life. While Chapter Three highlighted the hard physical work involved in ageing, here we have seen that it also involves hard psychological and emotional work. The chapters have highlighted the predominant success of the strategies and ways of coping in enabling participants to 'keep going' and 'stay me'. The next chapter shows that these strategies and ways of coping are deployed in the face of perceived threats to 'keeping going' and 'staying me', and a sense by participants that they are on 'the slippery slope' as they grow older.

FIVE

'The slippery slope'

"I want to keep myself as fit and independent as I can but I mean at 82 I'm on the slippery slope." (Harriet, interview 1)

Chapters Three and Four described and analysed practical strategies and cognitive ways of coping used by older people as they endeavour to manage changes and difficulties in their daily lives. This has conveyed a largely individualist view of ageing, with a predominant emphasis on personal strengths and coping styles. At the same time, particular beliefs and attitudes, which underpin coping efforts, are themselves heavily influenced by social and cultural constructions, as expressed, for example, in beliefs relating to individual responsibility and self-sufficiency. This chapter moves beyond the level of individual perspectives and behaviour to examine the resources and threats that respectively support or undermine older people's practical strategies (the 'keeping going' theme) and cognitive ways of coping (the 'staying me' theme). These are discussed at three levels: personal, social and community. Personal threats and resources considered include: health, finances, life experiences and perspectives. Social threats and resources are discussed in relation to the direct and indirect role played by social networks and dynamics within relationships. Community threats and resources are considered in terms of features of formal services that support or undermine coping and opportunities and obstacles within the wider community.

Although the previous chapters highlighted the predominance of 'strengths' talk within participants' accounts – for example, the focus on keeping busy and the underplaying of difficulties – there was nevertheless a clear sense of present and perceived future threat contained in their accounts. 'The 'slippery slope' conveys participants' perceptions of their tenuous hold on 'coping' and the implied threat of a time when they would no longer be able to manage. This chapter examines some of the factors that seemed to support or undermine their efforts to retain their hold on 'the 'slippery slope' of later life.

Personal threats and resources

Health and abilities

A key factor for participants, when giving an account of the nature and level of difficulties they experienced and their strategies for addressing them, was the state of their health. This is perhaps unsurprising, given that good health and the ability to carry out everyday tasks and routines are strongly associated with reported well-being and quality of life. This applies across ethnic groups (Grewal et al, 2004; Maynard et al, 2008). Bowling (2005) reported that almost two thirds of older respondents in her research agreed with the statement that there were 'few things more important than good health', while Hill et al (2007) found that health was the resource that older people valued most highly.

When asked a general question about their situation at the start of interviews, participants invariably selected health concerns to provide the context for their account of 'how things were'. Despite their assessed ineligibility for the provision of social services, some were facing a combination of health problems and/or quite serious conditions. These included serious heart conditions, stroke, rheumatoid arthritis, osteoarthritis, osteoporosis, angina, irritable bowel syndrome, incontinence, partial deafness and cataracts.

Some participants also expressed concerns about their mental health, in particular the current or future threats posed by memory loss and dementia. Barbara's husband had dementia for 10 years before he died so she both understood and feared it. In the third interview, she talked about her brother, who had dementia, and her sister, who she felt was also becoming confused. She said it worried her that she might 'go the same way', but she tried not to think about it. Harriet was very aware of her memory loss and had adopted strategies to try to deal with this:

> "The one thing that has affected me more than anything is my memory. I have absolutely no short-term memory at all. I just can't remember for five minutes what I was going to do or a telephone number or something I look up to watch on the television…. I have to write everything down." (Harriet, interview 1)

She was particularly concerned about exposing her physical and mental frailty to her friends:

> "Most of my friends are about 20 years younger than I am and so they are all independent, they've all still got their cars and I don't like to look as if I've lost it, if you know what I mean? I like to still feel independent with them. I don't want them to have to mother me. And so that's what I find difficult, it makes me feel stupid." (Harriet, interview 4)

Although participants often sought to avoid presenting a negative view of their situations or to be seen as complaining, as discussed in the previous chapter, they did reveal within the context of their narratives the extent of their health difficulties and the implications of this for them:

> "I can't stand and iron now whereas I used to be able to do a little bit, I can't do it now. And, well, I can't do much really. I do a bit of dusting and I hobble about a bit, you know, to get myself some exercise as

much as anything. But it's definitely got worse, definitely." (Patricia, interview 5)

The openness of participants to discussing health problems is interesting in the light of their strategies for self-affirmation discussed in the previous chapter. It is suggested that the close association of ageing with ill health may lead older people to deny health problems in order to distance themselves from a stigmatising social identity (Conway and Hockey, 1998). Participants in my study were willing to disclose health problems, although their impact tended to be minimised. Reference to health difficulties featured more in some participants' diaries than in interview accounts, perhaps because diaries were seen as having a different, non-social, function.

Health problems may precede older age rather than be concurrent with it. While Elsie's difficulties had arisen only recently in the context of a previously healthy and active life, for others problems were a continuation or accentuation of a lifetime of ill health. For example, as noted in her diary, Harriet had had rheumatoid arthritis since her mid 30s (so for nearly 50 years) and Patricia had suffered asthma and breathing problems since contracting tuberculosis when in her 20s. The assumption that ageing necessarily implies a progressive deterioration in health and abilities is also belied. During the three years of the study, while the health of some participants did unfortunately deteriorate to the point of their death (Winifred, Les and Ralph), the health of others improved. Barbara had a quadruple heart bypass operation and perceived herself as being significantly mentally and physically healthier at the conclusion of the study than when it started. She did not tire as easily, felt more energetic and was able to walk further. She felt that surviving the operation, which she had been told carried only a 10 per cent chance of recovery, had led her to re-evaluate her life, appreciate all of its positive aspects and opened up new opportunities as a result of her improved fitness. For others the path was less straightforward with recovery or improvement in some areas occurring alongside deterioration in others or the emergence of new problems. Roger, for example, recovered his mobility following a knee replacement operation, but found that because his heart condition was inoperable, his life expectancy was reduced to a year.

Whatever the nature and process of their illness or disability, it was clear that declining health and abilities were seen by participants as a significant source of threat to present and future well-being. Chapter Four described the impact of a knee injury on Gerald's perception of his own ability to cope, rapidly shifting him from a position of feeling in control to 'not knowing which way to turn'. Harriet used the expression 'being on the slippery slope' and her view was that ageing was a gradual process of sliding downwards:

> "I am better than I was but you never really get back to what you were before.... I do find that I am beginning to feel, not tired, weary. I find everything is a big effort these days.... I haven't got nearly the

stamina that I used to have. I still want to do it but I just can't do it."
(Harriet, interview 5)

Chapter Three described the ways participants 'pushed themselves' to deal with difficulties, but also their decisions about where the limits of 'pushing themselves' should lie, since this was often accompanied by anxieties about the potential consequences. Concerns about risks to health and ability were one area leading to decisions that 'pushing themselves' was no longer a viable strategy. In the fifth interview, Harriet talked about a fall she had sustained while shopping and how the fear of a recurrence of this incident had made her more cautious about walking to and from the town:

> "I still go out and do my shopping but I do definitely have to wait now for someone to pick me up. It's just so foolish to do it isn't it? I could easily have broken a leg doing that you see, you've just got to be sensible." (Harriet, interview 5)

Ill health or impairment could be the reason that people no longer felt able to engage in social activities. Ralph avoided using the telephone when his speech deteriorated following his second stroke. He was also reluctant to accept social invitations because of his incontinence problems:

> "I should have gone [to granddaughter's] last Tuesday but I said no, I didn't want to go. It's the waterworks that stops me.… The main reason I won't leave the house is because of the waterworks. I've got to have a toilet near. Like I said, I go out with my daughter see, and I can't control it, it's just if I can't get to a toilet, that kind of thing. It's awkward, it's just plain awkward. It can't be helped, these things happen." (Ralph, interview 2)

While incontinence may contribute to social isolation, mediating variables include self-esteem and personal attitudes, professional help and family support, mobility and access to facilities such as toilets, transport and finances (Godfrey et al, 2007). Following his stroke, Ralph had to use a wheelchair when he went out. His poor mobility, personal attitudes and lack of toilet facilities were all barriers impeding the management of his incontinence.

Linked with health and abilities, driving was an area that several participants defined as key to the retention of their independence. Perceived threats to continued driving included increasingly restricted mobility so that even getting in and out of the car was difficult (Alice) and diminishing confidence driving on busier roads (Barbara). Harriet had recently relinquished driving because of recurrent fainting and dizziness. She had just sold her car at the time of the first interview and the negative impact of this featured heavily in the interview:

"It's just left me completely stranded. I've always been used to doing everything for myself and going everywhere, it's just completely transformed my life." (Harriet, interview 1)

A small-scale study based on six in-depth interviews with older women who had given up driving found that adaptation to the cessation of driving was harder if this was a sudden change and if the decision had been imposed, rather than the woman's own choice (Bauer et al, 2003). It points out that a time of greater need for medical and support services may be accompanied by increased difficulties in accessing them. This study also highlights the psychological, as well as physical, implications of the discontinuation of driving. Other research has found that car ownership and car driving among older people is associated with a higher perceived quality of life, independently of the effects of wealth (Gilhooly et al, 2004). The continued ability to drive for the participants in my study appeared to have symbolic significance over and above its practical value in getting people from one place to another. For example, Harriet, who had been used to being mobile and self-reliant via her car, felt dependent and beholden to others when she no longer had this autonomy (see also Holland et al, 2005; Davey, 2007). For people who had driven for 50 or 60 years, driving was part of their identity as confident, competent and autonomous adults. As noted by Patricia's husband, Malcolm, giving up driving was seen as a permanent loss, a skill and asset that once relinquished would not be regained, hence the desire to preserve it for as long as possible.

Participants' thoughts about the future were tinged with anxieties about failing health. Even where participants perceived themselves as coping at the present time, they worried about how they would manage in the future:

"According to when I had the scan, they told me that it won't get any better, it will get worse. Well, since then it has got worse.... As I said, my back and my knees are gradually getting worse so in 12 months time, it's hard to say what I'll be like. Hopefully I'll be like this. I don't mind if I stay like this for another couple of years if I'm alive, but I can't see it staying like it is now." (Joyce, interview 1)

It was not the experiencing of ill health or disability in itself that concerned participants, but what this might signify in terms of the loss of the things they most valued, such as home, garden, activities and their status as independent.

"It's always there, of course, you're aware of the fact that it could come to an end tomorrow sort of thing but I don't let it worry me. I hope that I can keep going and not become an invalid as such, that's the worry that you've got when you get older." (Harriet, interview 5)

Participants who discussed death saw this as representing less of a threat than other losses. Harriet told me that her son, who was nearly 50, was going to be a father again:

> "They'd like to have a little girl, and I should be pleased to see a little girl, although it's come a bit too late because she won't be old enough for me to teach her anything, it will be too late I expect.... Let's put it this way, I hope I won't be here because, no, I don't want to be an old woman, someone who sits in the chair all day and can't do anything."
> (Harriet, interview 5)

Roger relayed his reaction when he heard from the heart specialist that an operation was not possible and he had about 12 months to live:

> "I wasn't surprised. My daughter, she was a little upset at the time but I told her, 'It's no good worrying at all', I said, 'I'd far sooner be like this and go quickly than hang about and you've got to nurse me for months'." (Roger, interview 5)

Despite his prognosis, Roger still saw himself as 'doing well' and he was determined to 'live his life out' and enjoy what remained of it. These extracts suggest that while service providers may be predominantly concerned with prolonging life, the main concern of many older people may be the quality of their life, as they define it, rather than its duration.

Financial resources

Lack of financial resources has direct implications for the enjoyment of basic human rights and social inclusion (Killeen, 2008). Low income prevents older people from accessing goods and services and denies them full citizenship (Craig, 2004). Participants' financial situations have to be understood within the broader context of poverty experienced by many older people (Parker, 2000). Particular factors predisposing to a low level of material resources include being a woman, living alone, being widowed, divorced or separated, having poor health, having a lower level of education and living in a deprived neighbourhood (Burholt and Windle, 2006).

Five of the participants were totally reliant on state benefits for their incomes (Elsie, Joyce, Ralph, Roger and Les). As mentioned previously, Roger conveyed clearly that he could 'manage' financially and he emphasised that he had never owed anyone anything. At the same time, comments he made suggested that his finances were limited and curtailed certain decisions. For example, he said he could not afford to have central heating installed or a new chimney fitted. At the time of the first interview, he was awaiting the outcome of an application for Attendance Allowance, but in the meantime finances were clearly a matter of some concern to him:

> "With the wife dying and all the funeral expenses and things like that, it's just about crippled me. And then the DHSS, they wrote back and told me when I sent the pension book back that if she'd been 60 or under, I would have had a £1,000 grant towards the funeral but as she was over 60 and drawing her pension, I'd get nothing." (Roger, interview 1)

He also talked about the worry caused by large unforeseen expenses:

> "I did have trouble with the sewer pipes from the toilet upstairs .... that was New Year and I had the chap out a couple of days later and he tried to unblock it and he couldn't and he cut a hole in the pipe and made a mess all over the window and everywhere else and said he couldn't do anything else for it. He charged me £150.... And hadn't sorted it out. And then I had to get a builder chappie and he came ... and he put me new pipes and he charged me £400 so that was a lot of money, £550 I had to find." (Roger, interview 3)

Other research on the impact of resources has indicated that the anxiety and difficulty posed by large unexpected expenditure can 'tip the balance' in terms of older people's ability to manage (Hill et al, 2009). Barbara described finances as 'a worry' – although she had some savings, she was aware that when she drew on these she had no way of replacing them.

Participants accrued new expenses when increasing impairments meant they had to pay for help with taken-for-granted, but necessary, tasks:

> I have to pay to have my hair washed and set weekly because I cannot wash or set it myself and have difficulty getting my arm up high enough to even brush or arrange it. (Alice, diary)

Roger paid someone to tend his solid fuel fire twice a day as he could no longer do this himself. Here the payment of Attendance Allowance was invaluable, not for the provision of 'care' as such, but for enabling participants to buy help to accomplish tasks they could no longer perform themselves. Patricia described as a 'godsend' the Attendance Allowance that enabled her to purchase private help around the house and this also gave her a feeling of security about further support if her difficulties increased:

> "And of course if I need help, even more help, at night or anything like that then they would increase it to another level. So that's fine at the moment." (Patricia, interview 4)

There are a number of significant barriers to older people claiming their benefit entitlements (Moffatt and Higgs, 2007). Initiatives that give them proactive help to make claims have been shown to increase their independence, both physical and psychological, facilitate their social participation and affirm identity in terms of according dignity and a sense of meeting social and cultural expectations (Craig, 2004).

Access to financial capital or occupational benefits meant that some participants could purchase equipment or services to help manage their illness or impairment. Ralph had bought an electric scooter, Gerald had purchased a 'top of the range' hearing aid and special shoes, and Alice had an electric garage door fitted so that she could open and close it without getting out of the car. Barbara was beginning to find driving difficult, particularly manoeuvres like parking and reversing, and she was weighing up whether she could afford to buy an automatic car with power steering. Both Alice and Patricia (the latter through occupational medical insurance) supplemented NHS physiotherapy with private services, including hydrotherapy and acupuncture. Clearly the option of purchasing these services was not available to all participants.

While it is argued that the market and consumerism allow multiple and diverse opportunities for the construction of identities and lifestyle choices (Higgs and Gilleard, 2006), having the financial means to participate in the market is only part of the picture. In my study, financial resources did not in themselves guarantee access to the support people felt they needed, as will be seen in the later discussion of experiences of formal service provision. The previous chapter described how Winifred was relatively affluent, but had 'an outlook of poverty' that meant she was unwilling to spend money, indicating that personality and attitudes are also significant factors in terms of how personal resources are deployed. Other examples of the influence of individual perspectives will be discussed later in this section. In the same way that access to financial resources does not necessarily imply access to adequate support or to subjective experiences of well-being, neither is there a direct relationship between lack of material resources and perceived poor quality of life. Burholt and Windle (2006) noted the 'satisfaction paradox' that the 'oldest old' people had low levels of material resources, but expressed higher levels of satisfaction. Roger can be seen as someone fitting within this category. Burholt and Windle suggest that the 'satisfaction paradox' may reflect psychological processes of adaptation, but stress that expressed satisfaction should not be taken to imply that older people's level of income is adequate to meet their needs.

Life experience

Chapter Four discussed specific life themes as representing an aspect of continuity for participants. Previous life experience was relevant to coping, not only in terms of continuity, but also the extent to which it equipped participants to deal with current difficulties. A recurrent theme for Joyce was 'living a hard life'. She talked of having worked at a brewery from the age of 14 until the brewery closed about 20 years previously (when she was 60):

"It was very heavy work, very wet.... We had to stack cases of drink and the empty bottles and help unload the lorries and what have you. It was very very hard, heavy work, very hard. And for ten shillings a week, and then you had your stoppages taken out." (Joyce, interview 3)

Although she saw herself as 'managing', life was still a struggle. Joyce lived in social housing and was in receipt of Income Support alongside her retirement pension. She apportioned her money carefully to pay her bills, but there was little money available for 'extras'. Life was also physically hard as she sought to continue to do her 'jobs' in the home despite the pain from her osteoporosis and arthritis. Although she had applied to social services for help with a shower, she had been on the waiting list for over a year. However, she saw her experience of living a hard life as an asset in preparing her for her current circumstances. In a similar way, Roger felt that his previous experience of running the household and looking after his wife had forced him to develop skills that helped him to cope in his present situation:

"I did everything for her until about the last two weeks when she was so ill she had to go into hospital.... But of course it made me so as I was used to doing the housework and the cooking and everything else, you see. It was only just that I missed her, you know.... Oh yes, people who've been relying on their wives to do every little thing for them and then they're suddenly gone, it's a terrible wrench then. No, I'd been doing it, you see, for a long long time." (Roger, interview 4)

Although previous life experience could, as with Joyce and Roger, equip participants to deal with problems they were encountering in later life, it could alternatively act as an obstacle if there was a disjunction between their previous experience and the knowledge and skills needed to manage their current situations. Some participants were ill equipped by their previous life experience to cope with new ways of managing. Harriet had driven all of her adult life so when she had to give up her car, she had no experience of using public transport. Her tendency to become dizzy, feelings of disorientation when out and poor memory all contributed to her feeling unable to make this adaptation:

"I couldn't cope with the buses, catching buses, getting the right time for the buses. I'm not used to travelling on buses. I've never done it, never had to do it so it's something that I find difficult, coping with buses. I haven't been anywhere on a bus by myself at all, not since I gave up the car. I just can't bring myself to do it on my own.... I don't

seem able to do it on my own. I feel lost. I've lost all my confidence,
I can't do it on my own." (Harriet, interview 4)

Other skills that acted as a resource or obstacle to coping with difficulties were
those concerned with employing and managing helpers:

"I've always been lucky with cleaners actually. When we lived at B
… I had someone who was marvellous and then when I had TB, I
had a wonderful woman…. I was completely bed-ridden you see."
(Patricia, interview 4)

"It used to be no problem. When I was younger, I always had someone
to come in and help, when I didn't really need it, back when the
children were little. I used to have someone to help on a regular basis
but now that I really need the help, I can't find it." (Harriet, interview 1)

Other participants such as Joyce and Les had no experience of employing domestic
help on which to draw when they needed these services. As Aronson (2002) notes
in her study of older women receiving home care in Canada, class and culture
divisions are directly relevant to ownership of the skills and resources to engage
and manage care staff.

New technologies and ways of doing things could also be perceived as a threat
by those who felt unable or unwilling to learn new skills. Elsie talked of her
grandchildren trying to show her how to use a computer:

"… my grandchildren understand all that but it's a mystery to me. My
grandson says, 'Oh, it's easy', and showed me the book and I said, 'It
might as well be in a foreign language'." (Elsie, interview 3)

Harriet had difficulty shopping now that she could no longer drive and she could
see that ordering purchases on the telephone would be a help to her. However,
she had never used a credit card:

"I refuse to have a credit card, I don't want to know about all these
cards. It's the same with metric measurements, I just don't want to
know about it…. I just can't be bothered, I don't feel I want to be
bothered with it…. I'm finding now on the television they don't
give you addresses. You are getting left behind." (Harriet, interview 3)

Perspectives

Chapter Four referred to the significance for participants of 'not going against the
grain' in terms of attitudes and values, thus reinforcing a sense of continuity and
personal identity. However, at another level the same attitudes and values could

represent threats to coping if they impeded the seeking and receiving of help. For example, Harriet did not feel she could ask friends for help as she saw this as undermining her independence. Roger and Joyce expressed views about not wanting to bother the doctor. Routine visits by the community nursing service had been replaced by a system of older people needing to telephone to request a visit. Joyce and Alice commented on the fact they now seldom saw the nurse as they didn't like to bother her:

> "You see the nurse doesn't come now. She used to come every month or so and now she expects you to ring her and of course I don't [laughs].… I don't want to bother them and I tend to think oh, it will go." (Alice, interview 4)

These attitudes may reflect individual personality traits, but they may also have a social class basis. One study of older people's experiences of health services found that concerns about not bothering or imposing on health professionals were particularly prevalent among working-class interviewees and that these views could contribute to their marginalisation from services (Wilson, 1995).

The tendency noted in Chapter Four for participants to 'look on the bright side' and to emphasise the positives of their situations could also militate against their receiving help. Seeking help and demonstrating eligibility require a 'problem-focused' narrative, as discussed in Chapter Two, whereas that of older people, as seen in the previous chapter, is more often geared to highlighting strengths and abilities. Patricia commented on the visit she received as part of the assessment for Attendance Allowance:

> "The man who came was such a nice man. He said, 'You didn't do yourself any favours on the form did you?'. Well, you don't like to complain too much do you?" (Patricia, interview 2)

Whether and when people seek to access welfare services is influenced by their perception of their role in relation to the state and market, as shown in Baldock and Ungerson's (1994) study. From their research with 32 people recovering from strokes, Baldock and Ungerson identified four models of participation in the care market: – 'consumerism', where no help was expected from the state but all care was arranged privately; 'privatism', characterised by a valuing of autonomy and a privatised lifestyle but a lack of ability to use the market for purchase of things other than consumer goods; 'welfarism', where individuals assumed an active role in trying to secure their entitlements from the welfare state; and 'clientalism', where people tended towards passive roles and attitudes of gratitude and acceptance. Joyce's attitudes, discussed in Chapter Four, about 'not sponging', restricted her requests for help, even when this help was potentially available. On the other hand, Gerald believed in his entitlement to services, his responsibility for finding out about these and claiming them, and this placed him in a stronger position when needing services. Gerald's approach straddles both the 'consumerist' and 'welfarism' models of participation identified by Baldock and Ungerson in that he was both active as a consumer in the private market and had expectations that the welfare state would and should meet certain needs. Joyce and Les, on the other hand, are better characterised in terms of 'clientalism' – they were not used to participating in the private care market and were passive and largely accepting of services provided (or not provided) by the state.

Les's 'clientalism' was an obstacle when he needed increased support as a consequence of his health difficulties. He had a serious heart condition and his daughter lived 30 miles away, also in social housing. He badly wanted his daughter to move nearer to him so that she could support him and his daughter also wanted this. However, they had repeatedly been told that they did not have sufficient housing 'points' for his daughter to be given a housing transfer. This was a decision that could perhaps have been challenged and further medical evidence obtained to support the need for the move. However, Les's personality and attitudes made him averse to pursuing this:

> "So that's my problem, really, my daughter not being able to move here.… I've never been one to stir up trouble, I always think people will see you as a troublemaker. But if I do get worse, and the doctor at the hospital told me it is getting worse, they will have to put someone in to help me or move me out and that doesn't bear thinking about."
> (Les, interview 1)

Both of Les's interviews (he died three months after the second interview) revealed attitudes of fatalism and passivity. This illustrates that however prevalent the policy rhetoric of consumer power and choice, in practice it is constrained for some people by entrenched attitudes and values of passivity, acceptance, self-reliance, shunning of 'charity' and so on. At a time when services are increasingly rationed, persistence, demands and challenge are often the order of the day to gain help. Some individuals will be disadvantaged in terms of their ability to access scarce resources in this environment, whether by lack of resources or ill health or by a particular 'generational habitus', that is, attitudes and experiences characteristic of that generation (Moffatt and Higgs, 2007).

This category of 'personal' threats and resources has comprised four dimensions of participants' situations that appeared to impair or boost their coping capacities, but none of these is entirely 'personal'; all are at some level created and maintained by social and economic parameters. Who becomes ill and disabled, how that is experienced, what resources are available to manage it, what previous experiences and current attitudes the person brings to dealing with the situation, all reflect social, economic and cultural differences and divisions (McLeod and Bywaters, 2000; Breeze, 2004; McMunn et al, 2006; Rose and Hatzenbuehler, 2009). They are issues that may be experienced as personal but which reflect deep-seated inequalities. Understanding older people's experiences of managing ageing has to encompass awareness of the significance of these factors.

Social network threats and resources

Social relationships are intrinsic to the themes of both 'keeping going' and 'staying me'. For example, as illustrated in the previous two chapters, the ability to maintain a sense of reciprocity and acceptable boundaries in relationships contributes to 'keeping going', while relationships also contribute to 'staying me' through supporting self-affirmation and experiences of continuity. In this chapter, the category of social network threats and resources refers to ways in which participants' social networks supported or undermined their efforts to manage difficulties. While Chapter Three highlighted the practical and emotional 'giving' by participants to their families and communities, the role of informal networks in supporting and enhancing older people's coping strategies also requires recognition.

Direct role of social relationships

There were numerous ways in which the family or friends of participants were involved in directly helping them to manage tasks they found difficult. These included routine help with household tasks such as shopping, changing beds, heavy cleaning and home maintenance tasks. This help was acknowledged with gratitude by those who received it:

> "She [sister] is very good. Anytime she goes out shopping she asks me if I want anything. She gets my pension for me usually and she brings me a few scones in. So she's very good and I go in for meals occasionally." (Alice, interview 2)

> "I mean I don't need home helps, my daughter comes over about four times a week for the odd hour when she can … occasionally when she comes over she'll cook me something, probably bring me a casserole, something like that and warm it up here. She's very good … she hasn't got any children and she takes all my washing back and changes the bed, things like that, you know, and does all that for me. I'm all right in that respect." (Roger, interview 5)

A common area of help provided by family and friends was transport, whether to the shops or supermarket or to the doctor's and hospital appointments. Even those who still drove tended to rely on transport provided by friends or family for anything other than local journeys. Les, on the other hand, had no means of private transport. Neither he nor his daughter had a car and in any case his daughter lived too far away to be able to take him to appointments:

"I've got this leaking heart valve and I'm often having to go to the hospital ... and when I go to the hospital, I've got no way of getting there, you see. When I went last week, I had to get one of the volunteer drivers to take me and I had to pay about £16 just to get there. My rent is £97 a fortnight so it doesn't leave a lot on my pension.... If you are going to be more than half an hour, they go off somewhere else and you ring them when you're ready to be picked up but then you've got to pay for a double journey." (Les, interview 1)

Another role played by family members was purchasing or organising equipment to help participants cope with impairments. Elsie was refused the installation of a walk-in shower and although the district council fitted an overhead shower as part of the general refurbishment of the property, she was unable to use this as she still could not climb in and out of the bath itself. Her son-in-law fitted rails to make this easier for her. Joyce had a long wait before the installation of her walk-in shower; in the meantime, her daughter bought her a cordless phone that she could take into the bathroom in case she needed to call for help. If she needed anything she could not afford, her daughter would lend her the money. Her daughter also bought her smaller pieces of equipment such as a grab stick that social services said they no longer provided. After Barbara had fallen out of bed and had been unable to summon help, her son fitted two telephones in the bedroom, one on either side of the bed. Patricia's son-in-law bought her and her husband a smaller car with power steering as her husband was finding it increasingly difficult to drive their existing car.

Members of the informal support network played a role in ascertaining information of value to participants and acting on it on their behalf. As Roberts and Chapman (2001) found, older people with families tend to be better equipped with information and more likely to know about their entitlements. When Roger was waiting for his knee replacement operation and was told he would have to go on a waiting list for a wheelchair, it was his daughter who contacted the Red Cross and arranged to borrow one:

"My daughter contacted them, she's very good. It's part of her work, she does doctor and hospital reports and things like that so she's quite knowledgeable and sorts things out for me." (Roger, interview 1)

Similarly, Ralph's daughter was directly involved in finding out about and arranging help for him following his stroke:

"Somebody was supposed to come in yesterday to have a look at the garden to see about doing it for me only they've postponed it until Monday.... It's from Age Concern or something.... My daughter, she found the number. I avoid the phone because of my speech and I'm hard of hearing." (Ralph, interview 2)

This role of family and friends in facilitating help seeking is also noted by Moloczij et al (2008) in relation to people recovering from stroke.

In addition to the more general seeking of information and support, family and friends performed an important monitoring and emergency response function for some participants. This included telephoning or visiting regularly and I witnessed this first hand on several of my visits:

> "[After answering the telephone] That was my daughter, just checking to see I'm all right. I usually phone morning and night but sometimes I forget, like this morning.... I do at times forget things ... so if I don't ring, she phones to check I'm all right." (Ralph, interview 2)

Although Les's daughter did not live locally, she nevertheless provided regular monitoring by telephone:

> "My daughter phones me every morning at 8.30 to check I'm all right. If anything's wrong, she's got a key – not that it would be any use if anything did happen with her being all over there." (Les, interview 1)

Most participants derived a sense of security from knowing that if they did need help, they had someone nearby they could call on:

> "I've got some lovely neighbours, I can't fault them. Mr T comes down most days to see if I'm alright. He'll say, 'I've called to see how the old girl is' [laughs], and I say, 'I'm telling the old boy I'm alright!'. And we have a laugh and a joke and it's nice.... And I know they're upstairs [in the flat above] and if there's anything I want done or anything I want fetched, I've only got to say." (Joyce, interview 3)

When participants did encounter problems, it was usually a family member who was contacted first and who then took responsibility for summoning help. Ralph described the morning he had his second stroke:

> "I tried to get up and I couldn't push myself up. This thing [lifeline] unfortunately went wrong. I managed to get my daughter on the phone.... She came round, she couldn't pull me up. She must have got the ambulance or phoned the doctor." (Ralph, interview 2)

As well as providing these forms of practical support, family, friends and neighbours were also involved in giving psychological and emotional support. In other words, they offer 'love' as well as 'labour' (Graham, 1983; Reynolds and Walmsley, 1998). The contribution of families to the emotional and social well-being of participants was readily apparent in the accounts of 10 of the 12 participants, and this will have been evident in many of the quotations already cited. The exceptions were

Winifred and Gerald who had no close family, but for them some aspects of this role was assumed by friends. Family members and friends demonstrated in the direct and indirect ways they gave support that they 'cared about', as well as 'cared for' (Graham, 1983). Combined with the 'caring about' that participants were able to do in return, this contributed a sense of self-worth, meaning and purpose.

Indirect role of social networks

Other people within the social network often play a crucial role in help seeking, whether from the statutory or independent sector (Qureshi, 1996; Clark and Spafford, 2001). We have already seen that friends and relatives of participants were instrumental in seeking help on their behalf or in putting them in touch with a relevant agency. The informal social network also served as an indirect resource for participants who were seeking help by virtue of the information circulated within the network as a whole. These informal sources of information proved more effective than formal channels. Whereas lists of agencies provided by social services were inadequate when participants were looking to purchase private domiciliary care, three participants eventually found help through contacts supplied by informal sources:

> "I asked everywhere, the surgery, the girls on the desk, and they didn't
> know anyone. So I was desperate really. I went to the pharmacy for
> my medicine, I said to the girl behind the counter, 'Do you know
> anyone?'. 'Oh yes', she said, 'I know one or two'." (Patricia, interview 3)

Harriet initially had great difficulty finding someone to help her in the house; she eventually found someone through a friend. When she decided she needed help with the garden, the person who helped in the house was able to recommend someone. Helpers found through informal sources therefore had the added bonus of coming with a personal recommendation, giving participants a greater sense of security about initiating the contact. If satisfied with the service, they could then in turn recommend the helper to others within their networks. If access to services is influenced by the level of information people have (Bartlett, 1999), and social networks are a prime source of information, it follows that this is one of the many ways in which social networks operate as a resource when older people are negotiating difficulties:

> "If it hadn't been for Marion [friend], I shouldn't have got anybody....
> I mean people that don't mix, they won't stand a chance of getting
> anybody in a village like this. She's out of the village, you see, and, yes,
> the importance of people being able to get out and about as well ...
> she doesn't mix at all, you see, so if she was trying to get somebody,
> you see, it would be hopeless." (Alice, interview 3)

As part of the surveillance (Seale, 1996) or keeping watch (Minichiello et al, 2000) function performed by friends and family, members of the informal social network seemed to play an important role in identifying or giving voice to problems that participants were experiencing. This then validated their own acknowledgement of difficulties and was instrumental in prompting help seeking:

"I'd been having them [pains in my chest] a long time, over 12 months, just as though I had an iron band closing in. I wasn't worried but my daughter was and she said, 'You've got to go to the doctor', and she took me down and she said, 'I'm coming in with you' ... and she came in with me and I was examined and I've got angina and they gave me tablets." (Elsie, interview 3)

"I've had sort of tinglings in my fingers and my daughter was ever so worried because they'd read something on the prescription her husband was having about, she was quite frantic that I'd got to see the doctor because it said if he'd got tingling in his fingers he must stop taking this medication immediately and see the doctor because he might be having a stroke and I thought, bless me, she's got enough to worry about, I'd better see about it ... I rang to get an appointment." (Alice, interview 3)

Of the four participants who had made the referral to social services themselves, three explained their help seeking as a response to the advice of others. Chapter Four discussed 'staying me' factors that can operate as obstacles to participants' acknowledgement of difficulties and help seeking, for example, beliefs about personal responsibility to 'put on a brave face' and 'not give in'. Given these forces acting against help seeking, identifying and addressing problems was perhaps rendered more acceptable if the need was identified or corroborated by someone else. If others take a key role in problem identification and help seeking, this allows older people to transfer responsibility for the decision to someone else, thereby avoiding potential social reprobation for being 'demanding'. It also allows them to retain intact a sense of their own coping if they see themselves as acting to alleviate the concern of others (Johnson, 1991).

The concerns of others in the social network may also encourage behaviour that reduces physical risk. Chapter Three described participants' concerns to avoid imposing psychological burdens on their families. Some participants similarly attributed their attempts to reduce risk to the anxieties of others:

"I don't worry; my daughter does because I've had these heart attacks, she made me have this thing [lifeline alarm] put in. And she says, 'When you go out again and start walking about, I'm going to get you a mobile phone'.... She does, but I don't, worry, I don't think about it, you know, I just keep going." (Roger, interview 1)

However, even here, participants did not just acquiesce to the concerns of others on their behalf, but made their own judgements based on their calculation of the risks involved and their evaluation of the benefits weighed against the potential consequences. As shown in Chapter Three, participants acted according to their own perception of risk rather than that of their families. This suggests that while the concerns of others may act as triggers to seeking help, validating participants' help-seeking actions, this occurs where participants themselves already at some level share the concerns. Where the anxieties of others are at variance with those of participants, they are more likely to dismiss them or engage in subterfuge, as illustrated by Elsie's comment:

> "I don't mind standing on stools but it's my daughter, she won't let me.... But I get up there to clean things, she doesn't know." (Elsie, interview 4)

There is a tension, then, between the need to preserve independence and the sense of desire or obligation to respond to the concerns of others (Moloczij et al, 2008). Research involving staff and older people in a day centre noted a potential conflict between staff members' preoccupation with physical risk and the older people's greater concern with social risks. Strategies by staff to reduce physical risk were observed to encourage older people's dependence and reduce their confidence and self-esteem (Ballinger and Payne, 2002). It is likely that within the private space of home, the participants in my study had greater power to resist the risk-avoidance pressures exerted by others. However, it seems that the anxieties of others, combined with older people's concerns not to 'overstep the mark' by imposing psychological as well as physical burdens on those close to them, can trigger help seeking and therefore reduce risk. On the other hand, if older people have a different perception of risk and lack the ability to resist the restrictions urged by others, the risk-minimising pressures within social networks could instead function as a threat rather than resource. This was illustrated by David's feelings of being stifled and over-protected by his family, described in Chapter Four.

Threats to social support

A corollary of the supportive role of social relationships is that the absence or loss of such relationships implies a threat to coping. Where family support is lacking, it may be that some of this role of providing direct support is assumed by friends, as in the case of Winifred, or by the potential to purchase support from the care market, as in the case of Gerald. However, the role of social networks in providing indirect support and in bolstering emotional and psychological coping suggests there are some facets of the role of close relatives and friends that are more difficult for other parties to assume. As well as considering 'gaps' in terms of the presence or absence of different types of support, it is also important to look at support in a more dynamic sense, recognising changes in levels of support over time.

There are particular factors in later life that may threaten the stability of social support, including the impact on relationships of ill health, disability and bereavement. Both Alice and Harriet talked of the importance of their relationships with friends, the difficulties of losing friendships through death and the increasing difficulty in maintaining friendships as they got older. For Harriet, having to give up driving meant that she could no longer visit friends as she used to and her arthritis meant that keeping in touch by letter was both difficult and painful. While participants' own health difficulties could impair their ability to sustain friendships, the ill health or disability of those close to them also threatened their support network. Patricia relied on her husband for both emotional and practical support and when he became ill, the fact he had to undertake caring tasks for her was a source of great anxiety:

> "My husband does everything at the moment but he's 81, he's got high blood pressure and he's on beta-blockers. I worry about the effect on him, I worry that he shouldn't be doing it and I feel guilty that I can't do it [becoming tearful at this point]." (Patricia, interview 1)

Alice's son-in-law had a serious health condition that meant her daughter's time was consumed in looking after him:

> "My son-in-law's still very poorly. I'm seeing less of them really. I haven't been for a meal for ages.... I never know when they're going to be able to pop in." (Alice, interview 3)

As Finch and Mason (1993) note, there are 'legitimate excuses', accepted on both sides, for family members not providing help, one of these being the ill health or disability of the potential helper.

In later life, there is a greater chance of bereavement, with the loss of close relationships such as partners, siblings and friends (Chambers, 2005). Nine of the participants in my study were widows or widowers and during the three years of the study, five of them experienced the deaths of brothers, sisters or friends, as recorded in some diary entries:

> Sad and lonely. Lost my friend.
> Lost another war-time comrade, that's three this month.
> Went to friend's funeral. Feel rather low. Came home and went to bed. (Les, diary)

> My older sister, E, died in September last year and we have missed seeing her and visiting her regularly and then my husband's sister died in January and although I have not been able to get over to see her so

much recently, I have missed talking to her on the phone. We lived in the same road for 34 years, almost opposite E and my mother-in-law, and we were quite close. (Alice, diary)

Friends often provided the basis for activities outside the home and the loss of these relationships then meant the loss of valued social activities as well. Barbara did not feel able to go on holiday on her own after the illness and death of her husband, but when she formed a new relationship, this again became possible for her. David had always loved dancing but did not feel able to go to dances when he moved from Scotland as he no longer had dancing partners. Social activity such as dancing may have a range of benefits for older people (Cooper and Thomas, 2002), and for David the cessation of this activity seemed to represent a physical, social and psychological loss.

As well as disruptions in social relationships, there are also 'blocks' to relationships fulfilling their helping potential. This was illustrated by Les's situation, discussed earlier in this chapter. The potential support his daughter could offer was blocked by seemingly inflexible housing policies, which meant she could not move to live nearer to him, and by poor public transport services. Although Les had no readily available family support, he did receive help from neighbours, who lived in the accommodation complex, so in some ways peers compensated for the deficit in family help. However, when his health deteriorated, this was inadequate to address his needs. Although his neighbours wanted to help at some level, there was concern, on both sides it seemed, about 'overstepping the mark'. A study of support provided by friends and neighbours suggests that what are perceived as excessive demands can jeopardise helping relationships (Nocon and Pearson, 2000). At the time of the second interview, Les had recently been discharged home after several weeks in hospital. He was taking 14 different sorts of tablets, had lost nearly three stone in weight and was very breathless (much of the tape recording of this interview was inaudible). He told me he thought that someone at the hospital was arranging meals-on-wheels and home care for him, but no one had yet visited. Although he had friends who lived in the housing complex who offered help with shopping and other tasks, he had no one to offer the flexible and more comprehensive help he needed or who would take responsibility for helping him to arrange this. This was in marked contrast to the situations of other participants, such as Joyce, Roger and Elsie, who had family members available to step into any breach in coping left by illness, frailty and the non-provision of services.

Another source of threat to coping was relationships characterised by conflict rather than support. While conflict in close relationships can, of course, feature throughout the lifecourse, it may have added implications in later life when the field of social relationships may be constricting, with fewer opportunities to develop new relationships, and when there are additional 'assaults to self'. When discussing the role of close friendships in helping to sustain a sense of stability and self-worth in Chapter Four, I cited the example of Gerald, whose close friend, Ann, lived in the same sheltered accommodation complex. In the same way that stable relationships could support participants' self-perceptions as 'managing', conflict within relationships appeared to contribute to a diminished sense of coping. At the third interview, when Gerald had just suffered a leg injury severely restricting his mobility, his relationship with Ann appeared to be in jeopardy. He had moved to the sheltered flats to be near to Ann and they had shared daily companionship and meals out since he moved in. However, Ann was considering returning south to her former home town. Gerald expressed anger and bitterness at what he saw as her proposed desertion:

> "She's decided when I was bad, started to be bad, she thought the best thing she could do was bale out.... I don't quite know what to do to be honest now because in a minute I'm going to need help and I don't know which way to turn.... I think she probably thought that I was going to be a lumber on her, that's all I can think of. I can't think of any other reason.... Because I'm so used to her about and she liked being with me, she told me so hundreds of times I should think.... I can see if I'm not careful this is going to be very lonely stuck in here. And I don't quite know what to do about it." (Gerald, interview 3)

Merely having family and neighbours is not an indicator of well-being; much depends on the quality of the relationships and whether they are a source of support (Cordingley et al, 2001; Bowling and Gabriel, 2007). Joyce told me in the first interview that her younger daughter had nothing to do with her – "She never asks if I've got two pennies or a slice of bread" – and that she had little contact with this daughter's two children either. She became tearful when talking about this and only spoke about it after the tape recorder was switched off. There was conflict between Ralph and his neighbours over their parking of their car in the space reserved for his scooter outside the house. He made the distinction,

> "There's no neighbours round here; there's people who live next door." (Ralph, interview 1)

Joyce and Elsie both talked about the difficulties they faced in their previous accommodation and their relief when the council finally gave them transfers to their present homes. Relationships with neighbours seemed to be the key factor. Joyce felt that the council 'dumped' people with problems in the flats and both she and Elsie felt they had little choice or control about moving. These situations seemed to feature not just an absence of support, but also the negative impact of hostility that in itself threatened to undermine some of the psychological aspects of coping discussed in Chapter Four.

Another important way in which relationships may compromise personal and social support, detracting from both 'keeping going' and 'staying me', is through abuse. Although this was not encountered in my study, it is vital to acknowledge the potential for abuse within relationships and the implications this may have for all aspects of older people's well-being (Penhale and Parker, 2008).

This category has identified different ways in which participants' social networks performed direct and indirect roles in supporting their efforts to manage difficulties. These include the giving of practical, financial, social and emotional support; providing information and arranging help; fulfilling a monitoring and crisis response function; triggering help seeking; and encouraging risk-minimising behaviour. It has also drawn attention to threats posed to informal support by disrupted relationships, blocks to potential helping and conflict within relationships.

Community threats and resources

This section moves beyond participants' immediate social networks to consider threats and resources contained within the wider community. It looks first at participants' experiences of seeking help from and using formal health and social care services before considering experiences of involvement and participation in communities more broadly.

Formal services

From participants' interview and diary accounts, a range of issues pertaining to formal health and social care services were identified. As noted in relation to personal resources, some participants were in a more advantageous position than others in terms of their access to financial resources, their attitudes and previous experience as care 'consumers'. However, even participants who had access to financial resources and who were 'consumerist' in their approaches were sometimes impeded in managing difficulties by the services they required not being available or not meeting their perceived need. These findings can be understood within the wider policy and practice context discussed in Chapter Two.

Service availability

The shift from experiencing a need for help to acknowledging that need publicly and seeking help from services, or from 'felt' to 'expressed' need, to use Bradshaw's (1972) terminology, is not straightforward. As has already been shown, participants' past experiences, attitudes and values are significant factors in determining whether they perceive a difficulty as a 'need' for which it is legitimate to seek help. Thus, Joyce was accustomed to her 'hard life', and she experienced difficulties in later life as a continuation of this, consistent with her earlier experiences and expectations. We have also seen that some participants did not want to be seen as 'vulnerable' or 'needy'. A referral for help that was made or triggered by others could feel more acceptable, but not all older people have someone to perform this role.

Non-referral for help could also reflect a lack of knowledge of the potential role of health and social care agencies. The provision of information by social services is itself a service and a legal duty, but a wealth of studies have documented the lack of effective information provision for older people and their lack of understanding and awareness of available sources of support (Clark et al, 1998; Littlechild and Glasby, 2000; Lloyd, 2000; Richards, 2000; Gott et al, 2007). It is not necessarily that information is not available, but rather that older people are not aware that it is available and do not know how to access it (Kerr and Kerr, 2003).

Participants' experiences indicated that their efforts to find help were hampered by lack of relevant information. For example, several participants identified lack of information about private home care services as a problem:

> "If I wanted a cleaner, I wouldn't know where to go to get one because I never let myself get that involved with things, sort of thing. I just live a quiet life, day to day.... I mean, so much is kept away from us, isn't it? You don't get enough information." (Joyce, interview 1)

At the first interview, Barbara said she knew that she needed some help but she 'hadn't a clue' what help was available or where to go for help. She had a hearing impairment so trying to find this out by telephone or even direct conversation was not straightforward. This relates to the earlier point about participants' previous life experiences acting as a resource or disadvantage when dealing with situations in later life. If they are encountering new areas of experience, the availability of clear information about how and where to access help and details of the terms and processes involved is a prerequisite for people to function as 'consumers'. Not knowing what provision would be available if their needs increased and who would provide this contributed to the sense of threat posed by their assumptions of deteriorating health, discussed earlier.

For some participants, however, non-referral to services seemed to indicate a realistic, rather than poor, understanding of available provision. Harriet, Barbara, Ralph, Les and Roger had all received help from social services in the past when caring for their spouses. This had given them some understanding of the restrictions on the help available and they had made or agreed to the current referral with little expectation that appropriate help would be forthcoming. The perception of several participants was that they would not receive a service, and even if they did, it would not address their needs as they saw them:

> "I couldn't afford to pay anybody. I mean, if I had a cleaner come in, from the council or what do you call it, these home helps, I mean, that's £7 an hour and ... they're not allowed to do this, they're not allowed to do that, so what the hell's the good of paying them to do something that you can do yourself. You want them to do things that you can't do, which will probably be the things they aren't allowed to do. Why bother with it?" (Joyce, interview 1)

The supply of aids and equipment was another area of unmet need for participants. Three participants had requested help getting in and out of the bath. The council regarded bathing as non-essential, unless a bath was required for hygiene reasons. As mentioned previously, Elsie was turned down for a walk-in shower, but a shower was installed over the bath as part of the refurbishment of the property, which had transferred from council to housing association management:

> "Well, eventually they fitted one [shower] but they fitted it the wrong end and it's hopeless because the side of the bath slopes and which ever way I tilt it, I can't get close enough to the water. Anyway, I've had trouble getting my leg over the side of the bath to get out and Len [son-in-law] said, 'You must have a grab rail' and they said they would fit one but I never heard anymore about it and eventually Len fitted one for me." (Elsie, interview 3)

The central role of equipment in supporting independence and the deficiencies in previous mechanisms of provision have been recognised in the implementation of a retail model for the supply of equipment (Care Services Efficiency Programme, 2008; Cutler, 2008). While this is based on the funding of community equipment services by local authority and health partnerships, Elsie and Joyce's experiences show the need for interconnection with housing agencies. Joyce, who also lived in housing association accommodation, had a similar experience of work being carried out that did not accord with her perceived needs. Her kitchen was refurbished as part of improvements carried out by the housing association, but this again failed to take account of her specific requirements:

> "When they did the kitchen, I told them how I wanted my sink and draining board and they've put it under the window. I can't reach my windows, I can't reach to open them or anything so they're never opened." (Joyce, interview 4)

She had to open the back door if she needed ventilation and she was very reluctant to do this in view of her concerns about security and crime. She was also unable to reach some of the cupboards that had been fitted high up on the wall, despite her request for them to be placed lower. And standing on a stool would expose her to the risk of falling.

Another issue this raises is the waiting times for receipt of a service. The service may be available eventually but resource shortages, rationing mechanisms or just the slow working of bureaucratic organisations may mean participants have to wait for them, their independence threatened in the meantime. One of the few grievances expressed by Roger was the length of the waiting time for various services; he had had to wait for social services to visit him, wait for a knee operation, wait for a wheelchair to be provided and wait six months before he could receive Attendance Allowance:

"Well, the only thing that annoys me really is this sort of gap in between, you know, you've got to wait for everything when really you want help within the first week or two of needing help." (Roger, interview 1)

By the end of the study Joyce had received two of the three services she had requested (a shower installation and a toilet seat), but she had had to wait over two years for them.

There is often a lack of understanding about processes of assessment and mechanisms for determining eligibility for services (Reed and Stanley, 2000). Several participants who had been refused services did not understand the basis on which these decisions had been made. This was particularly so for participants who had received an assessment only via telephone or letter. Neither Elsie nor Joyce, who had asked for shower installations, had been visited in response to the request. They were refused the service on the basis of a questionnaire that they completed and returned to social services. Help with bathing was only provided if it was seen as a health need, not as a social need (Twigg, 1997). For people accustomed to a daily bath, being told that bathing is not 'necessary' is difficult to comprehend and accept. Elsie revealed during the course of this interview that she had a longstanding gynaecological problem that required particular attention to hygiene. This might well have entitled her to a shower installation on medical grounds, but the questionnaire did not prompt her to reveal it so it was not taken into account in the assessment. Both Elsie and Joyce felt that sending a form was not an adequate way of finding out about their level of need:

"He [man from the district council] said, 'They say you're not disabled enough to have a shower fitted'. So I said, 'Well, the ones who have said that haven't seen how I get in and out of the bath, have they? So how can they judge?'. You can't judge if you haven't seen a person do it, can you? Not really." (Joyce, interview 3)

The modernisation of social work has increasingly separated out responsibilities for assessment, care coordination and review, and this fragmentation undermines the relationship-based dimensions of the practitioner's role (Tanner, 2009). One study based on documentary analysis and interviews with older service users, carers and care managers in seven different local authority areas in 2000-01 reported disruption in the continuity of relationships between service users and care managers caused by the fragmentation of the different tasks that constitute the care management process. It concluded,

There is a danger that the very personal service that is at the heart of care becomes disjointed rather than set into a relationship that develops trust and accountability. (Ware et al, 2003, p 425)

An increasing use of telephone screening through call centres (Coleman, 2009) adds further distance, discontinuity and impersonality to the initial assessment process. Winifred's friend was indignant on her behalf at the failure of social services to visit when she telephoned them for help. She felt that they had lost touch with people:

> "They said ... the policy is that we assess you over the phone.... I didn't believe it. I just could not believe how naïve people are, professional people. Why don't they get down to basics, they're so high up they forget what's underneath ... if they got off their backsides and made the journey to these people who are only within a few miles, it wouldn't have taken them 10 minutes if they'd come over, then they would see." (friend of Winifred, interview 1)

Being refused help on the grounds that their need was not severe enough could foster feelings of injustice and hostility towards those who did receive services:

> "A friend of mine phoned and she said, 'Remember so and so?', and I said, 'Yes'. She said, 'Well, she's got her shower fitted'. She lives in a bungalow and she's got a shower fitted. My friend said it's absolutely beautiful. I said, 'I didn't know she'd got anything wrong with her'. She said, 'She hasn't'. She said, 'All she does is sit at home and stuff her face and she's got too fat to get in and out of the bath so they've put her in a shower. She drives herself about in the car, she doesn't walk anywhere'. I said, 'My God, and here's folks bloody suffering, you know, to get in and out to have a shower and keep themselves clean and they look after people like that first'. It makes me so cross, it does. Oh it does make me cross." (Joyce, interview 4)

Similarly, Elsie talked of social services' refusal to install a walk-in shower:

> "I do not understand it. There are two people here who shall be nameless, fit as fiddles. I used to see one walking miles away, without sticks or anything, and she has a walk-in shower." (Elsie, interview 1)

Chapter Four discussed ways in which participants established reputations as deserving by positively comparing themselves with other people. While this appeared to support a positive self-evaluation and social presentation, social comparisons were also made in a way that suggested others were a threat. Situations where individual coping is felt to be in jeopardy, where there is a sense of being in competition for scare resources with others and where the basis for decisions is poorly understood can trigger or accentuate a sense of injustice and resentment towards others. Often it is other service users who are 'blamed', rather than deficiencies in health and social care systems.

Service qualities

This section considers participants' experiences of the quality of provision. One issue was whether the level of service available or provided was perceived as adequate. Three participants who had received home care when caring for their partners mentioned the inadequacy of allocated home care:

> "I had a little bit [of help] to help me out towards the end when my wife was very ill and, well, they were a help but not much. They used to come in the morning and help me get her up and get her washed and dressed and then I was left on my own all day long, the same as all night long. You see, you got no help with that." (Roger, interview 3)

Other examples cited where the level of service was felt to be insufficient related to healthcare provision, particularly chiropody services. Problems with foot care can create chronic difficulties for everyday living (Bowling et al, 1997) and contribute to the risk of falls (Menz and Lord, 2005), but NHS provision is restricted. Alice pointed out that NHS appointments at the foot clinic were not frequent enough for her needs and also difficult to access because home visits were very restricted. However, she was able to pay for private chiropody treatment to supplement what was available from the NHS.

Most studies report a high level of satisfaction and gratitude expressed by older people about professionals and services (Bury and Holme, 1991; Richardson and Pearson, 1995; Myers and MacDonald, 1996; Wilson, 1995; Henwood et al, 1998; Hey, 1999; Francis and Netten, 2004). Increasing age is associated with higher levels of expressed satisfaction (Reed and Gilleard, 1995), perhaps reflecting the decreasing expectations of people as they age. Hey's (1999) study found that the accounts of the frail older people she interviewed reflected both minimal expectations of external sources (for example, the community and the state) combined with maximum aspirations of their own ability to cope. The tendency of some participants to 'look on the bright side' was noted in Chapter Four. A situation often has to be 'drastic' before older people will complain (Roberts and Chapman, 2001). Of the older participants in my study, none of them had considered complaining about the refusal of services or dissatisfaction with services received. As in the Roberts and Chapman research, this seemed to be partly about the pejorative associations of being a 'complainer' and partly about their understanding and acceptance of the constraints on services. Roger's account of recent encounters with his GP demonstrated dissatisfaction with the service when promised visits by the GP or nurse did not materialise. However, he was reluctant to complain about this. Although recognising that the response was inadequate, he sought to make allowances for his GP, setting the deficiencies within the context of the positive aspects of the care he received generally and his understanding of the pressures faced by the service:

> "They've always been very good to me but whether he's a bit forgetful,
> I don't know.... I don't like bothering them because they're busy
> people." (Roger, interview 2)

Other research on expressed satisfaction expressed with health services found that
even when dissatisfied, older people made allowances, saw no point in complaining
and gave positive responses to satisfaction questionnaires (Wilson, 1995).

Where services were still being received, it was possible that participants felt
the need to 'look on the bright side' and were less inclined to be overtly critical.
Strong criticism tended to relate to services they were no longer receiving. Patricia
and Barbara were both highly critical of the service, now terminated, that they
received from private care agencies and this revealed a number of dimensions of
'quality' shortfalls, such as unreliability, poor quality of work, lack of trust and the
failure to deliver what felt like a personal service. Barbara detailed her attempts
to find private help in her diary:

> Owing to angina attacks, felt I needed help with housework. Saw
> advert in local paper. They came to have a chat and I decided to try
> them fortnightly.
> [Later entry] Not very good – rushed though work, not at all impressed.
> Will give them another chance to get to know me and my ways and
> the flat which will be different to other places they work.
> [Later entry] Have given them fair trial. Still not satisfied. They say
> they have finished in 40 minutes and I pay them for the hour.... I
> [told them] now I am feeling better I can cope. (Barbara, diary)

In the interview following this entry, Barbara reported that the workers had broken
things, moved a cupboard and not put it back properly and the kitchen floor felt
sticky after they had mopped it. She also said she did not like having a team of
two people as they talked to each other rather than developing a relationship with
her. Patricia also disliked agencies' common practice of sending in two or three
carers rather than one, commenting on how intrusive this was in her small flat.

Important dimensions of a quality service are also demonstrated by participants'
descriptions of a service with which they were satisfied. Eventually, through
informal contacts in the village, Patricia found a woman who lived locally who
came in twice a week to help her:

> "She lives just at the back of us, in the houses along the road at the
> back. And she's a very open sort of person, you know, very clean, and I
> thought, 'Oh, she'll be all right'. And she got here and she's a gem. She's
> an absolute gem. She comes on Tuesday morning and Friday and she's
> perfect. She cleans everything from top to bottom. She's wonderful.
> Oh, it's made such a difference to me.... And she's marvellous.... I
> don't have to ask her, she just does it.... She's always on time. If she's

going to be five minutes late ... she always rings immediately and says I'm going to be a bit late.... She calls me Pat, I call her Kate. And she's like one of the family. She's absolutely great, she's a pleasant girl to have around." (Patricia, interview 4)

Harriet was very pleased with the service provided by the helper she recruited through her informal contacts. She pointed out the relief she felt, knowing that she had someone calling regularly to help with the jobs she could no longer do on her own:

"It makes you feel better, this is the thing. And of course, I'm so used to her, it's like a friend. We sit down and spend the first half hour having coffee as soon as she gets here, and that is as good as the physical help actually, just to have someone to talk to." (Harriet, interview 3)

Alice was pleasantly surprised by the high quality of care she received from council home care staff. She acknowledged the limitations of the service, such as lack of choice about when the carers could call, the difficulty of adherence to a fixed time, the short duration of the visits and the need to accept multiple carers rather than one regular helper. However, despite these shortcomings, she emphasised the positive benefits of the service rather than its limitations:

"I enquired about help to get me up in the morning. I'd enquired about it before but they couldn't come very early and I thought it wasn't very good. It wasn't any good for me really because I can't lie in bed once I wake up ... because of being in one place and I ache, I have to move. But somebody suggested ... that I get my breakfast ready the night before on a tray ... and just put my dressing gown on, which I've got used to now but was quite a problem, and sat and had my breakfast and then waited for them to come. And it's worked out ever so much better.... They're only here for half an hour but what they do is marvellous really. They see to the commode, they make the bed, they help me get washed and dressed and then I'm ready for off, you know." (Alice, interview 5)

Whereas in previous interviews, Alice had referred to the importance of having a regular carer who was familiar with her and her home, she now commented on the benefits of having different carers and how interesting and stimulating she found this:

"I mean really, it's been a big experience for me having these people in. It's amazed me, I thought I'd mixed and I thought I knew a lot but I'm amazed at these young folk ... their outlook is quite different to the older ones.... Yes, I'm thrilled.... I'm very very glad I took it up because it's helped me such a lot, apart from educating me about the youth of today [laughs]." (Alice, interview 5)

She sought to understand the service limitations and in this way could accept them:

"Before they came, I thought, oh, they're hopeless, sort of thing, and of course everybody wants them at the same time for different reasons....They're very good, I couldn't grumble about anything really. I mean, you've got to try and understand. As I say, they can't sort of give you any definite time but they try to, they do what they can." (Alice, interview 5)

Aronson's (2002) longitudinal study of older women receiving home care in Ontario suggests three different ways in which the women managed often inadequate home care provision and the responses of the participants in my study seems consistent with this. Harriet and Patricia both sought to 'take charge' of the service provided, moulding it in ways that met their perceived needs. Barbara's account of her experience seems to illustrate the 'pushed over the edge' response in which care recipients feel out of control and that their identities are invalidated. In Alice's account, there are some elements of the 'restraining expectations' response, as she adjusted to the service shortfalls and made allowances for them. As Aronson points out, and as discussed in the earlier section on personal resources, class and culture are relevant to how older people engage with care staff and service providers. Harriet and Patricia both had previous experience of employing cleaners and were more inclined to be care directors than care recipients, acting authoritatively to ensure that the service met their requirements.

Harriet voiced a preference for receiving help 'on a paying basis' so that she could exercise control over what tasks were done:

"I would rather have someone privately if I can who would do what I want them to do ... with the home helps, they're not allowed to clean windows and things like that but those are the jobs that you need, that's why I want to get someone privately if I can because those are the things I can't do." (Harriet, interview 1)

Although care received from the council would also, in effect, be 'on a paying basis' since she would be charged for it, she felt she would only be able to exercise the required level of choice and control by buying services from the private sector. Other studies have noted older people's concerns about the lack of flexibility of domiciliary care and also concern about poor communication and relationships with care staff (Langan et al, 1996; Henwood et al, 1998; Bartlett, 1999; Nocon and Pearson, 2000; Francis and Netten, 2004; CSCI, 2006). There is some support for Harriet's view that paying for private help increases the exercise of choice in areas such as the times of visits and the tasks performed (Roberts and Chapman,

2001). However, there are still barriers to the development of positive relationships between older people and home care staff, for example, resource shortages and the need for brief, task-focused visits, high staff turnover and organisational policies (Leece and Peace, 2009). Alice's experience demonstrates that positive relationships can develop where there are multiple carers involved, if there is some consistency of staff. However, continuity of care staff is difficult for providers in both the statutory and independent sectors to achieve (Glendinning et al, 2000; Clark and Spafford, 2001; CSCI, 2006).

A major barrier to consumerism in practice is that the majority of 'users' of social care services are among the most disadvantaged and marginalised members of society. They frequently lack information, have little sense of entitlement, have few clear-cut rights and are in difficult situations that are not conducive to the expression of 'voice' or choice to 'exit' when faced with unsatisfactory arrangements (Walker, 1993; Caldock, 1994; Barnes, 1997; Higgs, 1997; Means and Smith, 1998b). As in Les's situation, choice tends to be confined to the refusal of services offered (Hardy et al, 1999; Hey, 1999). Direct payments and individual budgets, discussed in Chapter Two, increase the potential for service users to exercise choice and control about staff employed to provide help. However, Barbara, who had experienced social services help in the past, but was now receiving less than satisfactory help from a private agency, stated her preference for help provided directly by social services. This was because she had more confidence in the recruitment processes, training and support given to council staff. The significance of home as a private space was discussed in Chapter Four, and it is important that older people who may already feel vulnerable are confident about the trustworthiness of those coming into their homes (Clark et al, 1998). Some participants commented on feeling anxious about inviting strangers into their homes, even if care staff were provided through agencies. There was a sense of, as Barbara put it, 'never knowing who you are getting'. In this context, personal recommendation from informal contacts gave an increased sense of security and confidence.

Community participation

The local community can function as a resource in the management of difficulties or, conversely, as a source of threat. Barnes (1997) argues that the focus in 'community care' on receiving services should be replaced by a concern with community participation. This draws attention to broader goals and more generic aspects of social life that are necessary for older people to participate actively in communities (see also ODPM, 2006).

Community resources

There were a number of features of 'ordinary' community provision that appeared to support participants as they aged. One aspect referred to already is religious activity. As noted in Maynard et al's study, 'Religion has generally been ignored as a resource for older people', yet for many it is an integral part of their lives (Maynard et al, 2008, p 117). As the latter research with women from different ethnic groups shows, religion is intricately bound up with issues of identity, culture and ethnicity. Although there are some commonalities of themes across religious groups, there are different emphases and meanings both between and within them (Cohen et al, 2008). It needs to be borne in mind that participants in my study were all of white UK ethnic origin and an ethnically more diverse sample would have generated other issues. However, in general terms, older people's religious beliefs appear to be associated with perceptions of well-being and quality of life (Nilsson et al, 1998; Coleman et al, 2002). Although religious belief can be regarded as supporting personal coping, religious activity can also be seen as a resource at the community level, facilitating social engagement and community participation. Elsie, Alice and Patricia all talked about their participation in various ways in the lives of their church communities. As mentioned earlier, Elsie had until recently been on the flower rota at her church, delivered the church magazines and given talks to visitors on the history of the church. Alice took care of the financial accounts of her church and other members of the church played an important role in her social network. They attended meetings in each other's houses and went on trips and holidays together. These three participants felt able to seek and accept help from the church leaders and membership since this was consistent with normative expectations within their religious communities. Joyce did not attend church, but described herself as having a strong religious faith. This was practised in the private space of her own home in the context of offering healing to others. This gave her social contact, a sense of being useful and of fulfilling religious expectations. The benefits of religious activity do not necessarily cease therefore when mobility declines and religion is practised more privately (Godfrey et al, 2004; Maynard et al, 2008). In relation to 'keeping going' strategies, discussed in Chapter Three, participants' religious activity generated individual busyness, was a source of social contact and a significant part of weekly routines. With regard to 'staying me' coping mechanisms, discussed in Chapter Four, it may represent aspects of continuity and support self-affirmation strategies through a sense of spiritual well-being (Coleman et al, 2002).

Various other ordinary aspects of the community infrastructure supported participants' management of difficulties. Alice mentioned the disabled facilities available at the local supermarket. There were wide parking spaces, staff would assist with the packing of the shopping, carry it to the car and telephone across to the adjacent petrol station so that someone was available to help her refuel. The cashback facility at the supermarket was also appreciated, removing the necessity of a separate journey to the bank. Another service valued by several participants was the prescription collection service offered by some pharmacists, although not everyone was aware the service was available. For Ralph, a valued service was the mobile library that visited his village every fortnight. This allowed him to maintain his hobby of reading, even when he was obliged to relinquish other activities. Three participants used a local service that delivered frozen meals at reasonable cost. These could be kept in the freezer and microwaved when required. The service was available to all, so was non-stigmatising, and did not involve any paperwork in the form of invoices or the writing of cheques. All it took was a telephone call to place the order.

However, some aspects of community services appeared to undermine efforts to preserve independence. Community participation often depends on transport, yet transport has been identified as a frequent problem for older people (Langan et al, 1996; Bartlett, 1999). Particular concerns include the safety of using public transport in the evening or at night (Gilhooly et al, 2004) and lack of access to transport in rural areas (Wenger, 2001). The latter was evident in my study. In this context, it is easy to understand why participants attached so much importance to continuing to drive and why relinquishing driving signified such a loss of independence. Even where public transport is available, difficulties such as reduced mobility and poor vision or hearing can make using it problematic. The availability of transport could make a significant difference to people's management of everyday tasks such as shopping. For participants who lived in or near the town, there was a special bus that ran to the retail outlet where a large supermarket was located and this service was greatly valued. Les described in the first interview how he was able to do his own shopping using this bus service, buying lunch in the supermarket café before returning home. Accessible and affordable transport can thus enable older people to maintain or extend their participation in social and community life, reinforcing experiences of independence (Hill et al, 2009).

Earlier in the chapter, the lack of accessible information about formal services was identified as one aspect of service inadequacy. Similar points can be made about more general community resources. As has been shown, these can make a significant difference to the daily lives of older and disabled people and facilitate their involvement in community life, but only if the people who would most benefit from them have knowledge of them. This point was made by Harriet:

> "There was one thing that I was thinking, that often there are little things that you wouldn't dream of going to Citizens' Advice Bureau, just little things that you're not aware of or things you probably haven't updated yourself with, you know. It would be nice if there were someone, if occasionally someone visited you, just to chat to you and that you could ask little things.... There are lots of things that you don't know about, for instance, it's difficult for me to get prescriptions, my doctor is at the other side of town. I can't walk that distance so it means a vehicle. I've always got to go and ask someone to pick up my prescription and take it to the chemist for me … and then I found out that they can collect the prescription for you, they collect them from the doctor's. But there is no one to tell you that. I could have been making use of that service for years but there is no one to tell you. You don't know what is available, you've got to find out

yourself.... That's what I find is missing, information about facilities that are available in your area." (Harriet, interview 5)

These examples highlight ways in which 'ordinary' community services and infrastructure bolster older people in relation to both 'keeping going' and 'staying me', by virtue of easy access to non-stigmatising means of support.

Community threats

The rhetoric of 'communities' and 'community care' can mask their potential for harm (Barnes, 1997). As well as offering certain valued resources to participants, the community was also perceived by some as a source of threat. Key aspects of this were specific environmental hazards, discrimination and vulnerability to crime.

The local environment was perceived as containing threats to well-being. Physical features such as the condition of roads and pavements contributed to participants' anxieties about going out. Impairments such as decreased mobility and failing eyesight heightened the risk in terms of both increasing the likelihood of a fall and increasing the potential severity of the consequences:

> "I do use a stick but it's more or less a safeguard because the paving stones in [the town] are so uneven, I don't feel safe ... some years ago I caught my heel in one and broke my wrist. When I got to the hospital the nurse said, 'We have dozens, broken ankles, broken wrists, broken legs and even a broken hip'." (Elsie, interview 4)

Barbara was pursuing a claim for compensation against the district council for injuries she sustained when she tripped over uneven paving stones when out shopping. Sometimes the measures taken to adapt to changes in health or ability brought new perceived threats:

> After my fall in March I feel nervous of walking in the High Street. The pavements are disgraceful – I know of a number of people who have fallen. Now I go down the village with a four-wheel trolley to give me support and give me more confidence walking down the road but I feel embarrassed – it accentuates the little old lady! (Barbara, diary)

This leads to a second area of threat, discriminatory attitudes and behaviour. While questioning older people directly about age discrimination may not capture its extent and subtlety, more may be revealed by listening to their personal experiences about accessing and receiving services (Levenson, 2003). There were several examples of perceived age discrimination in the healthcare participants had received, confirming other findings (Minichiello et al, 2000; Roberts et al, 2002; Godfrey et al, 2004; Age Concern England, 2007). Elsie referred to her doctor's refusal to put her on the list for a gynaecological operation:

"I've asked to be stitched up but they wouldn't put me on the list. I said to the doctor, it's because I'm old and you think I'll die any minute. He said, 'No it's not' and put me on the list. But next time I saw him, he said he had had to take me off the list. He didn't say why but I know.... It's because I'm old." (Elsie, interview 1)

Roger had also experienced what he felt to be ageism from his GP:

"Well you see he made me mad because when I went down to see him.... I had this breathing trouble and he said, 'Oh, it's old age'. Anyway, the last time I went to see him I said, 'Now don't you start telling me it's old age again, I'm not having that'." (Roger, interview 3)

When Barbara fell out of bed, she had been unable to crawl to summon help for several hours. She said that the doctor had been unsympathetic, telling her "it's all in the mind". After a second fall when out shopping, she had been taken to hospital but had received no follow-up from her GP. She said she felt health problems were 'shrugged off' when people became old, the attitude being, 'What do you expect, it comes to us all?'.

Participants also perceived there to be age discrimination in their more general dealings with people in the community. The extract from Barbara's diary, cited above, and other comments from participants suggested that they perceived others as making ageist assumptions and they then reacted to those perceptions. Thus, Barbara resisted using the trolley even though it made her feel more secure physically. When Elsie injured her leg in a fall, she was very concerned to correct any assumption people might make that the fall was related to her age:

"I was in the garden looking at the pool and ... I just caught my heel and had an awful fall on my leg.... Because I'm 91, people think it was because I'm old but I've never fallen in my life. I can touch my toes with the greatest of ease." (Elsie, interview 1)

A third aspect of threat within the community was perceptions and experiences of vulnerability to crime. A high fear of crime is linked with higher rates of depression and anxiety and reduced social activity (Stafford et al, 2007). Participants differed in relation to how safe they felt in their homes and communities. Ralph commented on feeling that his local area was a safe place:

"It [village] had a bad name but not now. I feel safe." (Ralph, interview 1)

Joyce, on the other hand, saw both the block of flats where she lived and her local community as a source of potential harm. Between the second and third interviews, she had her handbag stolen when she was shopping at the supermarket.

She believed that another resident in the block of flats was taking drugs and that he invited other drug users back to the flat. She felt threatened by this and took care to keep her doors locked. She was therefore both a victim of crime and experienced a more general fear of crime. It has been found that older people who are victims of burglary suffer a decline in health faster than non-victims of a similar age. Two years after a burglary, the older victims were found to be 2.4 times more likely to have died or to be in residential care than their non-burgled neighbours (Donaldson, 2003). However, other factors mediate between the event itself and its impact. During the course of the study, Elsie returned from a holiday with her family to find she had been burgled and that jewellery had been stolen. However, she was stoical about this loss:

> Elsie: "I was grieved because I lost the things that were given to me but I've not been worrying about it, they've gone."
>
> Interviewer: "Has it made you nervous at all, the break-in?"
>
> Elsie: "Oh no, I'm not the nervous type. I was in the back row when nerves were given out." (interview 5)

It is the perception of threat and its impact on the individual concerned that is of relevance rather than the event or threatened event. Personality is one mediating factor, as shown in Elsie's comment that she is 'not the nervous type'. Elsie was also closely involved in the life of her local community and it is suggested that higher levels of social integration may mitigate the fear of crime (Clark et al, 1998).

Conclusion

Whereas Chapters Three and Four supported a view of participants as resourceful, resilient, creative and 'managing', this chapter interjects a more cautionary note, conveying a clear sense of threats, both experienced and perceived, to current and future well-being. At the same time, it highlights factors that can bolster participants' strategies and ways of coping.

As has been shown, later life may be characterised by frequent change arising, for example, from deteriorating health and abilities and disruptions within social support networks. Such changes are often experienced as beyond the individual's control (Hill et al, 2009), prompting 'reorganisation', that is, attempts to manage the disruptions in roles, activities and routines that ensue (Ray, 2000). This chapter has demonstrated that while participants perceived themselves as, to a large extent, individually responsible for the success or otherwise of this 'reorganisation', there is a range of external factors that intervened to support or undermine their efforts to 'keep going' and 'stay me'. These factors have been categorised as operating at the levels of personal, social and community. These levels are not, however, discrete. Factors within each level have implications for the other levels. For example, deteriorating health may act as a threat at the personal level of coping, but also impair the capacity to perform accepted roles within a social network and the ability to access community resources. Or fear of crime at the community level may inhibit social activity and contribute to isolation and depression at a personal level. Equally, resources in one or even two of the levels will not necessarily facilitate managing if the other level is deficient. For example, participants may be well-equipped in terms of personal resources, such as finances, life experience and attitudes conducive to consumerism, but be thwarted in their coping efforts by a lack of community resources, such as care services (as shown by the situations of Harriet and Patricia). On the other hand, community resources may be available, but inaccessible because of low personal resources, such as ill health, frailty, poverty or attitudes of 'clientalism' (as shown, for example, by Les). Equally, participants may have high levels of both personal and community resources but lack social networks to provide crucial roles such as monitoring, risk minimising or emotional support (as demonstrated by Gerald).

It seems that there are two main ways in which personal, social and community resources operate to support or undermine older people's abilities to manage ageing. From their two rounds of interviews with older people, carried out two years apart, Hill et al (2009) observed that resources functioned as a 'managing mechanism', helping older people to deal with change when it occurred. Resources also acted as a 'protective force', preventing or mitigating the impact of change. Both of these processes have been described in this chapter, for example, the many illustrations of ways in which resources, including informal support networks and formal services, help older people to manage when difficulties occur. At the same time, it has been shown that financial resources accrued earlier in the lifecourse and certain attitudes and perspectives could serve as protective factors when difficulties are encountered, buffering their impact.

These three chapters have discussed issues arising from the grounded theory and narrative analyses of participants' interview and diary accounts, relating these to other evidence. The next chapter examines the interrelationships between the three key themes identified – 'keeping going', 'staying me' and 'the slippery slope' – and connects them to a core theme, 'sustaining the self'.

SIX

'Sustaining the self'

> A person's identity is not to be found in behaviour, nor – important
> though this is – in the reactions of others, but in the capacity *to keep a
> particular narrative going*. The individual's biography, if she is to maintain
> regular interaction with others in the day-to-day world, cannot be
> wholly fictive. It must continually integrate events which occur in the
> external world and sort them into the ongoing "story" about the self.
> (Giddens, 1999, p 54, original emphasis)

The aim of this chapter is to derive some meaning at a broader level from the
analysis presented in the previous chapters. To facilitate this process, this chapter
begins with a review and summary of the themes discussed in the previous three
chapters. This is followed by discussion of how these connect to the wider theme
of efforts to sustain a sense of self. A model of key processes involved in managing
the ageing experience is proposed and compared with other models of response
to ageing and illness. Finally, the chapter considers how the theme of 'sustaining
the self' relates to wider theories concerned with self and identity.

Review of themes and categories

Analysis of the interview transcripts and self-completed diaries produced three
themes, each with related categories and sub-categories. These are shown in
Figure 6.1.

While all of the categories and sub-categories of the 'keeping going' theme refer
in some way to what participants describe themselves as doing and can be seen to
be doing, the second 'staying me' theme encapsulates more about who they 'are',
in other words, existential or 'being' mechanisms. Following Bury (1991), I have
referred to these cognitive processes as ways of coping, to distinguish them from
the action strategies of keeping going. Clearly this is to some extent a permeable
distinction since, as will be discussed later in this chapter, what participants 'do'
constitutes personal and public representations of who they 'are'. The third theme,
'the slippery slope', acknowledges that those consequences and meanings are
mediated by external factors. This theme incorporates those factors that appear to
support or undermine older people's strategies of keeping going and staying me.

The next section explores the interrelationships between the three themes,
their related categories and sub-categories and their relationship with the broader
theme, 'sustaining the self'.

Figure 6.1: Summary of themes, categories and sub-categories

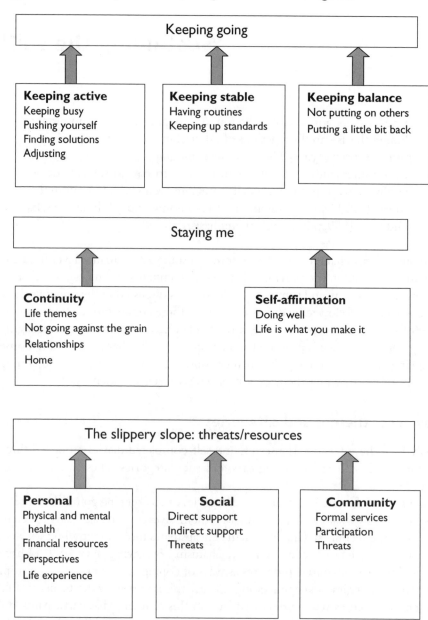

Towards a synthesis

The themes of 'keeping going', 'staying me' and 'the slippery slope' may be integrated to produce a more coherent understanding of how older people manage the experience of ageing. These practical strategies and cognitive ways of coping can be seen as efforts to sustain a sense of self. The third theme, 'the slippery slope', bears a slightly different relationship to the core theme since it refers to factors that support or undermine participants' strategies and ways of coping. The threats and resources occurring at the three levels of the slippery slope – personal, social and community – are seen as playing a mediating role between difficulties and how they are managed.

Figure 6.2 shows that the impact of threats and resources is on the practical and psychological strategies of 'keeping going' and 'staying me', rather than directly on 'sustaining the self'. To illustrate this with examples, sensitive and appropriate services can support the maintenance of standards within the 'keeping going' category while not undermining an older person's ability to find their own solutions or push themselves; experiences of ageism may threaten a positive sense of self by representing discontinuity with the past self and by contradicting the cognitive strategies involved in self-affirmation (for example, undermining the sub-category of doing well). Figure 6.2 also indicates that the relationship between the 'keeping going' and 'staying me' themes is mutually interactive. For example, keeping up valued activities will support feelings of continuity as well as facilitating positive comparison with others, thereby supporting self-affirmation.

Figure 6.2: Processes of sustaining the self

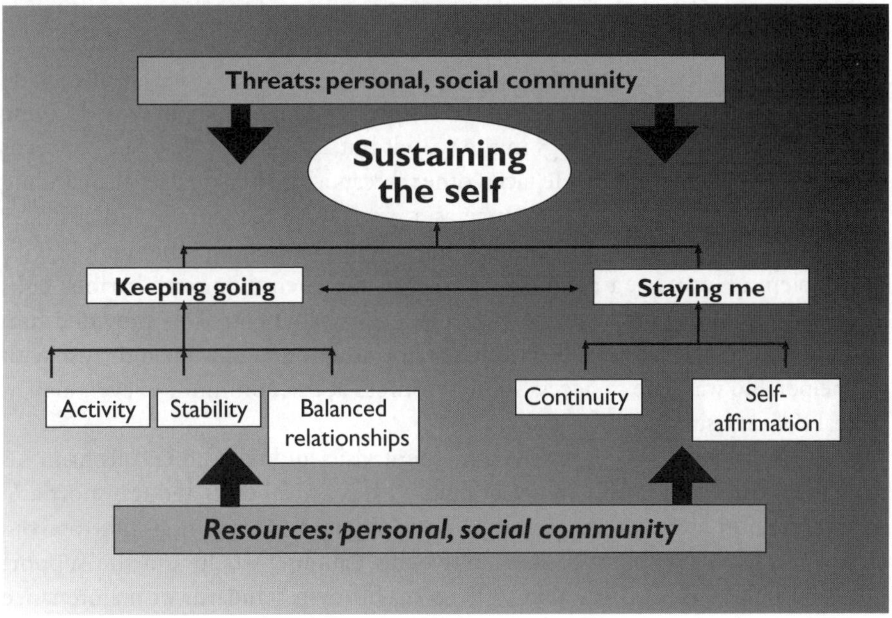

The danger of presenting a model in this way is that it inevitably simplifies highly complex processes and suggests the different dimensions are fixed and discrete. The purpose of offering it here is to clarify, rather than explain. Relating the model to the participants' circumstances facilitates understanding of the different levels of 'managing' they exhibited and experienced. It assists understanding of factors that have contributed to more positive experiences of managing as well as to more negative experiences and perceptions of not managing. Brief examples are now given of each, based on participants' circumstances, as discussed in previous chapters.

'Keeping going' and 'staying me': Roger

On my last visit to Roger, he told me that the heart specialist had told him that a further operation on his heart was not possible and he would be unlikely to survive another 12 months. While this might be expected to seriously threaten Roger's coping, he seemed to manage to sustain a positive sense of self throughout the five interviews. To try to understand why this is, it is worth exploring his situation in terms of the three themes of 'sustaining the self'.

At the personal level, Roger experienced a range of health problems during the study. He had a number of hospital admissions during this time, including a knee replacement operation, treatment for severe anaemia and injuries sustained in a fall. He had already had two operations to repair a leaking heart valve. Despite this he could still perform most everyday tasks and kept busy by regularly walking his dogs, cooking his own meals and doing jobs in the garden. He had adapted in various ways to his health problems by, for example, 'slowing up' and purchasing special equipment to help him with jobs in the garden. He presented himself as finding his own solutions, for example, deciding when to telephone the doctor and when to ask the person who helped him to increase her visits. He also made his own decisions about risk, for example, despite his daughter's concerns, deciding that he would still walk his dogs in the woods but agreeing to allay her concerns by wearing a personal alarm. He faced other threats at the personal level, including restricted finances, lack of experience as a private care consumer and attitudes about being independent, not complaining and not burdening other people with his problems. However, a neighbour had agreed to help him with various tasks once or twice a day on a private basis for a reasonable cost. This provided him with flexible and responsive help and a relationship of friendship and trust with the helper. He was able to access some resources at the community level, such as a meal delivery service.

At the social level, Roger received frequent visits and telephone calls from his daughter, who was a source of direct help with practical tasks and transport and indirect help in terms of triggering help seeking and encouraging him to avoid risks. With his own ability to keep active, his daughter's help and the support of a paid helper, Roger was able to keep up his own standards of maintenance of the home and, especially, his garden. He limited the help he would accept from his daughter and he was able to maintain a sense of independence through paying for help from the neighbour. This, together with giving to his community through loaning a wheelchair to others in the village and opening his garden to raise money for charity, enabled him to maintain what he felt were acceptable boundaries within helping relationships and to 'put a bit back' into his community. In relation to 'staying me' categories, he was able to preserve key dimensions of continuity, for example, his home, village and associated memories of his wife as well as a life theme of independence. He demonstrated all of the sub-categories of doing well, that is, making positive comparison between his situation and that of others, qualifying 'problem talk', modifying what he expected of himself and perceiving himself as fortunate. He maintained a sense of personal responsibility for keeping on the go and 'looking on the bright side'.

'Giving up' and 'giving in': Les

Les provides perhaps the starkest example of a self not sustained in terms of the model. Sadly he died after the second interview. His status as a 'self not sustained', as I am presenting it, is interesting in that there are some similarities between his situation and that of Roger. Both had serious heart conditions, close relationships with their daughters, limited financial means and similar attitudes and values in respect of wanting to be independent and not a bother to others. Whereas Roger was able to 'keep going' and 'stay me', this was not the case for Les, however.

Les faced threats at each level, personal, social and community. At the personal level, his serious heart condition had direct consequences for 'keeping going' categories, in particular, for his ability to keep busy and maintain stability in terms of routines and standards. In the first interview he showed me around his flat with some pride, and told me of the standards he adhered to when cleaning, such as always moving all the furniture aside when vacuuming. By the second interview, even walking slowly and talking were a struggle for him because of his extreme breathlessness. While previously he had been able to use the free bus to the supermarket to do his shopping or, on a good day, ride his bicycle, doing his own shopping was now out of the question. His limited income was another source of personal threat as were his lack of experience as a 'consumer' of care in the private market and his attitudes about not 'causing bother' and not wanting to be seen as a troublemaker. These attitudes impinged on the finding solutions sub-category as this would have meant confronting the council about their refusal to agree to a housing transfer for his daughter. This was in effect a 'blocked' relationship in that his daughter was willing to help him and he wanted her help, but housing policy prevented this. His attempt to persuade the council to rehouse his daughter had failed and he was now feeling powerless and lacking in all hope that this would be resolved in the future. His daughter living some distance away constituted a threat at the social level, as he had no sources of informal support to provide direct or indirect help at the level he needed. While this could potentially have been offset by the provision of appropriate services, threats at the community level meant this did not happen. As mentioned, Les had neither the experience nor financial resources to purchase private care and social services had not put in place the services he thought they had agreed to provide. His poor health and 'habit of the heart' about not complaining meant that he did not question or challenge this.

In terms of 'staying me' categories, some aspects of continuity were preserved, in particular, his home environment and desire not to be seen as a troublemaker. However, these aspects of maintaining continuity in respect of 'staying me' in some ways militated against accessing the resources required to support 'keeping going'. This shows that while the themes often operate in a way that support each other, they can also work in opposition. In relation to the category of self-affirmation, Les was no longer able to sustain a sense of doing well, a sense of personal control over his situation or an ability to construct it in positive terms.

Figure 6.3 summarises the relevant aspects of the model that facilitate understanding of Roger and Les's situations. The threats and resources within 'the slippery slope' can be seen as relevant to understanding both the factors experienced as difficulties and the resources available to address them. As mentioned in the previous chapter, some threats operate across levels so that poor health, for example, constituted a threat at the personal level but was also one of the factors limiting Les's ability to seek help at the community level. From this figure, it can be seen that while Roger and Les experienced similar threats at the personal level, Roger fared much better in terms of access to resources at the social and community levels. The availability of these resources supported his functioning in relation to the themes of 'keeping going' and 'staying me'. In contrast, Les faced a lack of resources at the social and community levels. This threatened his ability to 'keep going' and 'stay me' and consequently undermined his sense of self.

Subjective influences on coping

The two themes of 'keeping going' and 'staying me' have been presented as concerned with practical strategies and cognitive coping respectively. These can be seen as two broad types of processes by which a sense of self is maintained in the face of the changes and losses accompanying ageing – processes which may be supported or, conversely, undermined by factors in the personal, social and community environments. Intrinsic to this analysis is the view that there is no straightforward relationship between objective circumstances in later life and how individuals experience them. Quality of life is recognised to comprise both objective conditions (health and function, socioeconomic status) and subjective conditions (life satisfaction and self-esteem) (George and Bearon, 1980). However, George (1998) later developed this work, arguing that in terms of their implications for measures of quality of life the two dimensions are not necessarily congruent:

> ... rather than examine quality of life as having both objective and subjective requirements, my more recent work focuses on (1) the conditions under which perceived quality of life remains high despite unfavourable environments and/or capacities and (2) the social and psychological processes that seem to be more important determinants of perceived quality of life than objective conditions. (George, 1998, p 42)

Figure 6.3: Applications of the 'sustaining the self' model

Roger

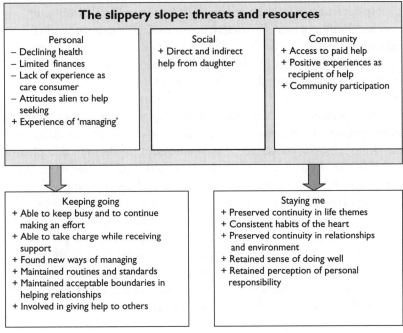

The slippery slope: threats and resources

Personal	Social	Community
− Declining health − Limited finances − Lack of experience as care consumer − Attitudes alien to help seeking + Experience of 'managing'	+ Direct and indirect help from daughter	+ Access to paid help + Positive experiences as recipient of help + Community participation

Keeping going
+ Able to keep busy and to continue making an effort
+ Able to take charge while receiving support
+ Found new ways of managing
+ Maintained routines and standards
+ Maintained acceptable boundaries in helping relationships
+ Involved in giving help to others

Staying me
+ Preserved continuity in life themes
+ Consistent habits of the heart
+ Preserved continuity in relationships and environment
+ Retained sense of doing well
+ Retained perception of personal responsibility

Les

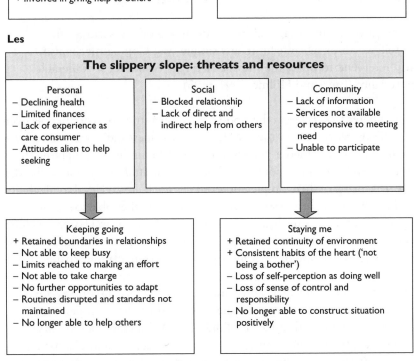

The slippery slope: threats and resources

Personal	Social	Community
− Declining health − Limited finances − Lack of experience as care consumer − Attitudes alien to help seeking	− Blocked relationship − Lack of direct and indirect help from others	− Lack of information − Services not available or responsive to meeting need − Unable to participate

Keeping going
+ Retained boundaries in relationships
− Not able to keep busy
− Limits reached to making an effort
− Not able to take charge
− No further opportunities to adapt
− Routines disrupted and standards not maintained
− No longer able to help others

Staying me
+ Retained continuity of environment
+ Consistent habits of the heart ('not being a bother')
− Loss of self-perception as doing well
− Loss of sense of control and responsibility
− No longer able to construct situation positively

Quality of life is thus complex, multidimensional and individually mediated:

> ...the meaning that individuals give to the quality of their later life is probably determined by their life context: by the political, economic and cultural influences of the society in which they live; by individual lived experiences across the life course; by their current expectations, attitudes and values and by the context in which they reflectively provide this account. (Bond and Corner, 2004, p 104)

Research on experiences of illness offers some insights into the role of subjective factors in mitigating the negative impact of adverse circumstances. Adaptation to chronic illness has been shown to be as much about psychological as physical processes. I referred at the end of Chapter Four to the parallel between Bury's (1991) distinction between strategies and coping and the keeping going and staying me categories concerned with the ways participants managed difficulties. Bury (1991, p 462) identified a further component of illness management, 'style', that is, the 'cultural repertoires' people use in their response to and presentation of their illness and I shall return to this concept of 'styles' later in the chapter. Other work by Bury attests to the role of cognitive factors in adaptation to more general changes accompanying ageing, not just illness. Bury and Holme (1991) conclude from their research with older people over the age of 90:

> ... negative or unanticipated events do not produce serious effects on self-worth or self-esteem in any simple way. Coping mechanisms may intervene to offset the impact of events or bolster a vulnerable personality. (Bury and Holme, 1991, p 95)

Johnson and Barer (1997) begin their book based on a study of older people over the age of 85 by reflecting on the puzzle that the 'oldest old' appeared to have adapted and to have retained a perception of well-being in seemingly negative circumstances. Indeed, in the course of their six-year study they noted that the subjective well-being of their sample improved despite increased levels of disability and hardship. They pose the question, 'By what means are they able to sustain well-being despite seemingly insurmountable odds?' (p 4). Johnson and Barer conclude that as social activity and control over other areas of life diminish, emotional and cognitive processes become more significant as ways of managing change:

> To control the emotional consequences of change, discourses are used as an adaptive strategy that helps individuals develop personal meanings about significant areas of their lives. While their bodies may be disabled, their minds continue to actively examine and interpret their predicament in a process that can perhaps alleviate distress and forestall demoralisation. The subjective life, consequently, can serve not only to sustain mood and motivations, but also to give the very

old some control over the emotional consequences of their losses. (Johnson and Barer, 1997, pp 224-5)

In this way they suggest that older people control the emotional consequences of significant events by being 'active manipulators of a self-concept moulded to be compatible with their status' (Johnson and Barer, 1997, pp 161-2).

Social and psychological processes play a key role in sustaining the self and each of the sub-themes of 'keeping going', 'staying me' and 'the slippery slope' encapsulate objective and subjective elements. For example, there is a direct relationship between the 'doing' strategies of keeping busy and pushing yourself and attitudes and beliefs contained within the staying me theme, in particular, attitudes about not asking for help and beliefs that life is what you make it. When discussing the situation of David in Chapter Four, the point was made that although his physical needs were well addressed by his family and he could therefore be seen to be coping well at an objective level, there were deficiencies in terms of the 'staying me' categories of continuity and self-affirmation. From the opposite perspective, Chapter Five described how Alice had become physically less mobile and needed increased help from formal services, but constructed the situation positively in terms of the social benefits she gained from her relationships with the team of care staff. These different dimensions of coping are illustrated in Figure 6.4, which includes examples of study participants who can be seen as falling within each quadrant.

Figure 6.4: Objective and subjective dimensions of coping

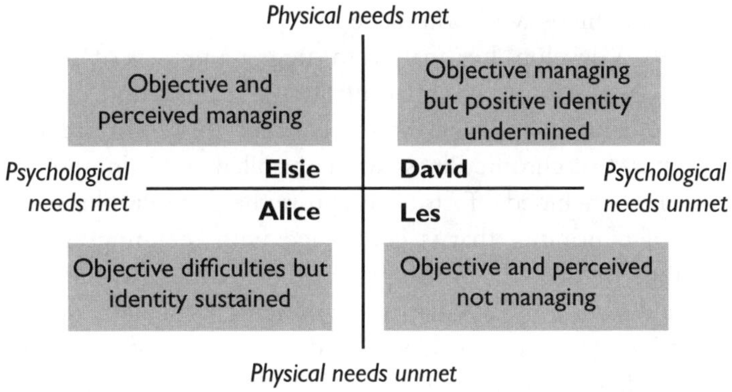

Comparison with other models

In this section the model presented in Figure 6.2 is compared with other models, first, a model concerned with experiences of illness and its relationship to selfhood and, second, those concerned more directly with experiences of ageing.

Illness as a threat to selfhood

There is empirical support for the identity threats posed by illness and disability. Charmaz (1983) describes the ways chronic illness acts as an assault on the self through four processes: restricting the individual's life, socially discrediting them leading to social isolation and causing them to become a burden on others. Based on interviews with men who were chronically ill, Charmaz (1997) outlines the processes involved in their response to their condition. First, awakening to the possibility of death and responding to the consequences could lead to validation of identity as the importance of the ill person is demonstrated by the love and concern expressed towards them by others. For example, in my research, Elsie, although loathe to dwell on her illnesses and declining mobility, took pleasure in remembering and recounting the number of cards she had received from family and friends when in hospital. Second, accommodating uncertainty could mean either 'bracketing' the uncertainty in a way that protected personal and social identities or 'epiphanies' bringing major changes to lifestyles or habits with enduring implications for identity. The efforts of participants in my study to keep busy, find solutions and maintain routines and standards can be seen as efforts to set limits and boundaries around the potential invasion of threatening forces, while their adaptation strategies reflected recognition of, rather than resistance to, changed circumstances. Third, Charmaz notes that the ways that illness and disability were defined – as an enemy, an ally, an invader or a harbinger of opportunity – were related to identity management strategies. Similarly, the ways in which individuals in my study constructed their situations were significant in sustaining a positive sense of self, as illustrated in the self-affirmation categories of 'doing well' and 'life is what you make it'.

Charmaz (1997) develops her analysis to suggest a process of 'preserving self', defining this as 'maintaining essential qualities, attributes and identities of this past self that fundamentally shape the self concept' (p 49). In order to preserve the self, the impact of chronic illness was controlled and minimised by a range of strategies. These included efforts to recapture the past self. This resonates with my category of continuity that is concerned with retaining and reaffirming core dimensions of the self, encompassing life themes, attitudes and values, relationships and environment. Charmaz comments particularly on the potential threat to identity posed by dependency and on the role of others in engaging in 'an elaborate dance around dependency' (1997, p 53) to help the individual negotiate this hazard safely. There was some evidence of this process in respect of the maintenance by Ralph of a positive and 'powerful' identity within the family despite his increasing physical dependency on his daughters for practical support. Closely linked with recapturing the past self are strategies to preserve a public identity when changes are occurring in the private sphere, and Charmaz suggests that these efforts are founded on maintaining gendered expectations. In Chapter Five I discussed the significance for Barbara's gender identity of a close relationship where she was both 'nurturer' on the one hand and 'protected' on the other. The emphasis given by Elsie to her role as family lynchpin and carer and by Gerald to his capacity as manager and benefactor are also examples of public identities influenced by gender. Charmaz calls the third type of strategy 'preserving self', using this to refer to individuals' efforts to continue with social and work activity despite chronic illness:

> They draw upon both taken-for-granted actions and explicit strategies to preserve their earlier selves and thus, maintain or recreate public and private identities. Their strategies involve careful considerations of timing, pacing, and staging to maintain appearances to others, and often, to self. (Charmaz, 1997, p 55)

There is, then, much in Charmaz's analysis of individuals' responses to chronic illness to support the discussion here of the centrality of sustaining the self in older people's management of the experience of ageing. Both studies highlight practical strategies and cognitive coping processes directed at maintaining a positive identity. This is perhaps unsurprising given that the main source of difficulties faced by participants in my study was illness and disability, rather than age itself. However, my study also encompasses a broader range of difficulties faced in later life and seeks to address the question posed, but unanswered, by Charmaz, 'What conditions shape whether a man [sic] will reconstruct a positive identity or sink into depression?' (p 57). The model presented in Figure 6.2 suggests key processes to be considered in attempting to answer this question.

Models of the ageing experience

Brandtstädter and Greve (1994) put forward a model of ageing that concerns itself specifically with processes by which a sense of self is stabilised and protected and I shall discuss this model by comparing it with the 'sustaining the self' model presented earlier (see Figure 6.2). Brandtstädter and Greve discuss what they see as the essential attributes of an individual's self-concept and three key attributes are identified. First, continuity and permanence refer to self-beliefs that are relatively stable over time. In Chapter Five I presented the 'staying me' theme as containing the category of continuity, which in turn included sub-categories concerning enduring life themes and perspectives. The second key attribute of an individual's self-concept noted by Brandtstädter and Greve is discriminative relevance, that is, the dimensions that the person believes distinguish them from other people. Brandtstädter and Greve suggest that individuals 'may actively select perspectives of comparison that enhance a sense of distinctiveness or uniqueness with respect to personally desired qualities' (p 54). The self-affirmation category of 'staying me' included ways in which participants in my study positively compared themselves and their situations with those of others. It was suggested that this could be seen as constituting a mechanism for affirming a positive view of self. Similarly, the narratives of participants reflected core life themes that were seen as representing a key element of their identities; these themes were what made them 'them', as distinct from anyone else. The third essential attribute of self-concept, according to Brandtstädter and Greve, is biographical meaningfulness, that is, elements that the individual considers important to his or her biography. Again, this is reflected in the 'staying me' category of continuity in terms of the significance of life themes, relationships and environment.

Brandtstädter and Greve suggest that understanding the significance of these dimensions of an individual's self-concept indicates those changes and events that are likely to create difficulties in later life. They suggest that problems are likely to arise in the following situations:

- When an individual's beliefs about themselves are threatened by incongruent evidence. For example, in David's situation, excessive support threatened his sense of autonomy and independence.
- When traits or qualities valued by the individual are lost or lose their value in distinguishing the individual from others. For example, despite being 93 (at the conclusion of the study), Elsie prided herself on 'not being old', like her (chronologically) younger sister; to her this meant being physically and socially active. If these abilities were lost, this would be likely to represent a significant threat to her self-concept.
- When elements that represent continuity are disrupted.

Brandtstädter and Greve conclude:

> To account for the apparent resiliency of the ageing self, we have to look for mechanisms and activities that are capable of dampening the detrimental impact of these problems on the individual's construction of self and personal continuity. (Brandtstädter and Greve, 1994, p 55)

They proceed to outline three ways in which a positive identity in later life may be maintained and these mechanisms can be compared with suggested processes for sustaining the self.

Brandtstädter and Greve suggest that a positive identity may be maintained by assimilative activities or 'problem-directed action', that is, actions aimed at changing situations so that they accord with the values and goals that are key to that individual's identity. This mechanism is therefore concerned with actions that closely reflect the 'keeping going' categories discussed in Chapter Three. For example, keeping busy, pushing yourself, maintaining standards and routines and maintaining relationship boundaries all concern action directed at managing situations in a way that retains cherished values and goals. The extent to which someone is able to act on situations is influenced by personal, social and community resources so there is also a close connection here with the categories contained within 'the slippery slope' theme discussed in Chapter Five.

A second way of maintaining a positive identity suggested by Brandtstädter and Greve is by accommodative processes or 'self-evaluation adjustments'. Here the focus is not on changing situations but on adjusting individual values and goals so that they are congruent with the situation. Brandtstädter and Greve propose that this mechanism tends to be invoked when assimilative processes are no longer possible or effective. They argue that it is important to be able to relinquish unattainable goals to avert demoralisation and depression. In this sense, disengagement from social goals would be seen not as resignation, but an adaptive mechanism to maintain a positive identity. Longitudinal case study research has suggested that the dominant strategy is assimilation rather than accommodation (Coleman et al, 1999). There were not many examples in my study of accommodative changes in underpinning values, but there were examples of participants adjusting their goals in line with changing abilities. For example, in the 'keeping going' sub-category of adjusting, discussed in Chapter Four, I cited instances of participants substituting a new activity in line with their changed abilities for one they could no longer manage. The underpinning values of a belief in keeping active remained the same. When discussing this category in Chapter Three, I referred to Baltes and Carstensen's (1996) 'selective optimisation with compensation' model and there are parallels here with Brandtstädter and Greve's model in that both make the distinction between changing goals and values on the one hand ('selection' and 'accommodative processes' as described in the respective models), and adjusting behaviour in order to retain existing goals on the other ('compensation' and 'assimilative activities' respectively). Brandtstädter and Greve discuss specific mechanisms of these accommodative processes: disengagement from blocked goals; adjustment of aspirations and self-evaluative standards; self-enhancing comparisons; and palliative interpretations (1994, pp 62-7). Again there are close parallels with categories derived from my analysis.

The third process for maintaining a positive identity suggested by Brandtstädter and Greve is immunising processes or the 'self-representation level'. This refers to ways in which individuals process information to defend themselves against threats to a positive self-concept. These mechanisms, it is suggested, come into play when self-enhancing interpretations consistent with an individual's beliefs are no longer available. Mechanisms here include the judicious selection of data to enhance a positive sense of self and the exclusion of other data. Dwelling on past achievements and downplaying present difficulties would be one example of this and there are suggestions of such processes in my study in terms of some participants' tendencies to mitigate 'problem talk' and engage in positive thinking.

The processes outlined by Brandtstädter and Greve are useful in both confirming and in some respects enhancing the understanding derived from my analysis of how the self is sustained. Assimilative activities can perhaps be seen as the first level of recourse when difficulties are faced, that is, attempts to continue to engage in important activities and to uphold significant beliefs and values, but to negotiate different ways of doing this in the light of changing circumstances. Many of the examples of participant behaviour discussed in the 'keeping going' theme can be seen as efforts at assimilation. Where assimilation is not possible, the next level in trying to manage difficulties is the accommodative, that is, making changes to goals and values because it is no longer possible to achieve or uphold them. For example, strong themes within Joyce's interview accounts were pushing herself, the value of struggle and the fulfilment of her personal responsibility in doing all of her own housework. By the final interview, she had reached the point of finding someone else to come in and 'do' for her every fortnight. This constituted a challenge to the values communicated in earlier interviews. This is where the third process of immunisation is relevant, in terms of the self seeking to defend itself against potentially damaging discordant evidence. In Joyce's case, she blocked discussion of the help she was now receiving by changing the subject, thus excluding data potentially damaging to her sense of self. Other examples from the interviews suggest that it is not just immunising processes engaged in by the self that are relevant to maintaining a positive identity, but also immunising by significant others. Thus, Ralph, Roger and Alice all received increasing levels of help during the course of the study that could potentially have threatened their view of self. However, others gave this help in ways that facilitated their retention of a positive sense of self. This has implications for service delivery, as discussed in the next chapter.

It is not suggested here that processes of assimilation, accommodation and self-evaluative adjustments occur in a one-directional linear way; the processes may be engaged in simultaneously and in any order, although there seems to be some evidence that attempts to 'manage' by adapting cognitions and values (secondary control) occur when efforts to change the environment (primary control) are unsuccessful or not possible (Heckhausen and Schulz, 1993). The central point of the discussion lies in recognition of the significance of cognitive coping mechanisms alongside practical strategies. Steverink et al (1998) put forward another model consistent with this view. Their model also concerns the ways older people seek to attain individually meaningful goals and how they negotiate changes in the resources available to them to do this. It is based on the notion that people are goal-directed and resourceful and able to adapt to changes and constraints in their circumstances, a view upheld by the findings of my study. It is premised on the existence of two universal goals, physical and social well-being. Physical well-being includes the first order instrumental goals of comfort (the meeting of basic needs) and stimulation, while social well-being encompasses the instrumental goals of affection (being loved by self and others), behavioural confirmation (being valued for what one does) and status (being valued in comparison to other people). The model proposes that as the resources available to older people diminish, they strive to minimise these losses by processes of substitution and compensation. If one instrumental goal is no longer attainable, another instrumental goal within that domain may be substituted. For example, it could be argued that as Elsie became more restricted physically and less active in the local community, her family became more significant as a source of self-affirmation. In other words, affection began to be substituted for behavioural confirmation. Similarly, the loss of certain resources may be compensated by other resources. For example, the reduction in social support faced by Alice as her mobility decreased was compensated by the social stimulation provided by the team of home carers. In this way,

> The process of ageing can be characterised as a changing balance between gains and losses (in resources) in which losses increasingly outweigh gains. With regard to delaying and mitigating this changing balance, the substitution or compensation of resources and instrumental goals is considered to be the central mechanism of successful adaptive behaviour in ageing individuals. (Steverink et al, 1998, p 455)

Cognitive processes are recognised as important in supporting behavioural adaptations. Looking at how far the model assists understanding of 'giving up' and 'giving in' in my study, the extent to which one instrumental goal can adequately substitute for another seems uncertain. For example, David's relatively high level of comfort did not adequately compensate for the loss of stimulation he experienced in moving to his flat; equally, the increase in affection (since he was now living nearer to his children) did not compensate for the reduction in behavioural confirmation and status. It is, perhaps, cognitive processes that bridge this gap in explaining when substitution and compensation 'work' for individuals. The model has important implications for preventive intervention since Steverink et al note that a 'critical phase' occurs when there are few remaining opportunities for substitution of goals and resources. Indeed, it may be that it is only when this critical phase is reached and there are few if any perceived options for managing difficulties that many older people consider seeking help. The implication is that supportive interventions should focus on creating or bolstering a range of possibilities to facilitate substitution of goals and resources.

The models considered here resonate closely with the model of sustaining the self presented in Figure 6.2 and with the themes discussed in the previous three chapters. In particular, shared themes include: the resourcefulness of older people in adapting to loss and change; the importance of understanding the individual significance of goals; and the significance of psychological or cognitive coping as well as practical strategies to maintenance of a positive identity in later life. However, it is worth noting that the models examined are predominantly psychological in orientation. They pay limited attention to two areas of interest arising from my analysis: first, the role of external forces in supporting or undermining these identity management processes (that is, 'the slippery slope' theme) and second, the question of why particular values and goals are significant to positive identity in the first place.

These dimensions are encompassed in a sociocultural model put forward by Godfrey (2001). This model is highly relevant to the policy context discussed in Chapter Two, since it concerns ways in which preventive measures can support successful ageing. Godfrey adopts Baltes and Baltes' (1990) model of successful ageing, and develops this to incorporate three dimensions significant to my study. First, she highlights that the meaning of losses incurred are mediated by the resources available to the individual to manage those losses, as well as by cultural norms and expectations. For example, lack of financial resources for older people from certain minority ethnic groups may have particular significance in terms of their being unable to fulfil religious and cultural expectations required of respected elders, such as paying for family funerals back home or giving gifts (Grewal et al, 2004). Second, the model reflects the significance of cultural norms and expectations in influencing the goals that are valued and pursued. For example, as discussed in Chapter Two, the goal of independence reflects dominant political and social discourses in western societies. Third, the model addresses the importance of access to resources that support the pursuit of valued goals in determining how an individual adapts to loss. For example, it was shown in Chapter Five that some participants had the financial resources to purchase services and equipment to compensate for functional impairments while others did not.

The role of resources in influencing both the significance of loss and processes of adaptation to loss are reflected in 'the slippery slope' theme. The importance of wider cultural values and expectations to individual perceptions and behaviour has been noted at a number of junctures in the previous three chapters, but further attention is now given to this dimension of 'self' in order to develop further understanding of processes by which the self is sustained. In doing this, the relevance of broader theoretical understanding about self and identity is considered before the focus is narrowed to application to the study findings.

Theorising self and identity

It is argued that in our rapidly changing and fragmented world, 'achieving a secure sense of self has become one of the biggest challenges of later life' (Phillipson, 1998, p 51). A central issue in debates on identity in later life concerns the extent to which individual experience is determined by social and economic factors, as suggested in structured dependency theories (for example, Townsend, 1981; Walker, 1993), or whether individuals should be seen as agents, actively choosing and creating their own meanings and identities, as put forward in postmodern approaches (see, for example, Gilleard, 1996). While the former approach emphasises the negative aspects of old age as an experience dominated by socially constructed disadvantage, the latter tends to promulgate a more positive view, highlighting the creative potential of later life. However, it is argued that this division between structure and agency is a false binary. Giddens (1979), for example, argues for the duality of structure and action, structure bearing directly on action and being reconstituted by it. More recently, it is suggested that postmodernist understandings may enable us to 'socialise the individual' rather than 'individualise the social' (Taylor, 1998, p 331). This section examines particular theoretical approaches to identity that straddle this division, recognising both the part individuals play in constructing their own situations, but also the influence of social and cultural factors in those constructive processes.

To understand how the meaning given to situations and behaviour supports or threatens an individual's sense of self necessitates examining how meanings are construed in the first place. Within the general framework of symbolic interactionism, discussed in Chapter One, Goffman's (1961) work on 'presentation of the self' and 'impression management strategies' is particularly relevant to understanding processes of sustaining the self. Although Goffman's concern with 'micro' interactions has been seen as underplaying the role of structural factors, this criticism is not entirely justified. Indeed, it is argued that Goffman is more concerned with structural constraints than the individual self. Collins (1988, p 48) argues, 'For Goffman, the self is not so much a private, individual attribute, as a public reality, created by and having its primary existence in public interaction'. Similarly, Giddens (1988) refutes the view that Goffman is concerned only with individual actors, arguing rather that the motivation of individual actors 'derives from the internalisation of some sort of overall normative consensus, which is then applied in the situations of face-to-face interaction' (Giddens, 1988, pp 278-9). Although in previous chapters the meanings attributed by individuals to their experiences have been described and analysed, these are not individual meanings in the sense that to understand them it is necessary to look at broader structural factors. Thus, while it is important to listen to older people's stories:

> ... such stories are themselves embedded in wider layers of meaning, these emerging from social and economic practices at large within society. People search for meaning and reinforcement of their stories "outside" as well as "inside" themselves. People age "from within" in a double sense: "within" themselves and "within" society. The crisis of social ageing essentially concerns the disjunction between the two, with the social meanings attached to growing old in tension with ageing as a psychological and biographical event. (Phillipson, 1998, p 108)

Identity, then, has both social and individual dimensions; it is about the 'intensely personal and the necessarily social' (Hekman, 1999, p 6). It concerns sameness and difference (Jenkins, 1996), encapsulating an ontological dimension, a sense of oneself as a coherent and unique individual (difference) but also categorical dimensions, a sense of oneself as a member of particular social categories (sameness) (Taylor, 1998). This dual aspect of identity is apparent within the 'staying me' theme, with individuals revealing a sense of their uniqueness in terms of particular life themes and habits of the heart but also their sense of membership of different social groupings. These two aspects are inextricably linked in the construction of identity:

> The paradox of uniqueness and sameness is easily resolved, of course, by recognising that individuals as unique selves are only formed within

social relations between others and through the participation in and construction of social categories. There is no pre-social individual "squatting outside" social relations. I only recognise my sameness by virtue of my difference and only my difference by reference to a common standard I share with others. (Taylor, 1998, p 345)

Similarly, Jenkins (1996) defines the self as:

... each individual's reflexive sense of her or his own particular identity, constituted vis à vis others in terms of similarity and difference, without which we would not know who we are and hence would not be able to act. (Jenkins, 1996, pp 29-30)

Jenkins argues that the private, internal self and the public, external person are intimately related to each other 'in one ongoing social process of identification' (p 30):

The self is, therefore, altogether individual *and* intrinsically social. It arises within social interaction. It is constructed within the internal– external dialectic of social identification. It draws upon the external social environment of people and things for its content. Even though it is the most individualised of identities – we might call it customised – selfhood is absolutely social. It depends for its ongoing security upon the validation of others, in its initial emergence and in the dialect of continuing social identification. (Jenkins, 1996, p 50)

Given the integration of the private self and the public person, negative social attitudes contain direct threats for sense of self: 'Public image may become self-image. Our own sense of humanity is a hostage to the categorising judgements of others' (Jenkins, 1996, p 57). This is important in understanding the threats to selfhood posed to older people by social perceptions of them as old, dependent and burdensome, and consequently in appreciating their recourse to self-protective strategies. As later life is likely to entail a range of threats to identity, the need to preserve a positive presentation of self may be particularly acute. A further key point is that identity must be understood as a process, as something that is continually renegotiated, involving 'trajectories of being and becoming' (Giddens, 1999, p 75).

The social nature of identity and the way it is continually renegotiated in the interaction between self and others is significant for understanding both sustaining the self and the more detailed identity management processes discussed in the 'keeping going' and 'staying me' themes. It is not possible here to present a comprehensive critique of the extensive literature relating to self and identity, but I shall refer to particular perspectives that assist understanding of the processes involved in sustaining the self. These include Bourdieu's concept of the habitus; Foucault's writings on power, governmentality and 'techniques of the self'; Biggs' notion of masquerade; Giddens' work on the reflexive self; and Leonard's discussion of the reflexive capacity of individuals to resist contradictory discourses.

Older people's experiences of ageing both shape and are shaped by dominant social and cultural values (Heikkinen, 1996), and Bourdieu's notion of the 'habitus' is one way of understanding this dynamic. Bourdieu sees the habitus as addressing the issue of conscious/unconscious behaviour and as bridging the divide between an account emphasising structural factors and one centred on the individual subject. The habitus refers to the socially constituted nature of behaviours that *appear to be driven* by conscious goal-directed reasoning. They are 'objectively adjusted to the situation', but are, in fact, not based on reason but on 'feel for the game':

> This "feel for the game", as we call it, is what enables an infinite number of "moves" to be made, adapted to the infinite number of possible situations which no rule, however complex, can foresee. (Bourdieu, 1994, p 9)

Bourdieu argues that behavioural regularities created by the habitus are not deduced directly from rules since 'the habitus goes hand in glove with vagueness and indeterminacy' (p 77). This contrasts with Goffman's depiction of interaction as governed by actors' awareness of and adherence to rules, a view contested by Jenkins (1996) who argues, in keeping with Bourdieu, that social life is often unscripted, requiring actors to improvise. This seems to be the case for many of the situations encountered by the study participants as they attempted to negotiate new experiences of loss, illness or disability. Even where these events had been encountered before, they were experienced differently because of participants' changed circumstances; old scripts could not be relied on and new ones had to be devised. For example, when he was virtually immobilised while awaiting a knee replacement operation, Roger recounted his experience of a broken back that had kept him in bed for a year. However, at this time in his life his wife was alive to look after him and he had material resources at his disposal that were lacking in this later situation. There were few pre-existing 'rules' that governed his help seeking with neighbours and family; these had to be negotiated. As detailed in Chapter Three, at a general level there appeared to be shared views about the importance of relationship boundaries and reciprocity that guided these interactions and these could therefore be seen as part of the habitus. However, how these general attitudes translated in practice was different for each participant and also varied across time as their circumstances changed. It seems more appropriate to see these as social values mediated by individual personality, attitudes, beliefs and circumstances rather than as commonly understood interactional rules.

The role of an individual in social situations is, according to Bourdieu (1994), that of 'the practical operator of the construction of objects' (p 13); the strategies he or she pursues are the product of their construction of objects, or their 'feel for the game':

The habitus as the feel for the game is the social game embodied and turned into a second nature. Nothing is simultaneously freer and more constrained than the action of the good player. He quite naturally materialises at just the place the ball is about to fall, as if the ball were in command of him – but by that very fact, he is in command of the ball. The habitus, as society written into the body, into the biological individual, enables the infinite number of acts of the game – written into the game as possibilities and objective demands – to be produced; the constraints and demands of the game, although they are not restricted to a code of rules, *impose themselves* on those people – and those people alone – who, because they have a feel for the game, are prepared to perceive them and carry them out. (Bourdieu, 1994, p 63, original emphasis)

The habitus thus transcends both pure structuralism and pure agency; individuals neither freely choose their behaviour nor are they compelled into it, but rather they,

... merely need to let themselves follow their own social "nature", that is, what history has made of them, to be as it were "naturally" adjusted to the historical world they are up against. (Bourdieu, 1994, p 90)

Individuals are active agents in constructing their understanding through the habitus but, at the same time, the habitus predisposes the individual towards certain attitudes, values and ways of behaving:

To speak of habitus is to assert that the individual, and even the personal, the subjective, is social, collective. Habitus is a socialised subjectivity ... the human mind is *socially* bounded, socially structured.... Social reality exists, so to speak, twice, in things and in minds, in fields and in habitus, outside and inside of agents. And when habitus encounters a social world of which it is the product, it is like a "fish in water"; it does not feel the weight of the water, and it takes the world about itself for granted. (Bourdieu and Wacquant, 1992, pp 126-7, original emphasis)

Bourdieu discusses the way that the habitus achieves a 'fit' between aspirations and what is realistically possible. Individuals are induced, 'to make a virtue of necessity', that is, 'to refuse what is denied them anyway and to want what is in fact inevitable' (Bourdieu, 1990, p 54). This helps to make sense of the cognitive ways of coping discussed in Chapter Four, for example, modification of self-expectations. It is also consistent with findings from Johnson and Barer's (1997) study of the 'oldest old' who, it is suggested, redefine their goals and expectations to accommodate their changed circumstances.

Throughout Chapters Three and Four I have referred to practical strategies and cognitive ways of coping that participants deployed to manage difficulties, and I noted in Chapter Four that these are not necessarily conscious processes. Bourdieu argues that while strategies are behaviours directed towards achieving certain ends, this does not necessarily mean they are exercised consciously. Indeed, Brandtstädter and Greve (1994) also note this in relation to their model of adaptive strategies: 'the changing self does not require an intentional actor who changes the self' (p 73). The habitus can also help to explain tension and conflict between individuals' ways of thinking and the demands of their environment. Bourdieu sees the habitus as relatively durable as perceptions are channelled through categories already constructed by experience. He argues that as people age, there is an increasing closure of responses to external stimuli and conditioning experiences: 'the mental and bodily schemata of a person who ages becomes more and more rigid, less and less responsive to external solicitations' (Bourdieu and Wacquant, 1992, pp 133-4).

This contrasts with Biggs (1999, p 81), who views identity as more fluid and identity management as becoming more sophisticated in later life. Maturity is seen as endowing older people with an increased ability to protect the core self by deploying different aspects of identity (Phillipson and Biggs, 1998). Bourdieu, however, invokes the notion of habitus to account for some of the difficulties experienced in later life. The habitus, the accepted, taken-for-granted ways of thinking, perceiving and behaving, may be discordant because it has to apply to different social conditions from those in which it was derived. For example, older people who have always believed that welfare benefits constitute 'charity' are likely to be reluctant to initiate claims, even when their current circumstances indicate need and entitlement (Moffatt and Higgs, 2007). As discussed in Chapter Two, current social services provision is tightly bound by eligibility criteria and a high level of need has to be demonstrated for services to be provided. Gilleard and Higgs (2005) refer to a 'generational habitus', that is, engagement with a particular generation-related cultural field, as distinct from an age cohort effect. The generational habitus of participants in my study reflected concern with self and social perceptions of independence, which signified they were 'doing well'; these concerns are not conducive to a problem-based presentation of self required to seek and obtain help from social or other services (see also Baldock and Hadlow, 2002). Equally, a 'welfare' generational habitus, rooted in ideas about social citizenship, will not equip older people to exercise 'independence, choice and control' as exhorted within current policy (Moffatt and Higgs, 2007).

Bourdieu's writing on the habitus and strategies has been criticised on a number of grounds, including its determinism and 'more than passing resemblance to structural functionalism' in the emphasis placed on the 'fit' between individuals and their social environment (Jenkins, 1996, p 81). Jenkins (1996) also argues that, despite his claim to move beyond a dualism between objectivism and subjectivism, Bourdieu is trapped in an objectivist standpoint and does not fully recognise the ability of individuals to act consciously and rationally. Nevertheless, Jenkins acknowledges that Bourdieu is 'good to think with' (1996, p 11). Habitus is a useful concept in facilitating understanding of the influence of social and cultural forces in shaping participants' perceptions and behaviour. For example, beliefs about the importance of independence, maintaining acceptable boundaries in relationships and putting on a brave face can all be seen as part of the habitus, social influences embodied in the individual. The notion of habitus helps to explain older people's ability to adapt to changing situations, to continue to feel like 'a fish in water' on the one hand, yet also accounts for the disjunction between their knowledges, practices and what the situation appears to demand on the other.

The centrality of power to the knowledges and practices of individuals is a key feature within the work of Foucault. Like Bourdieu, he recognises the social dimensions of self:

> The subject constitutes himself in an active fashion by the practices of self (but) these practices are nevertheless not something that the individual invents by himself. They are patterns that he finds in his culture and which are proposed, suggested and imposed on him by his culture, his society and his social group. (Foucault, 1987 [2000], p 11)

However, the truths and knowledges, or discourses, that are internalised by the individual are not 'neutral' but intimately connected with relations of power. Power is not regarded as in the possession of or applied to particular individuals or groups but, rather, as diffuse:

> Power is employed and exercised through a net-like organisation. And not only do individuals circulate between its threads; they are always in the position of simultaneously undergoing and exercising this power. They are not only its inert or consenting target; they are always also the elements of its articulation. In other words, individuals are the vehicle of power, not its point of application.... The individual which power has constituted is at the same time its vehicle. (Foucault, 1980, p 98)

'Disciplines', or techniques for managing people, while not directly imposed, infiltrate every aspect of life and are instilled in individuals as particular habits and values; these then promote practices of self-surveillance and self-control as individuals regulate their own behaviour (Foucault, 1975). For example, participants' efforts to keep active can be understood in relation to the internalisation of dominant discourses about 'successful ageing' in which 'success' is defined narrowly in terms of the ability to participate and contribute socially (Nolan et al, 2001).

However, Foucault also maintains that where there is power, there is always resistance, and that this is manifested through strategies focused on specific struggles (Foucault, 1975). The individual is therefore not in any sense determined by the structural framework, as suggested in Bourdieu's habitus. Through 'techniques of the self', individuals internalise discourses but also 'act on themselves', working out how to 'conduct themselves' in relation to particular moral rules (Foucault,

1987). While in my study participants had internalised dominant cultural attitudes about independence, for example, this was then translated and interpreted by them in their own terms. For some participants, this meant preserving financial independence; for some it was interpreted as carrying on with their usual modes of living, while for others it was constructed in terms of not relying on other people. In addition, as the category of self-affirmation within the 'staying me' theme revealed, participants are also active agents in reconstructing their situations and behaviour to accommodate internalised moral codes.

Giddens (1999) argues that self-identity has to be understood not just in relation to everyday practices and resistances but also within the much broader context of globalisation. He refers to 'the reflexive project of the self', emphasising the active role of the individual in making choices and decisions from multiple and constantly changing options available within late modern society. The fragmentation and pluralism within late modernity mean that there are no 'givens' for the self so it has to be created and recreated by the individual in the face of changing experiences in order that a distinct identity can be forged. In Giddens' view, an integrated self exists as more than just fragments of diverse multiple selves, and it is the work involved in forging this identity that forms 'the reflexive project of the self':

> Self-identity, in other words, is not something that is just given, as a result of the continuities of the individual's action-system, but something that has to be routinely created and sustained in the reflexive activities of the individual.... Self-identity is not a distinctive trait, or even a collection of traits, possessed by the individual. It is *the self as reflexively understood by the person in terms of her or his biography*. Identity here still presumes continuity across time and space: but self-identity is such continuity as interpreted reflexively by the agent. (Giddens, 1999, pp 52-3, original emphasis)

> A person's identity resides 'in the capacity *to keep a particular narrative going*' (Giddens, 1999, p 54).

Leonard (1997) takes a similar view on individual reflexivity, linking this with the will to resist. He refers to the 'contradictory consciousness' (p 48) that exists when there is a gap between dominant discourses and the individual's actual circumstances and experiences. The individual experiences this as discomfort or conflict, as forces towards both compliance and resistance are juxtaposed:

> This dialectic of the incorporation and repulsion of dominant discourses may explain how some forms of resistance may be expressed and also suggest how significant to the subject of late capitalism a reflexive ability might be. (Leonard, 1997, p 49)

This reflexive capacity of individuals to interpret events and behaviours in line with their 'ongoing story' seems pertinent to both the 'keeping going' and 'staying me' themes. Participants' efforts to maintain their usual routines despite deteriorating health and abilities, their creative adaptations to maintain goals and preserve acceptable boundaries in relationships and their cognitive ways of coping that constructed situations positively and in a way that preserved a sense of control and responsibility can all be seen as ways in which they sought to keep their own 'ongoing story' going. It is also possible to see aspects of these ongoing stories about the self as reflecting resistance to ageist assumptions and stereotypes, for example, constructions of the self as active, resourceful, independent and a giver of help to others.

Further understanding of processes of sustaining the self can be derived from the work of Biggs (1999). Unlike the previous writers, he examines identity specifically from the perspective of later life and he combines in his analysis a psychodynamic belief in the importance of a coherent sense of self with a postmodern understanding based on identity as fluid and fragmented. In common with Goffman, the 'performance' aspects of behaviour are central, but Biggs gives more emphasis to the agency of the individual in negotiating the public/private interface. He argues that identity:

> ... describes the way in which people represent an acceptable face to their social worlds, something that is constructed and maintained is an act of self-invention which also depends upon social context. It is, then, very much a concept at the crossroads of the personal and the social. It includes within itself props and associations that already exist in the social world, plus ideas, fantasies and desires that arise from an individual's inner being. (Biggs, 1999, p 3)

Biggs examines the relationship between the personal and the social in terms of the balance that can be achieved between hidden aspects of the self and those that can be expressed publicly. The concept of social mask or masquerade attests to the view that certain facets of the self have to be hidden because of a hostile social environment:

> The performance of masquerade, in other words, forms the link between the external social world and the internal desires of the performer, while at the same time shielding the inner life from external threat and assault. Social masking and its performance through masquerade become critical in the management of the boundary between self and other, and the permeability of that boundary reflects the possibilities latent in any one social space available for identity performance. (Biggs, 1999, p 131)

Identity performance is seen as a largely unselfconscious process in which identities discordant with dominant social expectations are concealed or underplayed. In this sense, 'rather than being seen simply as a form of inauthenticity, masque should be valued as an adaptive response to inhospitable settings' (Biggs, 1999, p 172). It is possible to see many of the participants' strategies discussed in the category of self-affirmation as a masquerade that seeks to conceal or minimise those aspects of the self that are socially devalued, principally those concerned with dependency, helplessness and an old age identity. According to Biggs, there is an inner self, internal to the individual, and a social space, which is external; identity is that ground in between where inner self meets social space. The notion of masquerade implies that individuals adapt their self-presentation in response to their assessment of the 'social space' in which they are located. In a supportive social space, aspects of self may be revealed that in hostile environments would be concealed. The individual, whether consciously or unconsciously, is making judgements about identity requirements or expectations in particular situations and then adjusting his or her masquerade based on this assessment. For example, while Harriet talked of her social embarrassment at her confusion when using buses and the strategies she used to conceal her poor memory from others, she revealed this in the 'safe' social space of the research interview.

All of the writers considered are concerned in some way with the interface between the individual self and the social structure, but there are significant differences in their views on the nature of this relationship. Whereas Biggs presents them as distinct entities, with masquerade forming the connection between them, Bourdieu sees them as merged, with one becoming part of the other. The individual does not have to work at presenting an acceptable social masquerade, but can do this readily because he or she has imbibed prevailing social and cultural values and expectations. For Bourdieu, these social and cultural expectations are relatively static and pervasive across situations, while for Biggs they are fluid and diverse. Whereas Biggs suggests that the success of masquerade lies in the ability of individuals to reconcile the hidden and the expressed, to balance presentation of their own inner needs and aspirations with the demands of the social space, Bourdieu sees habitus as about the 'fit' between the social and cultural elements embodied in the individual and the external environments in which they are actors. Foucault, on the other hand, while arguing that individuals internalise dominant discourses which then serve to regulate behaviour, sees these discourses as both more fluid and diverse than the habitus, but also as intimately connected to relations of power. He also stresses the actor's ability to resist and engage in 'techniques of the self'. Giddens similarly emphasises the creation and maintenance of the self as a reflexive project engaged in by the individual, rather than imposed by the social structure, but at the same time shows that what happens at the level of personal life is directly connected to the institutional order. Whereas Biggs views identity as the self that is presented socially and Bourdieu sees it as the self that is created socially, Giddens appears to place more emphasis on the individual's own interpretive processes in constructing and maintaining identity. The key task for individuals, according to Giddens, is to respond to changing conditions and reconstitute situations in a way that keeps a particular 'story' about the self going. For Biggs, the key task is to interpret and evaluate the social space and then decide on the appropriate aspects of identity to be presented.

Each perspective on the relationship between self and society, not surprisingly, suggests different forms of response in order to sustain a positive sense of self. While a central question in terms of masquerade is how a supportive social space can be facilitated, a key issue for the habitus is how its malleability and responsiveness to changing environments can be supported. In relation to Foucault's work, the questions posed include how we can help 'subjugated discourses' to be heard and how individuals' capacities for resistance can be strengthened. A central issue in relation to insights offered by Giddens is how individuals can be supported in their reflexive projects to preserve the coherence of their ongoing stories. The implications of these issues are considered further in the next chapter.

Sustaining the self: applying theoretical understanding

How then, do the theoretical perspectives on identity explored in this chapter facilitate understanding of processes by which older people sustain their sense of self? The perspectives converge in the view that the self cannot be understood outside of its social context, although they differ in their view on the nature, extent and direction of this influence. The study findings discussed in Chapters Three, Four and Five have highlighted the need to attend carefully to the social and cultural context within which participants attribute meaning to circumstances and behaviour.

To look first at practical or 'doing' strategies encompassed in the 'keeping going' theme, these behaviours are to a large extent directed by taken-for-granted beliefs and attitudes, for example, about keeping busy and pushing yourself, which could be seen as part of the habitus. In terms of categories within the 'staying me' theme, here too meanings have a social as well as individual significance. In the discussion of life themes in Chapter Four, I referred to Bury's (2001) definition of core narratives as incorporating a connection between cultural meanings and individual experience, giving the example of independence as a core narrative for some participants. Older people's views about independence cannot be dissociated from wider public discourses since notions of dependence are socially constructed (Symonds, 1998). Stereotypes of old age are highly relevant to understanding the construction of meanings. Hockey and James (1993) present an analysis of ways in which both older people and children are infantalised and constructed as dependent. They show how in western culture personhood is inextricably linked to perceptions of independence, with dependency seen as an identity rather than a temporary state. By contrast, in some societies dependence is viewed positively without associations of powerlessness or implications for how the 'whole person' is perceived (Hockey and James, 1993). The entanglement of independence with personhood helps to make sense of the prevalence within older people's discourses, in this and other studies, of themes that have at their heart the retention of independence.

However, while ageism inherent within western society would suggest that these attitudes are part of the habitus of older people themselves, and there is, of course, evidence of this, it is also clear from the study that many older people resist strongly an aged identity and its association with dependence. There may also be socially constructed gender differences in terms of the aspects of dependence most resisted and the more powerful alternative identities available that can be emphasised (Hockey and James, 1993). For example, Chapter Four referred to the high value that Gerald placed on financial independence and the emphasis placed on physical independence by Elsie. This may reflect traditional components of a masculine identity as 'the autonomous self' who is in charge, and feminine conceptions of the 'relational self' who nurtures others (Buker, 1999). Awareness of gender expectations may, then, facilitate understanding of why certain aspects of identity are more fiercely protected when under threat. At the same time, it is apparent that even in western culture, dependence is not inextricably linked with powerlessness or loss of personhood; a dependent status may be a way of exerting power within family situations (Biggs, 1993). For example, I described how Ralph became more physically dependent on his daughters over the course of the first two interviews, but nevertheless retained his status as head of the family. He and his daughter both constructed the situation in a way that preserved a sense of his position of power. This was shown in their use of language ("my daughters are not my slaves"; "he has us running around after him!"). This suggests that individuals have the power not only to resist dominant discourses (for example, that old age equates with powerlessness), but also to engage in 'techniques of the self' that exploit other dominant discourses ('the man is the head of the household') in such a way that a source of power (in this case, gender) is emphasised and positive identity maintained. While cultural values influence the constructs used to make sense of situations, individuals can nevertheless exercise agency in how they are interpreted and applied. In Chapter Three I referred to Gerald's preference for scheduling my visits on the morning of the residents' fortnightly meetings to give him an excuse to avoid attending them. While a professional perspective might view attendance at these meetings as evidence of inclusion and participation in valuable social activity, in Gerald's eyes it signified his belonging to the group of 'fuddy duddies' who lived in the sheltered accommodation complex. It was therefore an identity threat to be resisted, in contrast to his preferred activity, taking his friend out to pubs and restaurants, which confirmed his power and status as host and benefactor.

The strategies and coping mechanisms employed to manage the ageing experience are influenced by reflexive interpretations of what that behaviour conveys to others about the self (Goffman, 1961). Biggs (1993) invokes the concept of 'persona' to refer to the socially acceptable face or mask presented by people in order to conform to social expectations. The persona is, 'a device through which an active self looks out and negotiates with the world, to protect the self and to deceive others' (Biggs, 1999, p 76). Earlier in the chapter reference was made to Bury's (1991) distinction between coping, strategies and style. The concept of style is particularly relevant here since Bury uses this to refer to the cultural repertoires, reflecting variations in meanings and social practices that people draw on when responding to and presenting their illness. This concept is relevant when thinking more generally about the 'persona' of older people. As we have seen, one way of responding to identity threats is to use 'moral narratives' to establish one's personal worth (Bury, 2001). In western culture, the very notion of 'coping' or 'managing' implies moral worth and processes of self-affirmation, described in Chapter Four, show that participants' moral narratives reflect dominant cultural themes of being good for one's age (that is, defying expectations of agedness), putting on a brave face and not giving in. Not giving in is presented as an individual responsibility, residing within the control of individuals, a highly valued personality characteristic and a signal of moral worth. An interesting point is at what stage it becomes personally and socially acceptable to 'give in'. For example, Johnson and Barer's (1997) research suggests that there comes a time for the 'oldest old' when resignation and surrender, rather than resistance, are accepted adaptive strategies. From this it seems that while individuals engage in 'techniques of the self' to uphold their moral status, these are based on their reflexive interpretations and reconstructions, rather than being determined in any straightforward way by the habitus.

Interactions concerning the giving and receiving of help in informal relationships hold considerable significance for identity and moral worth. For example, research on obligations within families highlights the implications of the way that help giving and receiving is managed for personal and social identities:

> ... through negotiations about giving and receiving assistance, people are being constructed and reconstructed as moral beings.... A person's identity or reputation gets confirmed or modified as a result of the way in which they conduct themselves on each occasion. (Finch and Mason, 1993, pp 170-1)

So, too, Charmaz (1997) refers to the 'elaborate dance' of helper and helped to uphold established identities, as discussed previously. Research with people with advanced cancer also highlights the carefully negotiated balances of dependence/ independence as moral identities within caring relationships are constructed and recreated (Chattoo and Ahmad, 2008). In my study, participants' concerns with how their behaviour is perceived by others, for example, that they are not seen to be imposing practical or psychological burdens, illustrates that dominant discourses of independence and self-reliance are internalised and act as self-regulating mechanisms. At the same time, 'disciplinary techniques' of self-surveillance interact with surveillance by others in the social network. Seale's (1996) study of friends and relatives of older people living alone in the year before their death found that they were keenly aware of their moral identities as actual or potential helpers and that this included perceived duties of surveillance. These surveillance duties triggered corresponding identity management efforts on the part of those on their receiving end:

> The maintenance of a reputation of independence ... had to be demonstrated to neighbourly surveillance, by keeping up with regimes of housework and personal cleanliness, and by sustaining reciprocity in personal relationships. (Seale, 1996, p 84)

The way in which each party carefully negotiates the identity implications of helping encounters is also noted in a study of care giving involving people with dementia:

> ... each member reciprocally participates in the maintenance and transformation of the other's identity in social interactions. Further, each member, over time, develops an understanding of the boundaries of identity attributes. That is, negotiated boundaries emerge beyond which the person may not venture without the relationship becoming strained; newly formed boundaries are renegotiated. So long as each member continues to relate to the other as expected, he or she sustains and maintains the other's identity in taken-for-granted interactions. (Orona, 1997, p 183)

When established meanings are shaken and constitute a threat to identity, or there is 'contradictory consciousness' (Leonard, 1997, p 48), meanings may be resisted or reconstructed to diminish the threat. In Chapter Five I gave the example of Harriet's narrative reconstruction across the course of the study from a dread of being dependent on her friends for lifts to accepting and justifying this help on the basis of both past credit, that previously she gave lifts to other people, and also reciprocity, 'we all help each other'. Similarly, older people may render acceptable the receipt of help from their adult children on the basis of duties discharged in earlier parental roles (Bury and Holme, 1991). Clearly in some cultures, receiving help may not constitute an identity threat anyway; indeed, it may reinforce one's status as 'coming from a good family' (Grewal et al, 2004). This highlights the inextricable interconnection between moral dimensions of individual behaviour and perceptions and social and cultural meanings.

Assessments of the safety or threat contained with the social space influence how the self is presented, as Biggs suggests. Awareness of threats contained within the social space is shown in 'the slippery slope' theme of community, with some participants commenting on their experiences of being confronted with ageist or other discriminatory attitudes and behaviour. An expectation that they will be viewed or treated negatively if certain aspects of their 'selves' are revealed is likely to confirm the need for masquerade. This sense of responding to what is required by others is acknowledged directly in other accounts by older people:

> I have no duties, except to myself. That is not true. I have a duty to all
> who care for me – not to be a problem, not to be a burden. I must carry
> my age lightly for all our sakes…. Each day, then, must be filled with
> my first duty, I must be "all right". (Scott-Maxwell, 1968/1998, p 456)

Thus the sub-category 'putting on a brave face' indicated participants' assessment
of the need for a particular social presentation to preserve a positive social
identity. It suggests a perception that the social arena is not sympathetic towards
or does not value presentations of illness, unhappiness or dissatisfaction. Some
of these assessments may be out of line with current attitudes and values within
the environment if the habitus has become static and is not responsive to social
change. For example, older people's beliefs about the need to 'put on a brave
face' and conceal difficulties and unhappiness may be discordant with current
public discourses about the benefits of openly expressing problems and concerns
in various forms of counselling and therapy. 'Habits of the heart' about not
complaining conflict with expectations of the active consumer that underpin
community care policy, as discussed in Chapter Two. This underlines that it is
older people's own assessments of their behaviour and their own evaluations of
how other people view them that is significant in terms of sustaining the self.

The examples considered here suggest that each of the perspectives discussed
has a contribution to make to understanding processes by which the self is
sustained. Dominant social and cultural meanings are reflected in the beliefs,
attitudes and behaviour of study participants and these meanings are pivotal
in their self-evaluations and in their reflexive interpretations of how they are
viewed by others. However, they are also active agents in their capacity to
resist contradictory or hostile data and to respond reflexively to their changing
circumstances, manipulating meanings in ways that support a positive sense of
self. These capacities and opportunities for resistance and reflexivity are enhanced
by the range of resources available to individuals as they deploy coping strategies.
This aspect has been underplayed in the theoretical perspectives discussed here,
but was explored in relation to 'the slippery slope' theme in Chapter Four.

Conclusion

This chapter has considered theoretical perspectives on identity to assist
understanding of the dynamic between the social and individual components
of identity, the significance of social and cultural meanings and the reflexive
interpretations made by older people as they demonstrate and maintain their
sense of moral worth.

It has been argued that the sense of self does not emanate in any 'pure' sense
from an individual's thoughts, personality and behaviour, from how he or she
negotiates difficulties at a practical or psychological level, but that it reflects
meanings derived from social interaction with others. These relational elements
encompass messages about self that accrue from social interactions – for example,

perceptions of independence based on an ability to keep active and keep balance in relationships, contained within the 'keeping going' category, as well as reflexive interpretations based on how people believe they are perceived by others, for example, reported reflections of 'doing well' and 'life is what you make it' contained within the self-affirmation category of 'staying me'. These interpretive processes are mediated by dominant cultural meanings. The self that is sustained by the mechanisms described is therefore a sociological self, created and validated, not just revealed, through processes of interaction (Kelly and Dickinson, 1997). While at one level the study participants can be seen as autonomous 'subjects', exercising agency in the strategies they deploy to manage ageing, at another level they can be viewed as 'subjected' in that their identities are constituted by social and economic forces (Leonard, 1997).

The external world is important in terms of influencing the themes within an individual's 'ongoing story' and determining the resources available to support that story, but in both respects its significance lies in the sense the individual makes of it. This perhaps assists understanding of how the habitus may in some situations operate in such a way as to make an individual feel like 'a fish in water' and in others 'a fish out of water'. Where the individual is not able to integrate events and circumstances within 'the ongoing story of the self', perhaps by changing the situation (or using accommodative strategies in terms of the models discussed earlier), then the only option is to change the story itself (assimilative strategies). In relation to Johnson and Barer's description of 'the detached selves' of the 'oldest old', one could say that it is no longer possible for them to retain former stories about themselves as the discrepancy between this and their circumstances has become too wide. At this point there is a readjustment in their view of self. When individuals are not able to make this readjustment, tensions and difficulties are experienced as they become like 'a fish out of water'. This view suggests that the habitus is much more amenable to control and manipulation by the individual than as represented by Bourdieu. At the same time, it seems important not to shift too far in the other direction, regarding identity as a freely chosen 'pick and mix' selection (Hockey and James, 2003), but to recognise the way in which stories about the self are shaped by prevailing discourses. The central tension reflected throughout the chapter can be summed up as that between:

> ... individuals' capacity to make and remake themselves, to resist the penalties, constraints and imperatives of "social structure" and the ageing body, and their dependence upon "the social" as the source of who they experience themselves to be. (Hockey and James, 2003, p 199)

Having in this chapter examined the findings presented in previous chapters in terms of 'what does it all mean?', Chapter Seven considers 'in what directions does it take us?' (Wolcott, 1994), that is, the implications for social policy and practice.

SEVEN

Destinations and directions

To *feel* what it means to be old is to understand ageing from a completely different perspective and to be forever changed by that understanding. (R. Ray, 2007, p 63)

In Chapter Six I sought to integrate understanding derived from the analysis presented in Chapters Three, Four and Five. The chapter argued that the themes of 'keeping going', 'staying me' and 'the slippery slope' were related to a broader overarching theme of sustaining the self, examining this in the context of related research and theoretical perspectives. By exploring the wider meaning of the study findings, I thus began to address the question, 'What is to be made of it all?' (Wolcott, 1994).

This final chapter draws out the significance of the issues highlighted in the previous chapters for social care policy and practice. In particular, it considers how positive experiences of ageing can be promoted in two key areas: sustaining selfhood and creating a supportive social environment. Since the book's central thread is one small-scale research study, the chapter begins with brief critical reflections on this study.

Critique of methodology and process

There are a number of limitations and issues concerning the methodology and process of the study that need to be considered. First, the experiences and perspectives cited are those of 12 older people who were all of white UK ethnic origin. In Chapter Six I discussed the significance of dominant social and cultural values in shaping individual interpretations and behaviour. The particular values highlighted as significant in the study were those of independence and self-reliance, which are essentially western values. Cross-cultural studies suggest that there is a high degree of cultural specificity about constructions of activity, autonomy and successful ageing (Estes et al, 2003). Other themes, for example, faith and spirituality, might have had more prominence with a more ethnically diverse sample (Maynard et al, 2008). In addition, evidence of ethnic inequalities in economic and health status (Nazroo et al, 2004), and the significance of experiences of racism for black older people (Butt and Moriarty, 2004), suggests that the specific threats identified in 'the slippery slope' theme would have been different with a sample that included older people from minority ethnic groups. No assumptions can therefore be made about the wider validity of the more detailed categories and concepts discussed. However, there appear to be common themes, albeit differences in emphasis, in research with people from more diverse backgrounds. For example, Vernon (2002) noted that for younger (aged 18-40) Asian people with disabilities, the notion of independence meant choice and control, but also interdependence, 'being able to contribute to family life and reciprocate' (p 29). Independence and interdependence have also been found to be highly valued by older respondents from diverse ethnic backgrounds, although there were ethnic differences in the precise ways in which these concepts took shape in people's lives (Grewal et al, 2004). It may be that the higher level themes and categories have broader applicability even if the sub-categories require reworking to reflect the diversity of older people.

Second, there were a number of potential sources of bias intruding in various stages of the research process, particularly the selection of study participants. Delineating the sample in terms of older people who had expressed need to social services excluded older people who were experiencing need, but for various reasons not expressing it. Those who were identified as meeting the case requirements then self-selected into the study by responding to a written request to participate. This could potentially have excluded those unable to read English because of language differences, particular impairments or literacy issues. As the leaflet was seeking involvement in interviews, those people less comfortable with talking in a one-to-one situation or reluctant or fearful about inviting strangers into their home may also have been deterred from responding. When looking at the direction of bias constituted by these factors, it is possible that it worked in favour of the inclusion of older people in more advantageous physical, social and economic circumstances. The leaflet made clear that involvement in the study would not change the outcomes of decisions for individual participants, but might contribute generally to service improvements for older people in the longer term. Given the importance participants attached to 'putting a bit back' into their communities, discussed in Chapter Three, it is possible that framing participation in the study as a way of helping others may have attracted those with altruistic motivations.

Once people were recruited to the study, there were other influences on their continued participation. Three participants died during the course of the study and two others were unable to complete the full quota of five interviews because of health or other difficulties. A pertinent question is in what ways those who took part in all five interviews (and therefore contributed most 'data', in terms of quantity) differed from those who contributed less. It does seem to be the case that those who contributed more were those who were managing better at both objective and subjective levels, in the terms described in Figure 6.2 in Chapter Six. While it could be argued that this produces an overly positive view of older people's abilities to deploy effective strategies for managing ageing, I have also sought to apply the themes and model to those who fared less well in terms of managing, as shown in relation to Les and David. Understanding how older people manage the ageing experience also elucidates the factors that undermine their practical strategies and psychological coping.

Wolcott (1994) takes the view that quality in qualitative research concerns its ability to assist understanding, rather than to convince. The model and analysis presented in Chapter Six aims to summarise and elucidate dimensions and processes, not provide definitive answers. If generalisability is taken to mean the direct application of the findings to all older people, or even all those refused services by social services, then the findings are clearly not in any way generalisable. The small sample size, unrepresentativeness of the participants in terms of ethnicity and the various biases within the research process prevent any conclusions based on wider applicability of the findings. However, it is argued that the notion of generalisability is irrelevant when the concern is with the meanings of individual experiences (Janesick, 1998). When considering the appropriateness of generalisability in relation to evaluating her own research, Fook (2001) concludes:

> ... what we were doing was not devising a theory in order to *generalize* it across all populations, but rather developing an understanding ... which might be *transferable* to other situations, in that it might provide meaning in other contexts. Using theories developed in one context to explicate experiences in another context (transferability), is different, in this sense, from imposing the meaning gained from one context on another (generalizability). (Fook, 2001, pp 125-6, original emphasis)

While the themes and models presented in this book are not directly generalisable to older people in different situations, the understanding derived from the analysis may nevertheless be transferable – in Fook's sense of 'providing meaning in other contexts' – to other older people managing the experience of ageing.

Finally in this critique of methodology and process, I consider the role and contribution of research participants. Involving service users in research can challenge and change the research agenda, research processes and the way that findings are reported and acted on (Coghlan et al, 2007). Adopting an approach that sought to maximise the involvement of participants in the research process meant that to a considerable extent the older people themselves shaped the course of the study. The loosely structured nature of the interviews meant that participants played a significant role in determining what 'data' was revealed. Consequently, the central focus of the research shifted from concepts of eligibility criteria, needs and services, constructed and perceived through my social work practitioner/academic lens, to a concern with processes of sustaining a sense of self, constructed and perceived through an in-depth understanding of how older people manage the ageing experience. This echoes the disjunction noted by Baldock and Hadlow (2002) between the 'needs-talk' of professionals and the 'self-talk' of older people in assessment.

However, while the in-depth loosely structured interviews, by virtue of their open agenda, gave a wide filter for participant voices to be heard, the process of coding and constructing categories from this 'data' posed the risk of distancing participants and imposing my own interpretations. For example, participants talked of their efforts to keep up their routines, activities and interests, to manage tasks for themselves, and to avoid asking others for help; they did not talk of their efforts to sustain their sense of self. At various points in this study I attempted to involve participants in the process of 'making sense' of their own and others' experiences. The longitudinal nature of the study gave an opportunity not only for the data obtained from each interview to be verified with participants at the subsequent interview, but also for the preliminary analysis to be used as the basis of discussion with them. The analysis was therefore shared with participants during the research as well as at its conclusion. As noted previously, this led to a 'turning point' in the research process as I reviewed the approach taken to analysis and followed up the grounded theory-based analysis with a narrative approach. However, sharing the ongoing analysis with participants raised the question of reactivity, that is, the potential for processes of gathering data and analysis to change the data (Punch, 1998). It is possible that the content of later interviews was influenced by participants' understanding of the analysis shared with them. For example, the early analysis highlighted participants' determination and resourcefulness in finding strategies to 'keep going' in the face of difficulties. This may have reinforced the significance of positive social presentations, making it harder for them to acknowledge difficulties in later interviews.

Implications for theoretical understanding

This section addresses Wolcott's (1994) question, 'What is to be made of it all?' or 'So what?'. In terms of theoretical understanding, in Chapter Six I suggested that one way of making sense of how older people manage the experience of ageing is to interweave a number of other key strands with the central symbolic interactionist thread of meanings and interpretations. These include contributions from: postmodernism, highlighting the dynamic nature of identity and the capacity of individuals to respond reflexively to changing social conditions; lifecourse perspectives, highlighting the significance of enduring life themes; and narrative approaches, focusing on the significance of the construction of 'stories' for how individuals view themselves and present themselves to others.

Understanding the meanings older people attach to behaviour, events and situations is crucial for understanding the significance that particular difficulties and circumstances hold for their sense of self. However, the process of giving meaning can *only* be understood in relation to a particular social and cultural context since it is from within this context that meaning itself derives. At the same time, while meaning derives from a social and cultural context, it is also interpreted individually and reflexively, as individuals create, resist and manipulate the meanings of situations and experiences. Therefore, while understanding can be facilitated by awareness of the social and cultural context, no assumptions can be made about how this is interpreted at an individual level. These different aspects of theoretical understanding highlight the entanglement of the personal and social. This applies to the understanding of identity and stories of the self as well as processes by which a positive sense of self is undermined or supported. It is necessary to understand how individuals are influenced by social, economic and environmental factors and how dominant cultural concepts and values shape their sense of self. However, understanding also has to incorporate meanings and interpretations at the subjective level and how individual constructions can in turn create cultural and social change.

The research findings presented and analysed in this book also assist understanding of more specific aspects of theories of ageing. In relation to continuity theory (Atchley, 1989), Chapters Three and Four suggested that older people's identities comprise both stable and changing aspects. The self was seen as having some coherence and consistency, rather than being fluid, fragmented and constantly reconstituting. At the same time, identity evolves as circumstances change, for example, an identity as 'someone who gives lifts to others', to 'someone who is dependent on others', to 'someone who is part of a social network where everyone helps one another' (Harriet). However, these changes are negotiated and managed in ways that are as far as possible congruent with what is experienced as the core self. This is achieved by a range of mechanisms, discussed in the strategies of self-affirmation detailed in Chapter Four, including underplaying inconsistent messages and highlighting affirming messages. Thus, Harriet replaced her earlier talk of individual self-reliance with an emphasis on mutual reciprocity; and Ralph accommodated his changed circumstances by reinforcing a discourse of personal power (both he and his daughters presenting the dynamics of the relationship as featuring power on his side and subservience on theirs). This seems to support theories based on the narrative construction and reconstruction of self. However, in the same way that accommodative rather than assimilative strategies may be necessary when the situation cannot be changed and values and goals themselves have to be adjusted (Brandtstädter and Greve, 1994), when circumstances are flagrantly incompatible with the story, it may be necessary to change the story itself. This is found in studies of the 'oldest old' who have disengaged, no longer striving to maintain reciprocity or keep active (Johnson and Barer, 1997).

The importance of physical and mental activity to participants can be seen as providing some measure of support for activity theory (Havighurst and Albrecht, 1953). At the same time, it was shown that participants identified limits to 'pushing themselves' when this was no longer seen as a viable strategy and this, in turn, could be seen as suggesting some empirical support for disengagement theory (Cumming and Henry, 1961). However, such universalist theories of ageing fail to capture significant nuances of individual meaning, reflexive interpretation and narrative reconstruction. While discourses of activity, independence and so on may feature heavily in older people's accounts, these have diverse and continually renegotiated meanings at the individual level. For example, although research with older people who had moved to a retirement village found that themes of autonomy and security featured prominently in older people's accounts, these concepts had different meanings for different individuals:

> For some people, autonomy might mean having been able to lift the
> burden of care from family members; for others it might mean the
> freedom to take part in activities that they have always longed to do
> but have never been able to. (Bernard et al, 2004, p 53)

It is therefore necessary to explore individual meanings and interpretations of discourses and behaviour. To refer to one example, the relinquishing by Alice of certain social activities as her level of physical impairment increased could be interpreted according to disengagement theory as part of an inevitable process of withdrawal from social activity with advancing age. However, this would ignore the importance Alice attached to the many new relationships she formed with home care staff and to the significance of these relationships in preserving a key life theme of social activity, thereby facilitating her 'ongoing story of the self'. These relationships became part of a reworked social network, reflecting a process of re-engagement rather than disengagement.

Whether the self is perceived and presented in terms of activity or disengagement may, therefore, depend on the 'fit' between circumstances and the 'ongoing story about the self' (Giddens, 1999, p 54). When the story itself becomes insupportable and has to change, the individual may be able to adjust to the changed story of self; however, individuals may not always be able to negotiate with themselves and others a changed identity that they find acceptable. This seems to signify a time of particular vulnerability or 'critical phase' (Steverink et al, 1998), and the messages delivered by others could be crucial factors in easing or impeding the transition. This was illustrated in the situation of David who felt overprotected by his family and was not able to maintain his view of self as autonomous and geographically mobile, as enacted and symbolised in his entrapment in the first floor flat. The support available at both social and community levels in helping individuals maintain their story or, when this is not possible, helping them negotiate an acceptable alternative story, seems critical in understanding processes of managing in later life.

It is clear that older people have their own theory to contribute to this understanding. For example, this study has shown that their behaviour is motivated by explicit beliefs about what will benefit them and other people. Thus, keeping busy and 'pushing yourself' are believed to help them keep physically and mentally healthy; a cheerful social presentation and positive thinking are believed to contribute to social acceptance by others, as well as being beneficial for emotional and psychological health. Older people are aware of the threats facing them as they grow older and they have views about strategies of resistance. Acknowledging that older people theorise in this way is important, not just in extending traditional conceptions of what constitutes 'theory' (Gubrium and Wallace, 1990), but also in highlighting the need to engage this understanding of older people's own theories in how we support them. If older people believe that they need to keep active, it will not be helpful to them to provide a home carer to do their shopping and cook their meals if, with support, they could complete these tasks for themselves.

If they believe it is important to retain a measure of independence from their families, it will not be helpful to make assumptions about involving family and friends in providing 'care' in a way that breaches their own view of acceptable relationship boundaries. If older people believe it is important to think positively and present a cheerful social face, it will not be helpful to require them to focus only on 'needs' and problems in social work assessment.

Implications for social policy and practice

As discussed in Chapter Two and highlighted further in the remainder of the book, there are many discrepancies between the perceptions, requirements and lived experiences of older people and social care policy and practice. Phillipson and Biggs (1998) argue that a secure foundation for a mature identity is through:

> ... the creation of a protected inner core and an external environment that provides both an adequate material base while remaining sufficiently indeterminate to allow experiments with social identity. (Phillipson and Biggs, 1998, p 20)

This section explores the implications for social policy and practice of what has been learned from older people's experiences and perspectives in relation to these two aspects: protecting the core self and facilitating a supportive social space.

Protecting the core self

Supporting older people in sustaining the self depends, first, on some level of engagement with that 'self' and, second, on this understanding being actively and sensitively applied in the helping transactions that ensue.

Engaging with and respecting selfhood in assessment

'Need' is defined and experienced by older people in diverse ways and research findings discussed in previous chapters show that functional areas of difficulty, such as declining mobility, have wider psychological and emotional significance in terms of selfhood. The challenge for assessment policies and practices is to harness this understanding in the support offered to older people. As outlined in Chapter Two, the single assessment process guidance makes explicit reference to 'person-centred' assessment (DH, 2002b). However, Chapter Two also documented the difficulties of this being realised in practice, including the restricted opportunities for relationship-based practice, narrow and problem-focused assessment and the marginalising of service user stories. Older people's experiences of what helps them to 'keep going' and 'stay me' have implications for their relationships with assessors and the methods by which the assessment is carried out.

Even in relatively fleeting relationships, such as those with practitioners carrying out assessments, the interpersonal skills and demeanor of the person concerned play a key role in determining how older people evaluate their experience of the process (Powell et al, 2007). Practitioners' understanding of individual experiences and interpretations is contingent on a relationship of openness and trust in which reciprocal meanings can be constructed (Jordan with Jordan, 2000), yet relationships are too often regarded as a hindrance to the main business of rationing services (Jones, 2001). As noted in Chapter Six, the tasks of screening, assessment, care planning and review are increasingly fragmented in assessment and care management practice, undermining relationship-based practice. A related issue is the methods by which assessment information is obtained and the status it is accorded. If it is accepted, as argued here, that individual selves are revealed and presented through narratives, it is necessary that the 'gatekeepers' of support services engage with individual 'stories' and meanings (Rodger, 1991). That this is a skilled and sensitive task is illustrated by the self-affirmation strategies identified in Chapter Four. Older people may be inclined to present a positive picture of coping that may not marry well with assessment oriented to eliciting 'risks to independence'. Tightly prescribed predetermined assessment frameworks or telephone interviews via contact centres (Coleman, 2009) are unlikely to facilitate attentive listening to the service user's story or to capture diverse nuances of meaning.

Narrative approaches draw on the stories individuals tell about themselves and their lives, not just as a way of facilitating understanding but also as a way of producing change. As Parton and Marshall (1998, p 248) state, 'Talking not only helps people to understand their experiences, but also allows them to control, reframe and move on' (p 248). Gearing and Coleman (1996) argue the benefits of anchoring assessment in a biographical approach that elicits and utilises understanding of an individual's life story. The sensitive and flexible use of a biographical interview schedule, 'a route map of the territory to be explored' (p 273), is suggested as a means of enhancing the practitioner's understanding of the older person. Narrative and biographical approaches are respectful of and responsive to processes by which individuals construct and reconstruct their identities. If carried out in this way, the process of assessment could increase its intrinsic worth as a way of helping individuals maintain or change their 'ongoing story of the self', as well as being a route to determining service provision.

This is consistent with policy that views one of the purposes of assessment as being to assist individuals to 'gain a better understanding of their situation' (DH, 2002a, para 36). While delivery of the personalisation agenda places an emphasis on self-assessment, experience from the pilot sites suggested that traditional community care assessment systems were often being used alongside new individual budget assessments. Practices varied and while some individual budget assessments were seen as allowing scope for more in-depth information gathering, others were more restricted to resource allocation (Glendinning et al, 2008). Personalisation does not , therefore, offer a panacea for delivering assessment that is 'person-centred', not least because self-assessment removes the opportunity for individuals to benefit from the professional assessment itself.

Engaging with and respecting selfhood in help giving and receiving

Greater sensitivity is also needed to the implications of receiving services for selfhood. 'Help' can be provided in a way that either sustains or diminishes the sense of self:

> Offering and receiving care ... involves an interpersonal relationship which impacts on people's identity and sense of self, for both caregivers and those receiving care. The processes are value-laden and carry meanings and implications about roles and expectations, often at a very deep level. (Brechin, 1998, p 10)

'Help', as distinct from 'care', is about supporting older people's own strategies to live their lives according to their chosen routines and preferences. Supportive intervention is therefore not just about what services are or are not provided – primarily resource issues – but also about the processes through which help is channelled. Earlier chapters have illustrated the potential disjunction between action strategies to address difficulties and cognitive coping (Bury, 1991). Help provided by formal services or family may address the practical consequences of illness and disability but, in so doing, undermine a positive sense of self if key life themes, attitudes, values and self-concepts are contradicted in the process, and a changed identity acceptable to the individual cannot be renegotiated.

Looking first at informal care, one significant message is the need to understand older people's perceptions of acceptable relationship boundaries so that these normative expectations are not transgressed. This means taking account of older people's willingness to receive certain types of help from particular sources, not just on carers' willingness and ability to provide 'care' (Qureshi, 1996; McCann and Evans, 2002). One study found that receiving social support from adult children had psychological benefits for older people up to a certain level, but higher levels of support beyond this level reduced psychological well-being. A key factor was the degree of congruence between older people's expectations of support and the level of support received. Interestingly, the researchers found that receiving support that exceeded expectations was more damaging than support that was lower than expected (Silverstein et al, 1996). For example, if families intervene beyond the level that older people want and expect in the management of their finances, this can create stress in relationships and feelings of dependence and vulnerability (Tilse et al, 2007). The example of David's situation, presented earlier, confirms the view that support that exceeds individuals' preferences or expectations may result in feelings of loss of control, and consequently, negatively affect well-being (see also Seeman et al, 1996). A central issue appears to be not the amount of support received, but whether individuals are able to retain subjective perceptions of dignity and independence (Secker et al, 2003). While it may be expedient for care managers to assume or expect that family or friends will provide support, especially if these individuals themselves offer it, this may infringe beliefs and attitudes that underpin selfhood of the potential recipient.

Direct payments and individual budgets offer opportunities for older people to feel more in control in care transactions with family, friends or neighbours through the exercise of financial power. However, there may be less positive implications of these initiatives for caring relationships. Low rates of pay may make it difficult to recruit suitable staff, placing additional demands on family carers (Leece, 2010). There may be particular difficulties concerning the availability of PAs in rural areas (Manthorpe and Stevens, 2009). Family carers could feel obliged to step in and assume the role of PAs, even when neither they nor the older people concerned see this as an avenue for promoting their independence; or they could be put in the position of having to 'plug gaps' in care arrangements. Carers could also face additional demands through having to assume the task of managing direct payments or individual budgets (Ellis, 2007). The initial evaluation of individual budget pilots highlighted the need for sources of support independent of informal carers for those with complex needs, without access to family support or who prefer not to rely on their family (Challis et al, 2007).

Receiving care directly for cash carries many permeations of meaning within relationships, with implications for individual identity and interpersonal dynamics (Glendinning et al, 2000; Henderson and Forbat, 2002; Ellis, 2007). For example, paying family members for care could conflict with family, cultural or religious values about family roles and responsibilities. Interpersonal relationships are complex and the members of caring networks may have different and competing interests. It is argued that the individualistic model on which direct payments and individual budgets are based does not reflect these complexities (Glendinning, 2008). If personalisation is to play a role in 'protecting the core self', it is imperative that both service users and those who are part of their caring networks are central to its development and implementation in practice so that different needs and interests are taken into account (Beresford, 2009). The impact of the personalisation agenda on caring relationships is an important area for research.

Creating a supportive social space

Biggs (1999) highlights the significance of the social space in which 'self' meets 'other'. An important dimension of sustaining the self is through rendering the social space as more supportive. I consider the creation of a more supportive social space in terms of, first, reducing threats and augmenting resources, and second, the challenging of unhelpful social constructions.

Reducing threats and augmenting resources

As noted in Chapter Five, resources are significant as both 'tools' that help older people to manage difficulties, and as protective factors that buffer the impact of change and loss. This necessitates both more immediate interventions to ensure older people have access to appropriate support to deal with difficulties as they arise as well as longer-term strategies to build the reserves they can draw on as they age.

Throughout the book, the participants' determination to keep going in the face of difficulties and their creativity and resourcefulness in deploying strategies to enable them to do this have been highlighted. It has been shown that there is no straightforward relationship between level of difficulties and objective and subjective coping. In line with the model of 'managing' put forward in Figure 6.2 in Chapter Six, the questions raised for social policy and social practice are how the resilience of older people can be enhanced and supported. Rather than focusing on needs and risks, older people's well-being can be promoted through building resilience at the levels of the individual, family and environment. An understanding of these protective factors can be used as the basis of positive intervention to increase a sense of coping and promote control (Godfrey and Denby, 2004). It is not about eliminating risk or removing difficult situations, since these in themselves promote resilience, as reflected in the theorising of participants, discussed in Chapter Four. Ethically responsible research must be sensitive to its political outcomes (Wilson, 2001) and a concern is that this could be used to justify decisions to leave older people to their own devices on the grounds that this develops resilience and avoids the iatrogenic effects of becoming a social work or social care 'client'. Promoting resilience as suggested here is not a justification for non-intervention, but a proactive initiative to identify and bolster people's own coping and support mechanisms. In terms of the resources that support 'keeping going' and 'staying me' strategies, protective factors have been identified at all three 'levels'. At the personal level, these are: good health, adequate financial resources, experience and attitudes conducive to dealing with the difficulties faced and psychological coping mechanisms. At the social level, a key protective factor is having informal support mechanisms that perform both direct help-giving roles and indirect functions in terms of facilitating links with other resources, encouraging problem resolution and risk avoidance. At the community level, protective factors are access to adequate, available and acceptable formal care services and communities that provide support, and facilitate participation and inclusion.

In terms of how support can be provided in ways that sustain the self, it is relevant in the current policy and practice context again to consider the implications of personalisation. The focus on self-assessment, outcomes and control over resources that characterise the personalisation agenda offers opportunities for delivering support that is flexible and responsive to individual 'selfhood'. For example, there may be the potential for increased involvement in communities and for more equal relationships with 'carers'/supporters. Research comparing the experiences of direct payment users and their PAs with those of people receiving traditional home care and their home carers found that the former featured more reciprocal relationships. For example, direct payment recipients in the study made a birthday cake for their PA, looked after the PA's children and gave small gifts, as well as permitting more flexible working arrangements (Leece, 2010).

However, there are a number of concerns and challenges, both practical and ideological, raised by personalisation. Direct payment and individual budgets are based on the notion of individuals having clear information about the resources available and being assisted to develop a support plan that best achieves the outcomes identified (CSIP, 2007). In terms of older people's efforts to 'keep going', discussed in Chapter Three, this would support them to 'find solutions'. However, a research programme on the Modernisation of Adult Social Care (MASC), commissioned by the Department of Health, notes concerns about the adequacy of effective information and support mechanisms (Newman et al, 2008). Eligibility for services via direct payments and individual budgets is likely to remain restricted to those experiencing the highest levels of need, who are therefore likely to require considerable levels of support for processes of self-assessment, support planning and brokerage to be meaningful and effective (Clark et al, 2004; Henwood and Hudson, 2007). Also, those with complex needs require *ongoing* support to enable them to continue to exercise choice as their needs change (Glendinning, 2008).

Personalisation should also enable individuals to identify the outcomes that are most important to them and their preferred way of achieving these. However, it seems that there remains a tendency for support plans for older people to feature personal care needs, rather than needs related to occupation or social participation, 'restricting the scope for improvements in wider well-being' (CSIP, 2007, p 238). This suggests that while the mechanisms of assessment and care provision may be different, it is more difficult to shift professional culture and practice concerning the definition of 'need'. Another concern is that interviews with older people indicate that some experience the responsibility associated with planning and managing their support arrangements as burdensome (Glendinning et al, 2008). Any gains in control and flexibility may therefore be counterbalanced by anxieties about the responsibility inherent in an individual budget and the possibility that this will become another problem to be negotiated.

Concern has been expressed about the potential for heightened inequalities in a system in which lone purchasers are negotiating with private care agencies or individual PAs (Carmichael and Brown, 2002; Scourfield, 2005). For example, service users with greater needs or who are perceived in some way as being 'difficult' could be less attractive customers to organisations operating according to market principles (Glendinning, 2008). More broadly, certain social factors, for example, related to age, social class, gender, ethnicity, 'culture' and life experience, may make some individuals less able to adopt the consumer-citizen role envisaged in 'cash for care' schemes (Baldock and Ungerson, 1994; Moffatt and Higgs, 2007), thus accentuating rather than reducing existing social inequalities. As Scourfield (2007a, p 108) puts it, there is a danger that those who cannot fulfil the status of 'autonomous, managerial and enterprising individuals' become 'subordinated citizens'.

There are also questions about conflict between the flexibility of personalisation and the managerial concerns of a hitherto 'regulatory and centralizing state' (Scourfield, 2007a, p 111). An evaluation of individual budget pilot sites noted that both care managers and individual budget holders were uncertain about what it was legitimate to spend their publicly funded budget on, and the inherent tension between person-centred support and eligibility was highlighted:

> If a person can do without an element of the personal support they have been assessed as needing in order to free up money to spend elsewhere, can they still be seen as needing the personal care? Clearly an element of judgement is involved in resolving such dilemmas, but it points to a mismatch between the concepts underlying eligibility criteria and assessment practice, which focuses very tightly on clearly defined needs; and a personalised approach, which, in contrast, focuses on supporting quality of life and achieving a set of outcomes. (Glendinning et al, 2008, p 170)

There are also more fundamental criticisms of personalisation. It is argued that although it appears to respond to service users' requirements for increased choice and control, it is primarily about promoting the role of the private sector, rather than increasing the provider role of the public sector. The underpinning model is seen as that of individualised consumerism rather than collective citizenship (Pearson, 2000; Scourfield, 2007a; Beresford, 2008), a model that will not in itself tackle wider issues of powerlessness and inequality (Ferguson, 2007). On this note, Scourfield (2007a) argues that the direct payments and individual budgets rely on predominantly privatised solutions to socially constructed problems (such as 'old age'). While they may, at best, respond to some of the consequences of social and economic inequalities, they do not directly address them. It is important, therefore, to consider critically notions of giving older people choice and control in relation to their own care. On the one hand, the personalisation agenda supports closer engagement with older people as responsible citizens and experts in their own situations; on the other hand, it tends to obscure and restrict collective responsibilities for meeting individual and social need and risks marginalising and excluding those who are unable to function as citizens on the narrow terms in which this is constructed (Scourfield, 2007b).

With the tightening of eligibility criteria for access to social care services, discussed in Chapter Two, fewer older people qualify for social care provision, whether by an individual budget or otherwise, so reducing threats and augmenting resources are necessary at the wider community level, as well as at the level of care services. Access to information is important to older people at this broader community level as well as to 'service users'. Initiatives directed at improving information and access to community services appear to have substantial benefits for the health and well-being of older people, as well as for organisations in terms of cost savings and partnership working (DH, 2007b; Watt et al, 2007; Ritters and Davis, 2008).

There has also been considerable attention within social policy to promoting citizenship and this is another route to reduce threats and augment resources. Lister (1998) distinguishes between the status of citizenship, in terms of the rights that individuals 'have', and the practice of citizenship, that is, their active involvement in communities and wider society that is of benefit to themselves and others. Older people's accounts as relayed in this book and other studies highlight key themes of 'putting a bit back', interdependence and reciprocity in older people's practice of citizenship (Nolan et al, 1996; Reed et al, 2004; Breheny and Stephens, 2009). Wilkin (1990) adopts the following perspective: 'Where an individual is defined (by self and/or others) as having nothing of value to exchange, any claim made on others is evidence of dependence' (p 24). In these terms, 'promoting independence' is as much about recognising and facilitating exchange in relationships, or interdependence, as it is about encouraging non-reliance on others. This implies the need to support older people to be active participants and contributors to caring networks and communities, rather than confining their identities to that of recipients of care provided by others. There are a number of levels at which this may be addressed, including facilitating direct reciprocity, where older people are able to offer practical or emotional help to other individuals, or indirect reciprocity, where they are giving to their community or wider society more broadly.

Social policy accords older people active roles, both in relation to their own care and welfare and in terms of their civic responsibilities through prolonged working beyond the age of 65 and engagement in activities such as caring and volunteering (DWP, 2005). However, idealised constructions of active and engaged older people tend to homogenise later life (Biggs et al, 2006). The practice of citizenship may be much more diverse, indicating the need to enhance opportunities for older people to exercise active citizenship in ways that are meaningful to them. For example, meaningful political participation for older people includes activities beyond traditional voting, such as self-help, campaigning activities and having a 'voice' about issues of importance to them (Postle et al, 2005).

There are many ways in which older people have been involved as active citizens, for example through campaigning groups or organisations, service user consultations and advisory panels; involvement is at all levels, from local through to international (Barnes, 2005). Older people's motivation for participation is often based on 'making a difference' and 'getting things done' (Reed et al, 2006), so outcomes are important. The ability to be active and engaged as a citizen is directly related to social and economic influences on the lifecourse (Holstein and Minkler, 2007). A Social Exclusion Unit report, *A sure start to later life*, examined seven areas of social exclusion faced by older people: social relationships, cultural activities, civic activities, access to basic services, neighbourhood, financial products and material consumption (ODPM, 2006). Research on the social exclusion of older people in some of the most deprived urban areas of England highlighted the interrelationships between different aspects of exclusion (Scharf et al, 2004). For example, being poor adversely affected social relationships. Differences by age and gender were noted, with older people over the age of 74 and Somali and Pakistani older people being the most likely to face multiple forms of social exclusion. While most of the older people in the study were involved in civic activities, such as attending community or religious meetings, lack of material resources, language and literacy difficulties and anxieties about being the victim of crime were all identified as potential barriers to older people's civic involvement (Scharf et al, 2004). On this note, although older people's involvement was integral to the design and implementation of POPPs, discussed in Chapter Two, the evaluation observed the tendency for newly retired, healthy and better educated older people to be involved (Windle et al, 2009).

A project in Hull provides an example of an approach that aimed to develop the capacity of the local community (not just older people) to respond to its own support needs (Quilgars, 2004). Through facilitating community networks and fostering low level mutual support among residents, the project developed protective factors at the level of community resources. It also supported the protection of the core self by encouraging reciprocal help giving. The project report notes, however, that it did not reach the more vulnerable groups in the community. This suggests that additional measures might be needed to involve more marginalised older people in such initiatives. Promoting citizenship must involve removing barriers as well as creating opportunities.

One way of addressing barriers to citizenship is action to increase the take-up of welfare benefits. Craig (2004) demonstrated how increased access to welfare benefits enhanced the citizenship of older people, not only in relation to their physical well-being, but also their sense of choice, control, dignity and self-respect. The study focused on older people who might be deemed 'hard to reach', including people who lived in rural areas and older people from minority ethnic groups. Craig concluded that these people were not, once contacted, 'hard to reach'; the difficulty lay with services that were not set up to 'reach out'. He observes,

> ... it is the responsibility of those providing services to ensure that they are reached by all those entitled to do so and not to behave as if such services were only for the mainstream and not for those in some way at the margins. This reminds us that much social exclusion is involuntary, the result of the practices of agencies and organisations and that government, local authority and voluntary sector agencies have a particular responsibility to ensure that their services are accessible to just such populations. (Craig, 2004, pp 110-11)

Older people's involvement may also be limited by the particular type or range of mechanisms for participation that are employed. In a report examining forms or models of older people's involvement, Carter and Beresford (2000) conclude that there is no one 'best' model of involvement. They highlight the importance of forms of involvement that bring about real change in people's lives, are independent and inclusive and they advocate a range of forms of involvement so that there is choice for older people to select what best suits their needs and purposes. Barnes (2005) also notes the need for diverse forms of participation, but argues the case for 'new rules of engagement' if the full extent and value of older people's contributions is to be realised:

> If we understand public participation initiatives as arenas within which new discourses can be generated and circulated, rather than in which established identities and positions are expressed, then we probably need to be looking for other ways of constituting participative forums than by seeking representation from existing groups, and we need to be exploring other ways in which deliberation can be facilitated than by adopting rules and procedures which derive from existing institutional contexts. (Barnes, 2005, p 257)

For example, methods of involvement based on narratives and 'story telling' may be more inclusive and effective than public consultations and senior forums, especially for older people in poor health or with mental or physical impairments who are most likely to be excluded from traditional forms of participation (Help the Aged, 2008).

Reducing threats and augmenting resources therefore entails creating opportunities for interdependence and involvement, proactively supporting that involvement and promoting networks of support (Thornton and Tozer, 1994; Beresford and Trevillion, 1995). This has positive implications for the themes of 'keeping going' (practical management of difficulties), 'staying me' (continuity and self-affirmation) and 'the slippery slope' (building social and community resources). It operates at the level of personal empowerment as well as addressing societal oppression by challenging ageist stereotypes and promoting citizenship and inclusion.

Challenging discourse and changing values

'The slippery slope' theme, presented in Chapter Five, encompasses personal values and attitudes that may act as a resource or threat to coping, for example, individuals' beliefs about the need to be self-reliant and not 'put on' other people. Values and attitudes are also significant at a wider social level in relation to the category of community threats and resources, specifically, negative attitudes and behaviour that older people perceive to be directed towards them by virtue of their age, ill health, ethnicity, gender or disability. Chapter Six highlighted the connections between the individual, social and community levels since the meanings individuals ascribe to events and situations are embodiments of wider social and economic values and practices (Phillipson, 1998). As well as acting to increase resources and diminish threats, another way of creating a more supportive social space is by challenging and reconstructing certain social and cultural values that are problematic for maintaining a positive self-identity. For example, Grenier (2007) discusses the implications of the social construction of frailty for policy, practice and personal experience. She notes that in practice and much academic writing, frailty is related to physical deficits and risk, but that older women perceive and experience frailty in terms of a feeling of loss of control over their circumstances:

> While judgements primarily about the bodies of older women take precedence in professional care practice, older women's lived experiences point to the personal interpretations of physical changes. Such tensions challenge whether frailty is located in the body or in personal and emotional experiences.... While such socially and emotionally-defined experiences are subjugated in the dominant discourse, they are the primary themes in older women's accounts. Nonetheless, it is the dominant conceptualisations that shape the context of care, organisational practices, social representations and the lived experiences of older people. (Grenier, 2007, p 437)

Grenier maintains that the dominant construction of frailty is problematic because it gives priority to physical functioning, ignoring the way in which frailty in later life is structured by social and economic disadvantage across the lifecourse. Individual and cultural differences in the meaning and significance of physical frailty are discounted and negative attitudes and responses are generated by the linking of frailty with notions of pity, blame or burden (Grenier, 2007, p 438). Grenier argues that we need to shift from a narrow concern with physical frailty to a focus on preventing frailty and addressing subjective experiences of frailty.

Another dominant construction is the need to preserve independence; this has been shown to be a central concern for older people in terms of their view of self, social presentation and perception of others. Research findings considered in previous chapters demonstrate that attitudes regarding independence in some situations act as a barrier to acknowledging difficulties and seeking help. Equally, seeing oneself, and being seen by others, as someone in receipt of 'care' can undermine cognitive ways of coping. It has been argued that the negative construction of dependency can be seen as a particular cultural prescription and independence 'an ideologically induced illusion' (Leonard, 1997, p 54). The prevailing discourse of independence is, it is argued, warped, with dependence on the state demonised, but dependence on the market exhorted and reconceptualised as 'independence' (Leonard, 1997). User-focused research leads to the questioning of accepted notions of independence, and acknowledgement that this 'ideal' is socially constructed and not necessarily either desirable or attainable (Biehal,

1993: Morris, 1993). Independence defined in terms of self-sufficiency opposes accepted patterns of social relationships, creates an 'otherness' about the giving and receiving of care and ignores the reality that all human relationships are defined by some measure of interdependence and reciprocal caring (Wilkin, 1990; Barnes, 1997; Bytheway and Johnson, 1998; Henderson and Forbat, 2002). It is argued that to reflect the realities of people's lives, social policy should be formulated around the nature of relationships, rather than the notion of 'care' (Henderson and Forbat, 2002).

The findings discussed in earlier chapters show that receiving support from others can be rendered acceptable by the ability to reciprocate and that even very frail older people may be able to maintain a sense of reciprocity by, for example, offering emotional support to others or giving charitable help within their communities. However, it remains the case that at certain times people are unable to achieve in their relationships 'perfectly symmetrical reciprocity' (Froggett, 2002, p 124). While care-based discourses embrace this in their reinforcement of certain people as needing 'care' and the denial of interdependence based on wider notions of reciprocity, rights-based approaches challenge the 'reality' of dependency, but in so doing risk perpetuating negative constructions of the receipt of 'care' (Froggett, 2002). The challenge, according to this viewpoint, is to accept and value dependency:

> The consequences of this acceptance is a re-evaluation of vulnerability as so much an essential part of human learning and living that far from evoking pity or contempt, it is respected as an ingredient in the glue of interpersonal solidarity. (Froggett, 2002, p 125)

However, this does not mean losing sight of ways in which dependence is socially constructed:

> We need to accept that we are all *necessarily* dependent on others, but at the same time challenge the institutions, structures and social relations which render some groups *unnecessarily* dependent. (Williams, 1999, p 677, original emphasis)

Barnes (2006, p 117) argues that the social (not just personal) value of caring should be acknowledged. She proposes that policy and practice are based on an 'ethic of care' discourse. This involves seeing care as an intrinsic part of all relationships, yet also recognising that care giving is a form of citizenship that therefore has social rights attached to it. Barnes sees the 'ethic of care' discourse as a way of delivering social justice for both carers and people receiving care, but also as a route to recognising the contribution that caring itself plays in a socially just society. From this analysis, it follows that rather than formulating policy and practice on simplistic categorisations of 'care giver' and 'care receiver', we need to understand caring within its wider interpersonal context, delivered and experienced as an integral part of the relationships of 'ordinary living' (Finch and Mason, 1993; Henderson and Forbat, 2002), but also as an essential component of social justice (Barnes, 2006).

This opens up possibilities for the challenge of prevailing discourses at a wider social level, but also has more direct implications for social work and social care practice in terms of the potential to help older people who are 'cared for' to reconstruct their perceptions of care giving and receiving and to resist negative self and social attributions of dependence (Cox and Dooley, 1996). This connects with the point made earlier about the potential value of a narrative approach to assessment in reconstructing personal stories. A useful tool here could be Nolan et al's (2001) framework of the six senses. This acknowledges the same fundamental human needs of all parties, including the older person, 'informal carer' and care staff/professional, that is, needs for security, belonging, a sense of continuity, a sense of purpose, a sense of achievement and a sense of significance. This framework recognises the 'being' as well as 'doing' aspects of caring relationships, so it is readily compatible with the 'keeping going' and 'staying me' themes presented in the model in Figure 6.2 in Chapter Six.

A further challenge in terms of fostering a supportive social space is that of addressing ageism. Chapter Five discussed ageist attitudes as one source of threat at the community level. Rooting out age discrimination is Standard 1 of the NSF for older people and there are now specific initiatives to address age discrimination in health and social care services (DH, 2008b). However, Forder (2008) demonstrates that older people receive less social care support than younger people, and in a review of progress on achievement of NSF standards it was noted that although overt age discrimination in care services is rare, there remain 'deep-rooted negative attitudes and behaviours towards older people' (DH, 2006b, p 2). Minichiello et al (2000) show how the lived realities of older people are shaped by their internalisation of ageist attitudes. There is a range of other evidence, including that cited in earlier chapters, attesting to older people's dissociation from ageist stereotypes and from associated expectations of dependence (Thompson et al, 1990; Titley and Chasey, 1996; Tulle-Winton, 1999). While it is important to eschew ageist assumptions and practices, denial of the realities of ageing may perpetuate ageism rather than challenge it (Andrews, 1999), increasing the necessity for masquerade by older people (Biggs, 1999). The reconstruction of what it means to be an older person therefore has to be accomplished in ways that acknowledge the changes that accompany ageing, but without infusing these with negative meaning.

Challenging and reconstructing key concepts underpinning aged identities such as frailty, dependence and old age will facilitate a more supportive social space, while at the same time the supportive social space will promote positive assertions of ageing identities. Moreover, older people's understandings can drive this change if their 'theories' are voiced and heard, in the same way that, for example, disability activists have challenged and changed understandings of disability (see, for example, Morris, 1993; Oliver and Sapey, 2006) and mental health 'survivors' have reconstructed understandings of 'recovery' (Deegan, 1988; Wallcraft, 2005). In this way, '... small histories continuously and in multiple ways change the big historical picture' (Nielson, 1999, p 47). Leonard (1997) argues the need to recognise individual diversity while at the same time highlighting similarities in the structural factors that construct experiences of oppression. He argues that this approach,

> ... people's ...emphasizes a *potential solidarity* between the individual subjects of welfare. Emphasis on commonality, solidarity and interdependence serves not only to counteract self-invalidating and destructive internalising of shame and guilt, but also enables subjects to express individual resistance to domination and the possibility of participating in collective resistance in the pursuit of claims for welfare. (Leonard, 1997, pp 165-6, original emphasis)

While much of the focus of this book has been on individual experiences and identities of older people, it is important that the wider political context of those experiences is recognised and addressed, thus facilitating challenge and change.

A future research agenda

The issues discussed in this chapter indicate a number of areas for further exploration or development.

First, the conclusions reached have been based more on the experiences of older people who were able to 'keep going' and 'stay me' than on those who, for various reasons, were not able to 'sustain the self'. While it is important to promote positive views of ageing and to learn from older people's own ways of coping, it is also necessary to understand in detail the experiences of those who feel they are not able to manage the ageing experience. There is much to be learned from engaging with the experiences of a larger and more diverse group of older people, particularly using approaches that explore processes of managing over time. The aim would be to explore longitudinally the critical features of situations, events, experiences and perceptions that lead to 'giving in' and a loss of selfhood compared with those that support older people in 'keeping going' and 'staying me'. This is likely to lead to refinement or adaptation of the model of managing presented in Chapter Six and yield further messages for the promotion of older people's well-being.

Second, the wider applicability of the model could be investigated. The concept of personhood is central in research with other service user groups, for example, people experiencing mental distress. Further research on processes by which the self is sustained in situations of adversity could identify areas of difference, but also commonality. As mentioned in the earlier discussion of ways to create a more supportive social space, this could identify common concerns, forge alliances and establish shared bases for collective action between different service user 'groups'.

Third, existing knowledge about older people's practical strategies and cognitive coping processes can be harnessed in action research approaches that seek to develop interventions that support older people in sustaining selfhood. This could include exploring older people's evaluations of assessment processes that utilise a narrative approach and a specific focus on how such approaches can be integrated within single assessment procedures and the self-assessment that features centrally in personalisation. There is already considerable evidence about the factors that older people identify as important in promoting their quality of life and well-being and also about what they see as the defining features of quality services. There appears to have been less focus in research on how to use this evidence to inform the planning and provision of services that enhance the well-being of older people and build their resilience. For example, how can older people's desire for good interpersonal relationships with home care staff and continuity in these relationships be met in the context of service contracts with private domiciliary care agencies who have a high turnover of low-paid staff? What are the implications of personalisation for these interpersonal relationships? The psychological and emotional significance of 'low level' services has been demonstrated in research studies cited in this book, but how can this understanding be used to promote older people's well-being in the context of restrictive eligibility criteria and patchy initiatives to improve well-being at the community level? As noted previously, direct payments and individual budgets are only available to those who meet eligibility criteria. A key question for further investigation is how not only social care services, but also mainstream services and broader community resources, can be developed to support older people's own preferred practical strategies for managing and at the same time bolster their cognitive coping processes. Action research to grapple with some of these key tensions and to suggest ways forward is a priority.

Finally, as discussed in Chapter One, the research that forms the central thread of this book has involved older people in only a very limited way in key research processes such as analysis and theory building. It has, however, identified a number of issues to be considered in involving older people, including the need to utilise a range of methods and approaches and to enable different levels of involvement. Based on the arguments for involving service users discussed in Chapter One, it is vital that the older people are involved in all stages of the research process and that this experience is widely publicised so that others can learn from it. It is encouraging that older people have been involved in interviewing, analysing data and publicising findings in some of the projects carried out as part of the Economic and Social Research Council's (ESRC's) Growing Older Programme (Warren et al, 2003; Withnall, 2004) as well as in research funded by the Joseph Rowntree Foundation (Older People's Steering Group, 2004; Clough et al, 2006). However, there is still progress to be made in respect of the involvement of older people as equal partners in research and as managers or controllers of the research agenda and process.

Conclusion

Empirical research with older people has highlighted the relevance and limitations of existing theoretical perspectives in assisting understanding of how older people manage the experience of ageing. The research findings contribute to a 'sociology of old age' that is sensitive and responsive to both social structures and the activities and lifestyles of older people (Phillipson, 1998, p 138). The role of social and structural factors is recognised, first, in acknowledgement that individual stories and meanings are themselves socially embedded; second, in recognition that social and economic conditions are directly and incontrovertibly linked with the nature and level of difficulties experienced; and third, in the emphasis on the role of social, economic and structural resources and constraints in supporting or undermining practical strategies and cognitive ways of coping. Through detailed exploration of older people's experiences and perspectives, this book also contributes to the development of what Phillipson (1998, p 140) calls a 'sociology of resistance', that is, an understanding of how, usually in private spaces, older people are engaged in resisting the practical and cognitive challenges of ageing. While older people may experience various threats and losses as they age, they may also be able to deploy protective strategies to preserve the integrity of their core self (Phillipson and Biggs, 1998).

Older people's experiences and perspectives attest to their capacity to exercise control over their situations and to interpret meanings so that a positive identity is sustained. There is support for lifecourse perspectives in that older people seek to retain continuity in important dimensions of their lives while also engaging in continual change and readjustment in response to changing circumstances and abilities. They may have the capacity to reconstruct that identity when a given 'story of the self' can no longer be maintained. While Biggs (1999) highlights the significance of masquerade in negotiating the interface between personal and social space, older people's experiences show that they respond to their own understanding of social rules and expectations and how they see themselves to be perceived by others. They do not just react to their perception of threats in the social space by concealing aspects of identity through masquerade, but rather are proactive in managing and manipulating meanings in ways that enable them to experience and present a sense of self. The degree of their success in achieving this is influenced by their access to resources and exposure to threats in the personal, social and community environments, thus entwining the individual and the structural.

A pertinent conclusion is to see ageing identity as primarily concerned with 'sites of struggle rather than scenes of defeat' (Hockey and James, 1993, p 175). This book has offered some clues as to factors significant in this struggle, that is, factors that help to build resilience and resistance. Extensive research with more diverse populations (encompassing differences such as those relating to age, ethnicity, culture, gender and social class) would be valuable in further developing this understanding. The central focus on older people's efforts to sustain selfhood points to the need for social and community-based interventions to be directed at supporting these efforts. As argued in Chapter Two, many aspects of current social policy and practice appear to diminish the sense of self. The challenge is to develop strategies that sustain the self by supporting not just practical ways of managing difficulties, but also cognitive ways of coping. Since identity itself is fluid and diverse, so too must be the range of support options on offer and the way particular services are delivered. There is a potential tension in the idea of services designed to meet universal needs being responsive to individual differences, preferences and circumstances. Williams (2000) advocates a welfare system based on 'the politics of a differentiated universalism' (p 350), combining a commitment to the social inclusion and equal moral worth of all with a respect for individual diversity. Such an approach offers the potential to support both the 'core self' and foster a benign social environment. Coleman (2000) urges services for older people to switch their emphasis from deficit, decline, disability and dependency to well-being, activity and independence (for which we could perhaps substitute interdependence), and this is also a key theme from work undertaken by the Joseph Rowntree Foundation (Older People's Steering Group, 2004). In terms of promoting well-being, this would translate to a concern with healthy ageing, building resilience and capacity and the development of community resources. This is not about older people's access to care services as such, but about changing the nature of the communities they live in and their involvement in them, as participants in helping networks (Thornton and Tozer, 1994; ODPM, 2006). This stands to benefit not only older people themselves but also society as a whole (Barnes and Shaw, 2000). It is a more ethical approach compatible with promoting equal relationships among citizens, rather than dependency and subservience of a targeted sub-group (Barnes, 1997; Jenkins, 2001). There are resonances here with the stated objectives of personalisation. This offers creative possibilities, such as older people getting together and pooling their budgets, thus generating networks of mutual support, participation and community involvement, rather than reliance on individual 'carers' (DH/CSIP, 2007). However, there are concerns about the predominantly individualised model of care enshrined in personalisation and the risk that managerial restrictions will undermine its potential for creativity and flexibility.

Although the book's focus has been on older people, the issues arising from it have wider resonance and applicability to other service user 'groups' and individuals experiencing a wide range of difficulties and challenges. Much research and literature produced from a service user perspective has at its heart a concern with sustaining the self in the face of assaults on identity (understood as both personal and social in nature), where pivotal concepts underpinning selfhood include control, choice, privacy and dignity. Sustaining a sense of self is a universal human need. Having, for the purposes of this research, selected out and 'othered' older people, it seems appropriate at this point to reconnect them not only with other service users but also with the rest of humanity.

As Chapter One made clear, I did not set out on this journey to conduct or present work that could be seen as communicating essential truths about the ways older people manage the ageing experience. Rather, I hope that older people's experiences and perspectives have contributed insights that may facilitate our understanding and inform our response in certain situations. In this vein,

> ... it is highly unlikely we will ever establish a total picture of "the truth" about an individual or his or her aging. Rather, we will understand only fragments of the inner world of ageing individuals, as they are manifested in social arenas or in social communication. These fragments, tied together, might give us patterns of the experience and the symbolic relevance of different aspects of aging shared by some individuals. (Ruth and Kenyon, 1996, p 8)

The research findings presented in this book and the sense I have made of them have to be regarded as tentative understandings rather than established truths. The material presented is an inevitably selective and partial version of what transpired in my own study and what has emerged from other research. It remains the case that the 'whole of a story can never be told, no matter how much space or what devices are used to tell it' (Ely et al, 1997, p 95). My hope is that enough has been revealed to generate a better understanding of the processes by which older people negotiate changes they encounter as they age and that this will contribute to policy, research and practice that more effectively support their efforts to manage the ageing experience.

References

Age Concern England (2007) *Age of equality? Outlawing age discrimination beyond the workplace*, London: Age Concern England (www.ageconcern.org.uk/AgeConcern/Documents/ACE_DLR_report_FINAL_PDF.pdf).

Andrews, M. (1999) 'The seductiveness of agelessness', *Ageing & Society*, vol 19, no 3, pp 301-18.

Arber, S. and Evandrou, M. (1993) 'Mapping the territory: ageing, independence and the life course', in S. Arber and M. Evandrou (eds) *Ageing, independence and the life course*, London: Jessica Kingsley Publishers, pp 9-26.

Arksey, H. and Knight, P. (1999) *Interviewing for social scientists: An introductory resource with examples*, London: Sage Publications.

Aronson, J. (2002) 'Elderly people's accounts of home care rationing: missing voices in long-term policy debates', *Ageing & Society*, vol 22, no 4, pp 399-418.

Atchley, R. (1989) 'A continuity theory of normal aging', *The Gerontologist*, vol 29, part 2, pp 183-90.

Audit Commission (1986) *Making a reality of community care*, London: HMSO.

Audit Commission (1997) *The coming of age: Improving care services for older people*, London: Audit Commission.

Audit Commission (2008) *The effect of fair access to care services bands on expenditure and service provision*, London: Audit Commission/Commission for Social Care Inspection.

Baldock, J. and Hadlow, J. (2002) 'Self-talk versus needs-talk: an exploration of the priorities of housebound older people', *Quality in Ageing – Policy, Practice and Research*, vol 3, no 1, pp 42-8.

Baldock, J. and Ungerson, C. (1994) *Becoming consumers of community care: Households within the mixed economy of welfare*, York: Joseph Rowntree Foundation.

Baldwin, M. (2000) *Care management and community care: Social work discretion and the construction of policy*, Aldershot: Ashgate.

Ballinger, C. and Payne, S. (2002) 'The construction of the risk of falling among and by older people', *Ageing & Society*, vol 22, no 3, pp 305-24.

Baltes, M. and Carstensen, L. (1996) 'The process of successful ageing', *Ageing & Society*, vol 16, no 4, pp 397-422.

Baltes, P. and Baltes, M. (1990) *Successful ageing: Perspectives from the Behavioural Sciences*, New York, NY: Cambridge University Press.

Banerjee, S. and Macdonald, A. (1996) 'Mental disorder in an elderly home care population: associations with health and social service use', *British Journal of Psychiatry*, vol 168, pp 750-6.

Barnes, M. (1997) *Care, communities and citizens*, Harlow: Longman.

Barnes, M. (2005) 'The same old process? Older people, participation and deliberation', *Ageing & Society*, vol 25, pp 245-59.

Barnes, M. (2006) *Caring and social justice*, Basingstoke: Palgrave Macmillan.

Barnes, M. and Shaw, F. (2000) 'Older people, citizenship and collective action', in A. Warnes, L. Warren and M. Nolan (eds) *Care services for later life: Transformations and critiques*, London: Jessica Kingsley Publishers.

Bartlett, H. (1999) 'Primary health care for older people: progress towards an integrated strategy?', *Health and Social Care in the Community*, vol 7, no 5, pp 342-9.

Bauer, M., Rottunda, S. and Adler, G. (2003) 'Older women and driving cessation', *Qualitative Social Work*, vol 2, no 3, pp 309-25.

Beaumont, G. and Kenealy, P. (2004) 'Quality of life perceptions and social comparisons in healthy old age', *Ageing & Society*, vol 24, no 5, pp 755-69.

Bennett, K., Smith, P. and Hughes, G. (2004) *Older widow(er)s: Bereavement and gender effects on lifestyle and participation*, Economic and Social Research Council Growing Older Programme, Findings 6, University of Sheffield (www.shef.ac.uk/uni/projects/gop).

Beresford, P. (2001) 'Social work and social care: the struggle for knowledge', *Educational Action Research*, vol 9, no 3, pp 344-53.

Beresford, P. (2003) *'It's our lives': A short theory of knowledge, distance and experience*, London: Citizen Press in association with Shaping Our Lives.

Beresford, P. (2008) 'Whose personalisation?', *Soundings*, vol 40, Winter, pp 8-17.

Beresford, P. (2009) 'Personalisation, brokerage and service users: time to take stock', *Journal of Care Services Management*, vol 4, no 1, pp 24-31.

Beresford, P. and Trevillion, S. (1995) *Developing skills for community care: A collaborative approach*, Aldershot: Arena.

Bernard, M., Bartlam, B., Biggs, S. and Sim, J. (2004) *New lifestyles in old age: Health, identity and well-being in Berryhill Retirement Village*, Bristol: The Policy Press.

Biehal, N. (1993) 'Changing practice: participation, rights and community care', *British Journal of Social Work*, vol 23, pp 443-58.

Biggs, S. (1993) *Understanding ageing: Images, attitudes and professional practice*, Buckingham: Open University Press.

Biggs, S. (1997) 'Choosing not to be old? Masks, bodies and identity management in later life', *Ageing & Society*, vol 17, no 5, pp 553-70.

Biggs, S. (1999) *The mature imagination: Dynamics of identity in middle life and beyond*, Buckingham: Open University Press.

Biggs, S., Phillipson, C., Money, A. and Leach, R. (2006) 'The age shift: observations on social policy, ageism and the dynamics of the adult life course', *Journal of Social Work Practice*, vol 20, pp 239-50.

Blumer, H. (1969) *Symbolic interactionism*, Oxford: Oxford University Press.

Bond, J. and Corner, L. (2004) *Quality of life and older people*, Maidenhead: Open University Press.

Bornat, J. (1999) 'Introduction', in J. Bornat (ed) *Biographical interviews: The link between research and practice*, London: Centre for Policy on Ageing.

Bourdieu, P. (1990) *The logic of practice*, Cambridge: Polity Press.

Bourdieu, P. (1994) *In other words: Essays towards a reflexive sociology*, Cambridge: Polity Press.

Bourdieu, P. and Wacquant, L. (1992) *An invitation to reflexive sociology*, Cambridge: Polity Press.

Bowling, A. (2005) *Ageing well: Quality of life in old age*, Maidenhead: Open University Press.

Bowling, A. and Gabriel, Z. (2007) 'Lay theories of quality of life in older age', *Ageing & Society*, vol 27, no 6, pp 827-48.

Bowling, A., Grundy, E. and Farquhar, M. (1997) *Living well into old age: Three studies of health and well-being among older people in East London and Essex*, London: Age Concern.

Bradshaw, J. (1972) 'The concept of social need', *New Society*, 30 March, pp 640-3.

Brandtstädter, J. and Greve, W. (1994) 'The aging self: stabilizing and protective processes', *Developmental Review*, vol 14, pp 52-80.

Brechin, A. (1998) 'What makes for good care?', in A. Brechin, J. Walmsley, J. Katz and S. Peace (eds) *Care matters: Concepts, practice and research in health and social care*, London: Sage Publications, pp 170-87.

Breeze, E. (2004) *Inequalities in quality of life among people aged 75 years and over*, Economic and Social Research Council Growing Older Programme, Findings 1, Sheffield: University of Sheffield.

Breheny, M. and Stephens, C. (2009) '"I sort of pay back in my own little way": managing independence and social connectedness through reciprocity', *Ageing & Society*, vol 29, vol 8, pp 1295-313.

Brown, G. and Harris, T. (1978) *The social origins of depression*, London: Tavistock.

Buker, E. (1999) 'Is the postmodern self a feminist citizen?', in S. Heckman (ed) *Feminism, identity and difference*, Ilford: Frank Cass.

Burholt, V. and Windle, G. (2006) *The material resources and well-being of older people*, York: Joseph Rowntree Foundation (www.jrf.org.uk/bookshop/eBooks/9781859354230.pdf).

Burnette, D. (1994) 'Managing chronic illness alone in late life: sisyphus at work', in C.K. Riessman (ed) *Qualitative studies in social work research*, Thousand Oaks, CA: Sage Publications, pp 5-27.

Bury, M. (1991) 'The sociology of chronic illness: a review of research and prospects', *Sociology of Health and Illness*, vol 13, no 4, pp 451-68.

Bury, M. (2001) 'Illness narratives: fact or fiction?', *Sociology of Health and Illness*, vol 23, no 3, pp 263-85.

Bury, M. and Holme, A. (1991) *Life after ninety*, London: Routledge.

Butler, I. (2002) 'A code of ethics for social work and social care research', *British Journal of Social Work*, vol 32, pp 239-48.

Butler, R.N. (1963) 'The life review: an interpretation of reminiscence in the aged', *Psychiatry*, vol 26, pp 65-76.

Butt, J. and Moriarty, J. (2004) *Quality of life and social support among people from different ethnic groups*, Economic and Social Research Council Growing Older Programme, Findings 23, Sheffield: University of Sheffield (www.shef.ac.uk/uni/projects/gop).

Bytheway, B. and Johnson, J. (1998) 'The social construction of carers', in A. Symonds and A. Kelly (eds) *The social construction of community care*, Basingstoke: Macmillan, pp 241-53.

Caldock, K. (1994) 'Policy and practice: fundamental contradictions in the conceptualization of community care for elderly people?', *Health and Social Care*, vol 2, pp 133-41.

Caldock, K. (1996) 'Multi-disciplinary assessment and care management', in J. Phillips and B. Penhale (eds) *Reviewing care management for older people*, London: Jessica Kingsley Publishers, pp 28-59.

Caldock, K. and Nolan, M. (1994) 'Assessment and community care: are the reforms working?', *Generations Review*, vol 4, no 4, pp 2-7.

Carers UK (2006) *In the know: The importance of information for carers*, London: Carers UK (www.carersuk.org/Professionals/ResearchLibrary/Profileofcaring/1201108799).

Carers UK (2008) *Carers' Policy briefing: The National Strategy for Carers*, London: Carers UK (www.carersuk.org/Professionals/ResourcesandBriefings/Policybriefings.

Care Services Efficiency Programme (2008) *Transforming community equipment services: Efficiency delivery – Supporting sustainable transformation*, London: Department of Health (www.csed.csip.org.uk/silo/files/sbtces.pdf).

Carmichael, A. and Brown, L. (2002) 'The future challenge for direct payments', *Disability and Society*, vol 17, no 7, pp 797-808.

Carter, T. and Beresford, P. (2000) *Models of involvement for older people: Briefing report for the Steering Group, Older People's Programme*, York: Joseph Rowntree Foundation (www.jrf.org.uk/bookshop/eBooks/1859353215.pdf).

Challis, D., Davies, B. and Traske, K. (eds) (1994) *Community care: New agendas and challenges from the UK and overseas*, Aldershot: Ashgate.

Challis, D. et al, including Glendinning, C. and Wilberforce, M. (2007) *Individual budgets evaluation: A summary of early findings*, York: Social Policy Research Unit, University of York.

Chambers, P. (2000) 'Widowhood in later life', in M. Bernard, J. Phillips, L. Machin and V. Harding Davies (eds) *Women ageing: Changing identities, challenging myths*, London: Routledge, pp 127-47.

Chambers, P. (2005) *Older widows and the life course: Multiple narratives of hidden lives*, Aldershot: Ashgate.

Charmaz, K. (1983) 'Loss of self: a fundamental form of suffering in the chronically ill', *Sociology of Health and Illness*, vol 5, no 2, pp 168-95.

Charmaz, K. (1997) 'Identity dilemmas of chronically ill men', in A. Strauss and J. Corbin (eds) *Grounded theory in practice*, Thousand Oaks, CA: Sage Publications.

Chattoo, S. and Ahmad, W.I.U. (2008) 'The moral economy of selfhood and caring: negotiating boundaries of personal care as embodied moral practice', *Sociology of Health and Illness*, vol 30, no 4, pp 550-64.

Clark, H. and Spafford, J. (2001) *Piloting choice and control for older people: An evaluation*, Bristol: The Policy Press.

Clark, H., Dyer, S. and Horwood, J. (1998) *"That bit of help": The high value of low level preventive services for older people*, Bristol: The Policy Press.

Clark, H., Gough, H. and Macfarlane, A. (2004) *"It pays dividends": Direct payments and older people*, Bristol: The Policy Press.

Clarke, A. and Warren, L. (2007) 'Hopes, fears and expectations about the future: what do older people's stories tell us about active ageing?', *Ageing & Society*, vol 27, pp 465-88.

Clements, L. (2009) *Carers and their rights: The law relating to carers* (3rd edn), London: Carers UK (www.carersuk.org/Professionals/ResourcesandBriefings/Carersandtheirrights).

Clough, R., Green, B., Hawkes, B., Raymond, G. and Bright, L. (2006) *Older people as researchers: Evaluating a participative project*, York: Joseph Rowntree Foundation.

Clough, R., Manthorpe, J., Green, B., Fox, D., Raymond, G., Wilson, P., Raymond, V., Sumner, K., Bright, L. and Hay, J. (2007) *The support older people want and the services they need*, York: Joseph Rowntree Foundation (www.jrf.org.uk/bookshop/eBooks/1954-older-people-services.pdf).

Coghlan, A., Letherby, G., Tanner, D., Wilson, C. and Bywaters, P. (2007) 'Managing the process', in G. Letherby and P. Bywaters (eds) *Extending social research: Application, implementation and publication*, Maidenhead: Open University Press, pp 90-107.

Cohen, H., Thomas, C. and Williamson, C. (2008) 'Religion and spirituality as defined by older adults', *Journal of Gerontological Social Work*, vol 51, no 3-4, pp 284-99.

Coleman, N. (2009) 'This is the modern world! Working in a social services contact centre', in J. Harris and V. White (eds) *Modernising social work: Critical considerations*, Bristol: The Policy Press, pp 31-50.

Coleman, P., Ivani-Chalian, C. and Robinson, M. (1999) 'Self and identity in advanced old age: validation of theory through longitudinal case analysis', *Journal of Personality*, vol 67, no 5, pp 819-48.

Coleman, P., McKiernan, F., Mills, M. and Speck, P. (2002) 'Spiritual belief and quality of life: the experience of older bereaved spouses', *Quality in Ageing – Policy, Practice and Research*, vol 3, pp 20-6.

Coleman, R. (2000) 'Design for later life: beyond a problem orientation', in A. Warnes, L. Warren and M. Nolan (eds) *Care services for later life: Transformations and critiques*, London: Jessica Kingsley Publishers, pp 219-42.

Collins, R. (1988) 'Theoretical continuities in Goffman's work', in P. Drew and A. Wootton (eds) *Erving Goffman: Exploring the interaction order*, Cambridge: Polity Press, pp 41-63.

Conway, S. and Hockey, J. (1998) 'Resisting the "mask" of old age?: the social meaning of lay health beliefs in later life', *Ageing & Society*, vol 18, no 4, pp 469-94.

Cooper, L. and Thomas, H. (2002) 'Growing old gracefully: social dance in the third age', *Ageing & Society*, vol 22, no 6, pp 689-708.

Cordingley, L., Hughes, J. and Challis, D. (2001) *Unmet need and older people: Towards a synthesis of user and provider views*, York: Joseph Rowntree Foundation.

Coupland, J., Coupland, N. and Grainger, K. (1991) 'Inter-generational discourse: contextual versions of ageing and elderliness', *Ageing & Society*, vol 11, no 2, pp 189-208.

Cox, E. and Dooley, A. (1996) 'Care-receivers' perceptions of their role in the care process', *Journal of Gerontological Social Work*, vol 26, no 1/2, pp 133-52.

CQC (Care Quality Commission) (2010) *The state of health care and adult social care in England: Key themes and quality of services in 2009*, London: CQC.

Craig, G. (2004) 'Citizenship, exclusion and older people', *Journal of Social Policy*, vol 33, no 1, pp 95-114.

CSCI (Commission for Social Care Inspection) (2006) *Time to care: An overview of home care services for older people in England*, London: CSCI.

CSCI (2008a) *The state of social care in England 2006-7*, London: CSCI.

CSCI (2008b) *Cutting the cake fairly: CSCI review of eligibility criteria for social care*, London: CSCI.

CSIP (Care Services Improvement Partnership) (2007) *Evaluation of the self-directed support network: A review of progress up to 31st March 2007*, London: CSIP (http://individualbudgets.csip.org.uk/dynamic/dohpage14.jsp).

Cumming, E. and Henry, W. (1961) *Growing old: The process of disengagement*, New York, NY: Basic Books.

Curry, N. (2006) *Preventive social care: Is it cost-effective?*, Background paper, Wanless Social Care Review, London: The King's Fund.

Cutcliffe, J. and Ramcharan, P. (2002) 'Levelling the playing field? Exploring the merits of the ethics-as-process approach for judging qualitative research proposals', *Qualitative Health Research*, vol 12, no 7, pp 1000-10.

Cutler, P. (2008) *Transforming Community Equipment Services Programme: Review of the Outline Business Case*, London: Care Services Efficiency Delivery, Department of Health (www.csed.csip.org.uk/silo/files/tce-obc-review.pdf).

Dant, T. and Gully, V. (1994) *Coordinating care at home: Practical approaches to organising support for older people*, London: Collins Educational Press Ltd.

Davey, J. (2007) 'Older people and transport: coping without a car', *Ageing & Society*, vol 27, pp 49-65.

Deegan, P. (1988) 'Recovery: the lived experience of rehabilitation', *Psychosocial Rehabilitation Journal*, vol 11, no 4, pp 11-19.

Degnen, C. (2007) 'Minding the gap: the construction of old age and oldness amongst peers', *Journal of Ageing Studies*, vol 21, pp 69-80.

Denzin, N. (1989) *Interpretive interactionism*, London: Sage Publications.

Denzin, N. (1997) *Interpretive ethnography: Ethnographic practices for the 21st century*, Thousand Oaks, CA: Sage Publications.

Denzin, N. and Lincoln, Y. (eds) (1994) *Handbook of qualitative research*, Thousand Oaks, CA: Sage Publications.

Dey, I. (1993) *Qualitative data analysis: A user-friendly guide for social scientists*, London: Routledge.

DH (Department of Health) (1989) *Caring for people: Community care in the next decade and beyond*, London: HMSO.

DH (1990) *Community care in the next decade and beyond: Policy guidance*, London: HMSO.

DH (1992) *Memorandum on the financing of community care arrangements after April 1992 (October 2)*, London: DH.

DH (1999) *Caring about carers: A national strategy for carers*, London: The Stationery Office.

DH (2001a) *The National Service Framework for older people*, London: DH.

DH (2001b) *Improving older people's services: Inspection of social care for older people*, September, London: DH.

DH (2002a) *Fair access to care services: Guidance on eligibility criteria for adult social care*, London: DH.

DH (2002b) *The single assessment process for older people*, London: DH.

DH (2005) *Independence, well-being and choice: Our vision for the future of social care for adults in England and Wales*, Cm 6499, London: DH.

DH (2006a) *Our health, our care, our say: A new direction for community services*, Cm 6737, London: DH.

DH (2006b) *A new ambition for old age: Next steps in implementing the National Service Framework for older people*, London: DH.

DH (2007a) *Putting People First: A shared vision and commitment to the transformation of adult social care*, London: DH.

DH (2007b) *Description of successful Round 2 Partnership for Older People site projects*, London: DH (www.dh.gov.uk/en/SocialCare/Deliveringadultsocialcare/ Olderpeople/PartnershipsforOlderPeopleProjects/index.htm).

DH (2008a) *Carers at the heart of 21st century families and communities: A caring system on your side, a life of your own*, London: DH (www.dh.gov.uk/en/ Publicationsandstatistics/Publications/PublicationsPolicyAndGuidance/ DH_085345).

DH (2008b) *Standard One: Rooting out age discrimination*, Benchmarking tools (online), London: DH (www.dh.gov.uk/en/SocialCare/Deliveringadultsocialcare/ Olderpeople/OlderpeoplesNSFstandards/DH_4071271).

DH (2009) *Shaping the future of care together*, Cm 7673, Norwich: The Stationery Office.

DH (2010) *Prioritising need in the context of Putting People First: A whole system approach to eligibility for social care. Guidance on eligibility criteria for adult social care, England 2010*, London: DH.

DH/CSIP (Care Services Improvement Partnership) (2007) *Older people's services and individual budgets: Good practice – Examples and ideas*, London: DH/CSIP.

Dickinson, A. (2003) 'The use of diaries to study the everyday food life of older people', in B. Bytheway (ed) *Everyday living in later life*, London: Centre for Policy on Ageing.

Dittmann-Kohli, F. (1990) 'The construction of meaning in old age: possibilities and constraints', *Ageing & Society*, vol 10, no 3, pp 279-94.

Doel, M., Carroll, C., Chambers, E., Cooke, J., Hollows, A., Laurie, L., Maskrey, L. and Nancarrow, S. (2007) *Developing measures for effective service user and carer participation*, Position Paper 09, London: Social Care Institute for Excellence.

Donaldson, R. (2003) *Experiences of older burglary victims*, Findings 198, Research, Development and Statistics Directorate, London: Home Office (www.homeoffice.gov.uk/rds/pdfs2/r198.pdf).

Drakeford, M. (2006) 'Ownership, regulation and the public interest: the case of residential care for older people', *Critical Social Policy*, vol 26, no 4, pp 932-44.

DWP (Department for Work and Pensions) (2005) *Opportunity age: Meeting the challenges of ageing in the 21st century*, London: DWP.

Elliot, H. (1997) 'The use of diaries in sociological research on health experience', *Sociological Research Online*, vol 2, no 2 (www.socresonline.org.uk/2/2/7.html).

Ellis, K. (1993) *Squaring the circle: User and carer participation in needs assessment*, York: Joseph Rowntree Foundation.

Ellis, K. (2007) 'Direct payments and social work practice: the significance of "street-level bureaucracy" in determining eligibility', *British Journal of Social Work*, vol 37, no 3, pp 405-22.

Ellis, K., Davis, A. and Rummery, K. (1999) 'Needs assessment, street-level bureaucracy and the new community care', *Social Policy and Administration*, vol 33, no 3, pp 262-80.

Ely, M., Vinz, R., Downing, M. and Anzul, M. (1997) *On writing qualitative research: Living by words*, Washington, DC and London: Falmer Press.

Estes, C., Biggs, S. and Phillipson, C. (2003) *Social theory, social policy and ageing: A critical introduction*, Maidenhead: Open University Press.

Ferguson, I. (2007) 'Increasing user choice or privatising risk? The antinomies of personalization', *British Journal of Social Work*, vol 37, no 3, pp 387-403.

Fernandez-Ballesteros, R., Zamarron, M. and Ruiz, M. (2001) 'The contribution of socio-demographic and psychosocial factors to life satisfaction', *Ageing & Society*, vol 21, no 1, pp 25-43.

Finch, J. and Mason, J. (1993) *Negotiating family responsibilities*, London: Routledge.

Fisher, M. (2002) 'The role of service users in problem formulation and technical aspects of social research', *Social Work Education*, vol 21, no 3, pp 305-12.

Fletcher, P. (1998) 'Focus on prevention: back on the political agenda', *Working with Older People*, vol 2, no 3, pp 8-12.

Fook, J. (2001) 'Identifying expert social work: qualitative practitioner research', in I. Shaw and N. Gould (eds) *Qualitative research in social work*, London: Sage Publications, pp 116-31.

Fook, J. (2002) *Social work: Critical theory and practice*, London: Sage Publications.

Forder, J. (2008) *The costs of addressing age discrimination in social care*, PSSRU Discussion Paper 2538, Canterbury: Personal and Social Services Research Unit (www.pssru.ac.uk/pdf/dp2538.pdf).

Foster, M., Harris, J., Jackson, K., Morgan, H. and Glendinning, C. (2006) 'Personalised social care for adults with disabilities: a problematic concept for frontline practice', *Health and Social Care in the Community*, vol 14, no 2, pp 125-35.

Foucault, M. (1975) *Discipline and punish: The birth of the prison* (translated by Alan Sheridan, 1977), New York, NY: Pantheon Books.

Foucault, M. (1980) 'Two lectures: Lecture Two, 14 January 1976', in C. Gordon (ed) *Michel Foucault: Power/knowledge: Selected interviews and other writings 1972-1977*, Harlow: Pearson, pp 78-108.

Foucault, M. (1987 [2000]) 'Introduction to "The use of pleasure"', in P. du Gay, J. Evans and P. Redman (eds) *Identity: A reader*, London: Sage Publications, pp 360-70.

Francis, J. and Netten, A. (2004) 'Raising the quality of home care: a study of service users' views', *Social Policy and Administration*, vol 38, no 3, pp 290-305.

Froggett, L. (2002) *Love, hate and welfare: Psychosocial approaches to policy and practice*, Bristol: The Policy Press.

Gearing, B. and Coleman, P. (1996) 'Biographical assessment in community care', in J. Birren, G. Kenyon, J. Ruth, J. Schroots and T. Svensson (eds) *Ageing and biography: Explorations in adult development*, New York, NY: Springer Publishing, pp 265-82.

George, L. (1998) 'Dignity and quality of life in old age', *Journal of Gerontological Work*, vol 29, no 2/3, pp 39-52.

George, L. and Bearon, L. (1980) *Quality of life in older persons: Meaning and measurement*, New York, NY: Human Science Press.

Giddens, A. (1979) *Central problems in social theory: Action, structure and contradiction in social analysis*, London and Basingstoke: Macmillan.

Giddens, A. (1988) 'Goffman as a systematic social scientist', in P. Drew and A. Wootton (eds) *Erving Goffman: Exploring the interaction order*, Cambridge: Polity Press, pp 250-79.

Giddens, A. (1999) *Modernity and self-identity: Self and society in the late modern age*, Cambridge: Polity Press.

Gilhooly, M., Hamilton, K., O'Neill, M., Gow, J., Webster, N. and Pike, F. (2004) *Transport and ageing: Extending quality of life for older people via public and private transport*, Economic and Social Research Council Growing Older Programme, Findings 6, Sheffield: University of Sheffield (www.shef.ac.uk/uni/projects/gop).

Gilleard, C. (1996) 'Consumption and identity in later life: toward a cultural gerontology', *Ageing & Society*, vol 16, pp 489-98.

Gilleard, C. and Higgs, P. (2005) *Contexts of ageing: Class, cohort and community*, Cambridge: Polity Press.

Ginn, J. and Arber, S. (1993) 'Ageing and the cultural stereotypes of older women', in J. Johnson and R. Slater (eds) *Ageing and later life*, London: Sage Publications, pp 60-67. Glasby, J. and Beresford, P. (2006) 'Who knows best? Evidence-based practice and the service user contribution', *Critical Social Policy*, vol 26, no 1, pp 268-84.

Glasby, J. and Littlechild, R. (2009) *Direct payments and personal budgets: Putting personalisation into practice*, Bristol: The Policy Press.

Glaser, B. (ed) (1993) *Examples of grounded theory: A reader*, Mill Valley, CA: Sociology Press.

Glass, T., Mendes de Leon, C., Marottali, R. and Berkman, L. (1999) 'Population based study of social and productive activities as predictors of survival among elderly Americans', *British Medical Journal*, vol 319, pp 478-83.

Glendinning, C. (2008) 'Increasing choice and control for older and disabled people: a critical review of new developments in England', *Social Policy and Administration*, vol 42, no 5, pp 451-69.

Glendinning, C., Halliwell, S., Jacobs, S., Rummery, K. and Tyrer, J. (2000) 'New kinds of care, new kinds of relationships: how purchasing services affects relationships in giving and receiving personal assistance', *Health and Social Care in the Community*, vol 8, no 3, pp 201-11.

Glendinning, C., Clarke, S., Hare, P., Kotchetkova, I., Maddison, J. and Newbronner, L. (2006) *Outcomes-focused services for older people*, London: Social Care Institute for Excellence.

Glendinning, C., Challis, D., Fernandez, J., Jacobs, S., Jones, K., Knapp, M., Manthorpe, J., Moran, N., Netten, A., Stevens, M. and Wilberforce, M. (2008) *Evaluation of the individual budgets pilot programme: Final report*, York: Social Policy Research Unit, University of York.

Glynn, M., Beresford, P. with Bewley, C., Branfield, F., Butt, J., Croft, S., Dattani Pitt, K., Fleming, J., Flynn, R., Patmore, C., Postle, K. and Turner, M. (2008) *Person-centred support: What service users and practitioners say*, York: Joseph Rowntree Foundation (www.jrf.org.uk/sites/files/jrf/2173-person-centred-support.pdf).

Godfrey, H., Hogg, A., Rigby, D. and Long, A. (2007) *Incontinence of older people: Is there a link to social isolation?*, London: Help the Aged (http://policy.helptheaged. org.uk/NR/rdonlyres/4C31DB75-FF9D-4D67-8C0F-93F91015001C/0/ incontinenceisolation101007.pdf).

Godfrey, M. (2001) 'Prevention: developing a framework for conceptualizing and evaluating outcomes of preventive services for older people', *Health and Social Care in the Community*, vol 9, no 2, pp 89-99.

Godfrey, M. and Denby, T. (2004) *Depression and older people: Towards securing well-being in later life*, Bristol: The Policy Press.

Godfrey, M., Townsend, J. and Denby, T. (2004) *Building a good life for older people in local communities: The experience of ageing in time and place*, York: Joseph Rowntree Foundation.

Goffman, E. (1961) *The presentation of self in everyday life,* Harmondsworth: Penguin.

Gott, M., Barnes, S., Payne, S., Parker, C., Seamark, D., Gariballa, S. and Small, N. (2007) 'Patient views of social service provision for older people with advanced heart failure', *Health and Social Care in the Community*, vol 15, no 4, pp 333-42.

Graham, H. (1983) 'Caring: a labour of love', in J. Finch and D. Groves (eds) *A labour of love: Women, work and caring*, London: Routledge and Kegan Paul.

Granville, G. (2000) 'Menopause: a time of private change to a mature identity', in M. Bernard, J. Phillips, L. Machin and V. Harding Davies (eds) *Women ageing: Changing identities, challenging myths*, London: Routledge, pp 74-92.

Grenier, A. (2007) 'Constructions of frailty in the English language, care practice and lived experience', *Ageing & Society*, vol 27, no 3, pp 425-45.

Grewal, I., Nazroo, J., Bajekal, M., Blane, D. and Lewis, J. (2004) 'Influences on quality of life: a qualitative investigation of ethnic differences among older people in England', *Journal of Ethnic and Migration Studies*, vol 30, no 4, pp 373-61.

Griffiths, R. (1988) *Community care: An agenda for action* (The Griffiths Report), London: HMSO.

Gubrium, J. and Wallace, J. (1990) 'Who theorises age?', *Ageing & Society*, vol 10, no 2, pp 131-49.

Hardy, B., Young, R. and Wistow, G. (1999) 'Dimensions of choice in the assessment and care management process: the views of older people, carers and care managers', *Health and Social Care in the Community*, vol 7, no 6, pp 483-91.

Harper, D. (1992) 'Small Ns and community case studies', in C. Ragin and H. Becker (eds) *What is a case? Exploring the foundations of social inquiry*, Cambridge: Cambridge University Press, pp 139-57.

Harris, J. (2002) 'Caring for citizenship', *British Journal of Social Work*, vol 32, no 3, pp 267-81.

Harris, J. and Unwin, P. (2009) 'Performance management in modernised social work', in J. Harris and V. White (eds) *Modernising social work: Critical considerations*, Bristol: The Policy Press, pp 9-30.

Havighurst, R. and Albrecht, R. (1953) *Older people*, London: Longmans, Green.

Heckhausen, J. and Schulz, R. (1993) 'Optimisation by selection and compensation: balancing primary and secondary control in the lifespan', *International Journal of Behavioural Development*, vol 16, no 2, pp 287-303.

Heikkinen, R. (1996) 'Experienced ageing as elucidated by narratives', in J. Birren, G. Kenyon, J. Ruth, J. Schroots and T. Svensson (eds) *Ageing and biography: Explorations in adult development*, New York, NY: Springer Publishing, pp 187-204.

Hekman, S. (1999) 'Identity crises: identity, identity politics and beyond', in S. Heckman (ed) *Feminism, identity and difference*, Ilford: Frank Cass, pp 3-26.

Help the Aged (2008) *Voice: A briefing paper on the voice of older people in society*, London: Help the Aged (www.helptheaged.org.uk/NR/rdonlyres/734EBE2B-66E5-461F-A339-88AF3C4D43A7/0/voice_briefing_290708.pdf).

Henderson, J. and Forbat, L. (2002) 'Relationship-based social policy: personal and policy constructions of "care"', *Critical Social Policy*, vol 22, no 4, pp 669-87.

Henwood, M. and Hudson, B. (2007) *Evaluation of the self-directed support network: An overview of key messages*, Towcester: Melanie Henwood Associates.

Henwood, M., Lewis, H. and Waddington, E. (1998) *Listening to users of domiciliary care services: Developing and monitoring quality standards*, London: Nuffield Institute/ United Kingdom Home Care Association.

Hepworth, M. (1991) 'Positive ageing and the mask of age', *Journal of Educational Gerontology*, vol 6, no 2, pp 93-101.

Hewitt, J. (1994) *Self and society: A symbolic interactionist social psychology*, Boston, MA: Allyn and Bacon.

Hey, V. (1999) 'Frail elderly people: difficult questions and awkward answers', in S. Hood, B. Mayall and S. Oliver (eds) *Critical issues in social research: Power and prejudice*, Buckingham: Open University Press, pp 94-110.

Higgs, P. (1997) 'Citizenship theory and old age: from social rights to surveillance', in A. Jamieson, S. Harper and C. Victor (eds) *Critical approaches to ageing and later life*, Buckingham: Open University Press.

Higgs, P. and Gilleard, C. (2006) 'Departing the margins: social class and later life in a second modernity', *Journal of Sociology*, vol 42, no 3, pp 219-41.

Hill, K., Sutton, L. and Cox, L. (2009) *Managing resources in later life: Older people's experience of change and continuity*, York: Joseph Rowntree Foundation (www.jrf. org.uk/sites/files/jrf/older-people-resourcesSUMMARY.pdf).

Hill, K., Kellard, K., Middleton, S., Cox, L. and Pound, E. (2007) *Understanding resources in later life: Views and experiences of older people*, York: Joseph Rowntree Foundation.

Hill, M. (2002) 'Network assessment and diagrams: a flexible friend for social work practice and education', *Journal of Social Work*, vol 2, no 2, pp 233-54.

Hockey, J. and James, A. (1993) *Growing up and growing old: Ageing and dependency in the life course*, London: Sage Publications.

Hockey, J. and James, A. (2003) *Social identities across the life course*, Basingstoke: Palgrave Macmillan.

Holland, C., Kellaher, L., Peace, S., Scharf, T., Breeze, E., Gow, J. and Gilhooly, M. (2005) 'Getting out and about', in A. Walker (ed) *Understanding quality of life in old age*, Maidenhead: Open University Press, pp 49-63.

Holland, J. and Ramazanoglu, C. (1994) 'Coming to conclusions: power and interpretation in researching young women's sexuality', in M. Maynard and J. Purvis (eds) *Researching women's lives from a feminist perspective*, London: Taylor and Francis, pp 125-48.

Holstein, J. and Gubrium, J. (1997) 'Active interviewing', in D. Silverman (ed) *Qualitative research: Theory, method and practice*, London: Sage Publications, pp 113-29.

Holstein, M. and Minkler, M. (2007) 'Critical gerontology: reflections for the 21st century', in M. Bernard and T. Scharf (eds) *Critical perspectives on ageing societies*, Bristol: The Policy Press, pp 13-26.

Howarth, G. (1993) 'Food consumption, social roles and personal identity', in S. Arber and M. Evandrou (eds) *Ageing, independence and the life course*, London: Jessica Kingsley Publishers, pp 65-77.

Howe, D. (2008) *The emotionally intelligent social worker*, Basingstoke: Palgrave Macmillan.

Hughes, B. (1993) 'A model for the comprehensive assessment of older people and their carers', *British Journal of Social Work*, vol 23, pp 345-64.

IFSW (International Federation of Social Workers) (2002) *Definition of social work*, Berne, Switzerland: IFSW (www.ifsw.org/f38000138.html).

Information Centre for Health and Social Care (2009a) *Community care statistics 2007-08: Referrals, assessments and packages of care for adults, England*, London: NHS Information Centre (www.ic.nhs.uk/webfiles/publications/Social%20Care/RAP%20Full%20Report/2007-08/RAP%20Report.pdf).

Information Centre for Health and Social Care (2009b) *Community care statistics 2008: Home care services for adults, England*, London: NHS Information Centre (www.ic.nhs.uk/webfiles/publications/Home%20Care%20%28HH1%29%20 2008/HH1%20Final%20v1.pdf).

Janesick, V. (1998) 'The dance of qualitative research design: metaphor, methodolatory and meaning', in N. Denzin and Y. Lincoln (eds) *Strategies of qualitative inquiry*, London: Sage Publications.

Jenkins, M. (2001) 'Ethics and economics in community care', *Critical Social Policy*, vol 21, no 1, pp 81-102.

Jenkins, R. (1996) *Social identity*, London: Routledge.

Johnson, C. and Barer, B. (1997) *Life beyond 85 years: The aura of survivorship*, New York, NY: Springer Publishing.

Johnson, J. (1991) 'Learning to live again: the process of adjustment following a heart attack', in J. Morse and J. Johnson (eds) *The illness experience: Dimensions of suffering*, London: Sage Publications, pp 13-88.

Jones, C. (2001) 'Voices from the front line: state social workers and New Labour', *British Journal of Social Work*, vol 31, pp 547-62.

Jordan, B. with Jordan, C. (2000) *Social work and the third way: Tough love as social policy*, London: Sage Publications.

Katz, S. (2000) 'Busy bodies: activity, aging and the management of everyday life', *Journal of Aging Studies*, vol 14, no 2, pp 135-52.

Kellaher, L., Peace, S. and Holland, C. (2004) 'Environment, identity and old age – quality of life or a life of quality?', in A. Walker and C. Hagan Hennessy (eds) *Growing older: Quality of life in old age*, Maidenhead: Open University Press, pp 60-80.

Kelly, M. and Dickinson, H. (1997) 'The narrative self in autobiographical accounts of illness', *The Sociological Review*, vol 45, no 2, pp 254-78.

Kerr, L. and Kerr, V. (2003) *Older people doing it for themselves: Accessing information, advice and advocacy*, York: Joseph Rowntree Foundation.

Killeen, D. (2008) *Is poverty in the UK a denial of people's human rights?*, York: Joseph Rowntree Foundation.

Kleinman, A. (1988) *The illness narratives: Suffering, healing and the human condition*, New York, NY: Basic Books.

Langan, J., Means, R. and Rolfe, S. (1996) *Maintaining independence in later life: Older people speaking*, Oxford: Anchor Trust.

Lee, D., Woo, J. and Mackenzie, A. (2002) 'A review of older people's experiences with residential care placement', *Journal of Advanced Nursing*, vol 37, no 1, pp 19-27.

Lee, E. and Brennan, M. (2002) '"I cannot see flowers but I can smell them": the relation of age and gender to self-reported coping strategies among older adults with visual impairment', *Qualitative Social Work*, vol 1, no 4, pp 389-411.

Leece, J. (2010) 'Paying the piper and calling the tune: power and the direct payment relationship', *British Journal of Social Work*, vol 40, pp 188-206.

Leece, J. and Peace, S. (2009) 'Developing new understandings of independence and autonomy in the personalised relationship', *British Journal of Social Work*, Advanced Access, 14 October, pp 1-19.

Leonard, P. (1997) *Postmodern welfare: Reconstructing an emancipatory project*, London: Sage Publications.

Levenson, R. (2003) 'Institutional ageism', *Community Care*, 17-23 July, pp 42-3.

Lewis, J. and Glennerster, H. (1996) *Implementing the new community care*, Buckingham: Open University Press.

Lister, R. (1998) 'Citizenship on the margins: citizenship, social work and social action', *European Journal of Social Work*, vol 1, no 1, pp 5-18.

Littlechild, R. and Glasby, J. (2000) 'Older people as "participating patients"', in H. Kemshall and R. Littlechild (eds) *User involvement and participation in social care: Research informing practice*, London: Jessica Kingsley Publishers, pp 143-158.

Litwin, H. and Shiovitz-Ezra, S. (2006) 'The association between activity and wellbeing in later life: what really matters', *Ageing & Society*, vol 26, pp 225-42.

Lloyd, M. (2000) 'Where has all the care management gone?: the challenge of Parkinson's Disease to the health and social care interface', *British Journal of Social Work*, vol 30, no 6, pp 737-54.

Mandelstam, M. (2009) *Community care practice and the law* (4th edn), London: Jessica Kingsley Publishers.

Manthorpe, J. and Stevens, M. (2009) 'Increasing care options in the countryside: developing an understanding of the potential impact of personalisation for social work with rural older people', *British Journal of Social Work*, Advance Access, 27 March, pp 1-18.

Mauthner, N. and Doucet, A. (1998) 'Reflections on a voice-centred relational method: analysing maternal and domestic voices', in J. Ribbens and R. Edwards (eds) *Feminist dilemmas in qualitative research: Public knowledge and private lives*, London: Sage Publications, pp 119-44.

Maynard, M., Afshar, H., Franks, M. and Wray, S. (2008) *Women in later life: Exploring race and ethnicity*, Maidenhead: Open University Press.

Mayo, M. (1994) *Communities and caring: The mixed economy of welfare*, Basingstoke: Macmillan.

McCann, S. and Evans, D. (2002) 'Informal care: the views of people receiving care', *Health and Social Care in the Community*, vol 10, no 4, pp 221-8.

McKevitt, C., Baldock, J., Hadlow, J., Moriarty, J. and Butt, J. (2005) 'Identity, meaning and social support', in A. Walker (ed) *Understanding quality of life in old age*, Maidenhead: Open University Press, pp 130-45.

McLeod, E. and Bywaters, P. (2000) *Social work, health and equality*, London: Routledge.

McMunn, A., Breeze, E., Goodman, A., Nazroo, J. and Oldfield, Z. (2006) 'Social determinants of health in old age', in M. Marmot and R. Wilkinson (eds) *Social determinants of health* (2nd edn), Oxford: Oxford University Press.

Means, R. (2007) 'The re-medicalisation of later life', in M. Bernard and T. Scharf (eds) *Critical perspectives on ageing societies*, Bristol: The Policy Press, pp 27–44.

Means, R. and Smith, R. (1998a) *From Poor Law to community care: The development of welfare services for elderly people 1939-1971* (2nd edn), Bristol: The Policy Press.

Means, R. and Smith, R. (1998b) *Community care: Policy and practice* (2nd edn), Basingstoke: Macmillan.

Means, R., Morbey, H. and Smith, R. (2002) *From community care to market care? The development of welfare services for older people*, Bristol: The Policy Press.

Menz, H. and Lord, S. (2005) 'The contribution of foot problems to mobility impairment and falls in community-dwelling older people', *Journal of the American Geriatrics Society*, vol 49, no 12, pp 1651–6.

Miles, M. and Huberman, A. (1994) *Qualitative data analysis: An expanded sourcebook* (2nd edn), London: Sage Publications.

Milner, J. and O'Byrne, P. (2009) *Assessment in social work* (3rd edn), Basingstoke: Palgrave Macmillan.

Minichiello, V., Browne, J. and Kendig, H. (2000) 'Perceptions and consequences of ageism: views of older people', *Ageing & Society*, vol 30, no 3, pp 253–78.

Moffatt, S. and Higgs, P. (2007) 'Charity or entitlement? Generational habitus and the welfare state among older people in North-east England', *Social Policy and Administration*, vol 41, no 5, pp 449–64.

Moloczij, N., McPherson, K., Smith, J. and Kayes, N. (2008) 'Help-seeking at the time of stroke: stroke survivors' perspectives', *Health and Social Care in the Community*, vol 16, no 5, pp 501–10.

Moriarty, J., Rapaport, P., Beresford, B., Branfield, F., Forrest, V., Manthorpe, J., Matineau, S., Cornes, M., Butt, J., Iliffe, S., Taylor, B. and Keady, J. (2006) *The participation of adult service users, including older people, in developing social care*, Practice Guide 11, London: Social Care Institute for Excellence (www.scie.org.uk/publications/practiceguides/practiceguide11/files/pg11.pdf).

Morris, J. (1993) *Independent lives? Community care and disabled people*, Basingstoke: Macmillan.

Morrison, A. (2001) 'Improving the quality of written assessments: a participative approach', in V. White and J. Harris (eds) *Developing good practice in community care: Partnership and participation*, London: Jessica Kingsley Publishers, pp 34–48.

Moustakas, C. (1994) *Phenomenological research methods*, Thousand Oaks, CA: Sage Publications.

Mullen, P. (1993) 'Cutting back after heart attack: an overview', in B. Glaser (ed) *Examples of grounded theory: A reader*, Mill Valley, CA: Sociology Press.

Murphy, E. (1982) 'The social origins of depression in old age', *British Journal of Psychiatry*, vol 141, pp 135–42.

Musingarimi, P. (2008) *Social care issues affecting older gay, lesbian and bisexual people in the UK: A policy brief*, London: International Longevity Centre.

Myers, F. and MacDonald, C. (1996) '"I was given options, not choices": including older users and carers in assessment and care planning', in R. Bland (ed) *Developing services for older people and their families*, London: Jessica Kingsley Publishers, pp 97–111.

Nazroo, J., Bajekal, M., Blane, D. and Grewal, I. (2004) *Ethnic inequalities in quality of life at older ages: Subjective and objective components*, Economic and Social Research Council Growing Older Programme, Findings 11, Sheffield: University of Sheffield (www.shef.ac.uk/uni/projects/gop).

Newman, J., Glendinning, C. and Hughes, M. (2008) 'Beyond modernisation? Social care and the transformation of welfare governance', *Journal of Social Policy*, vol 37, no 4, pp 531–57.

NHS Confederation (2009) *Personal health budgets: The shape of things to come?*, London: NHS Confederation (www.nhsconfed.org/Publications/Documents/personal_health_budgets160109.pdf).

Nielson, H. (1999) '"Black holes" as sites of self-constructions', in R. Josselson and A. Lieblich (eds) *Making meaning of narratives*, Thousand Oaks, CA: Sage Publications.

Nilsson, M., Ekman, S. and Sarvimäki, A. (1998) 'Ageing with joy or resigning to old age: older people's experiences of the quality of life in old age', *Health Care in Later Life*, vol 3, no 2, pp 94–110.

Nocon, A. and Pearson, M. (2000) 'The roles of friends and neighbours in providing support for older people', *Ageing & Society*, vol 20, no 3, pp 341–67.

Nolan, M., Davies, S. and Grant, G. (2001) 'Integrating perspectives', in M. Nolan, S. Davies and G. Grant (eds) *Working with older people and their families*, Buckingham: Open University Press, pp 75–97.

Nolan, M., Grant, G. and Keady, J. (1996) *Understanding family care*, Buckingham: Open University Press.

O'Connor, P. and Brown, G. (1984) 'Supportive relationships: fact or fancy?', *Journal of Social and Personal Relationships*, vol 1, no 2, pp 159–75.

ODPM (Office of the Deputy Prime Minister) (2006) *A sure start to later life: Ending inequalities for older people. A Social Exclusion Unit final report*, London: ODPM.

Older People's Steering Group (2004) *Older people shaping policy and practice*, York: Joseph Rowntree Foundation (www.jrf.org.uk/bookshop/eBooks/1859352456.pdf).

Oliver, M. and Sapey, B. (2006) *Social work with disabled people* (3rd edn), Basingstoke: Palgrave Macmillan.

Orona, C. (1997) 'Temporality and identity loss due to Alzheimer's Disease', in A. Strauss and J. Corbin (eds) *Grounded theory in practice*, Thousand Oaks, CA: Sage Publications.

O'Shea, E. (2006) 'An economic and social evaluation of the Senior Help Line in Ireland', *Ageing & Society*, vol 26, pp 267–84.

Parker, H. (ed) (2000) *Low Cost but Acceptable incomes for older people: A minimum income standard for households aged 65-74 years in the UK*, Bristol: The Policy Press.

Parton, N. and Marshall, W. (1998) 'Postmodernism and discourse approaches to social work', in R. Adams, L. Dominelli and M. Payne (eds) *Social work: Themes, issues and critical debates* (1st edn), Basingstoke: Macmillan, pp 240-49.

Peace, S. (1998) 'Caring in place', in A. Brechin, J. Walmsley, J. Katz and S. Peace (eds) *Care matters: Concepts, practice and research in health and social care*, London: Sage Publications, pp 139-53.

Pearson, C. (2000) 'Money talks? Competing discourses in the implementation of direct payments', *Critical Social Policy*, vol 20, no 4, pp 459-77.

Pease, B. (2002) 'Rethinking empowerment: a postmodern reappraisal for emancipatory practice', *British Journal of Social Work*, vol 32, no 2, pp 135-47.

Penhale, B. and Parker, J. (2008) *Working with vulnerable adults*, London: Routledge.

Percival, J. (2002) 'Domestic spaces: uses and meanings in the daily lives of older people', *Ageing & Society*, vol 22, no 6, pp 729-49.

Phillips, J., Bernard, M., Phillipson, C. and Ogg, J. (2000) 'Social support in later life: a study of three areas', *British Journal of Social Work*, vol 30, no 6, pp 837-53.

Phillipson, C. (1998) *Reconstructing old age: New agendas in social theory and practice*, London: Sage Publications.

Phillipson, C. and Biggs, S. (1998) 'Modernity and identity: themes and perspectives in the study of older adults', *Journal of Aging and Identity*, vol 3, no 1, pp 11-23.

Phillipson, C., Bernard, M., Phillips, J. and Ogg, J. (2001) *The family and community life of older people: Social networks and social support in three urban areas*, London: Routledge.

Poland, B. (1995) 'Transcription quality as an aspect of rigor in qualitative research', *Qualitative Inquiry*, vol 1, no 3, pp 290-310.

Postle, K. (2002) 'Working "between the idea and the reality": ambiguities and tensions in care managers' work', *British Journal of Social Work*, vol 32, no 3, pp 335-51.

Postle, K., Wright, P. and Beresford, P. (2005) 'Older people's participation in political activity – making their voices heard: a potential support role for welfare professionals in countering ageism and social exclusion', *Practice*, vol 17, no 3, pp 173-87.

Powell, J., Robison, J., Roberts, H. and Thomas, G. (2007) 'The single assessment process in primary care: older people's accounts of the process', *British Journal of Social Work*, vol 37, no 6, pp 1043-58.

Pratt, M. and Norris, J. (1994) *The social psychology of ageing*, Oxford: Blackwell.

Punch, K. (1998) *Introduction to social research: Quantitative and qualitative approaches*, London: Sage Publications.

Quilgars, D. (2000) *Low intensity support services: A systematic review of effectiveness*, Bristol: The Policy Press.

Quilgars, D. (2004) *Communities caring and developing: Lessons from Hull*, York: Joseph Rowntree Foundation.

Qureshi, H. (1996) 'Obligations and support within families', in A. Walker (ed) *The new generational contract: Intergenerational relations, old age and welfare*, London: UCL Press, pp 101-20.

Radley, A. (1994) *Making sense of health and illness: The social psychology of health and disease*, London: Sage Publications.

Radley, A. and Billig, M. (1996) 'Accounts of health and illness: dilemmas and representations', *Sociology of Health and Illness*, vol 18, no 2, pp 220-40.

Ray, M. (2000) 'Older women, long-term marriage and care', in M. Bernard, J. Phillips, L. Machin and V. Harding Davies (eds) *Women ageing: Changing identities, challenging myths*, London: Routledge, pp 148-67.

Ray, M. (2007) 'Redressing the balance? The participation of older people in research', in M. Bernard and T. Scharf (eds) *Critical perspectives on ageing societies*, Bristol: The Policy Press, pp 73-87.

Ray, R. (2007) 'Narratives as agents of social change: a new direction for narrative gerontologists', in M. Bernard and T. Scharf (eds) *Critical perspectives on ageing societies*, Bristol: The Policy Press, pp 59-72.

Raynes, N., Temple, B., Glenister, C. and Coulthard, L. (2001) *Quality at home for older people: Involving service users in defining home care specifications*, Bristol: The Policy Press.

Reed, R. and Gilleard, C. (1995) 'Elderly patients' satisfaction with a community nursing service', in G. Wilson (ed) *Community care: Asking the user*, London: Chapman Hall, pp 113-25.

Reed, J. and Stanley, D. (2000) 'Discharge from hospital to care home: professional boundaries and interfaces', in A. Warnes, L. Warren and M. Nolan (eds) *Care services in later life: Transformations and critiques*, London: Jessica Kingsley.

Reed, J., Stanley, D. and Clarke, C. (2004) *Health, well-being and older people*, Bristol: The Policy Press.

Reed, J., Cook, G., Bolter, V. and Douglas, B. (2006) *Older people 'getting things done': Involvement in policy and planning initiatives*, York: Joseph Rowntree Foundation (www.jrf.org.uk/bookshop/eBooks/9781859354575.pdf).

Reynolds, J. and Walmsley, J. (1998) 'Care, support or something else?', in A. Brechin, J. Walmsley, J. Katz and S. Peace (eds) *Care matters: Concepts, practice and research in health and social care*, London: Sage Publications, pp 66-80.

Richards, S. (2000) 'Bridging the divide: elders and the assessment process', *British Journal of Social Work*, vol 30, pp 37-49.

Richardson, S. and Pearson, M. (1995) 'Dignity and aspirations denied: unmet health and social care needs in an inner-city area', *Health and Social Care in the Community*, vol 3, no 5, pp 279-87.

Ritters, K. and Davis, H. (2008) *Access to information and services for older people – The joined-up approach*, London: Department for Work and Pensions (www.dwp.gov.uk/asd/asd5/wp53.pdf).

Roberts, E., Robinson, J. and Seymour, L. (2002) *Old habits die hard: Tackling age discrimination in health and social care*, London: The King's Fund.

Roberts, K. and Chapman, T. (2001) *Realising participation: Elderly people as active users of health and social care*, Aldershot: Ashgate.

Rodger, J. (1991) 'Discourse analysis and social relationships in social work', *British Journal of Social Work*, vol 21, pp 63-79.

Rogers, A., Casey, M., Ekert, J., Holland, J., Nakkula, V. and Sheinberg, N. (1999) 'An interpretive poetics of languages of the unsayable', in R. Josselson and A. Lieblich (eds) *Making meaning of narratives: The narrative study of lives*, Thousand Oaks, CA: Sage Publications, pp 77-106.

Rose, S. and Hatzenbuehler, S. (2009) 'Embodying social class: the link between poverty, income inequality and health', *International Social Work*, vol 52, no 4, pp 459-71.

Ruth, J.-E. and Kenyon, G. (1996) 'Biography in adult development and aging', in J.E. Birren, G. Kenyon, J.-E. Ruth, J.J.F. Schroots and T. Svensson (eds) *Aging and biography: Explorations in adult development*, New York, NY: Springer Publishing, pp 1-20.

Ruth, J.-E. and Oberg, P. (1996) 'Ways of life: old age in a life history perspective', in J. Birren, G. Kenyon, J.-E. Ruth, J. Schroots and T. Svensson (eds) *Ageing and biography: Explorations in adult development*, New York, NY: Springer Publishing, pp 167-186.

Scharf, T., Phillipson, C. and Smith, A. (2004) 'Poverty and social exclusion – growing older in deprived urban neighbourhoods', in A. Walker and C. Hagan Hennessy (eds) *Growing older: Quality of life in old age*, Maidenhead: Open University Press, pp 81-106.

Scott-Maxwell, F. (1968/1998) 'The measure of my days' (reproduced in H. Moody) *Aging: Concepts and controversies* (2nd edn), Thousand Oaks, CA and London: Sage Publications.

Scourfield, P. (2005) 'Implementing the Community Care (Direct Payments) Act: will the supply of personal assistants meet the demand and at what price?', *Journal of Social Policy*, vol 34, no 3, pp 1-20.

Scourfield, P. (2007a) 'Social care and the modern citizen: client, consumer, service user, manager and entrepreneur', *British Journal of Social Work*, vol 37, pp 107-22.

Scourfield, P. (2007b) 'Helping older people in residential care remain full citizens', *British Journal of Social Work*, vol 37, pp 1135-52.

Seale, C. (1996) 'Living alone towards the end of life', *Ageing & Society*, vol 16, no 1, pp 75-91.

Secker, J., Hill, R., Villeneau, L. and Parkman, S. (2003) 'Promoting independence: but promoting what and how?', *Ageing & Society*, vol 23, pp 375-91.

Seeman, T.E., Bruce, M.L. and McAvay, G.J. (1996) 'Baseline social network characteristics and onset of ADL disability: MacArthur studies of successful ageing', *Journals of Gerontology: Social Sciences*, vol 51b, S191-S200.

Shaw, I. and Gould, N. (2001) 'The consequences of qualitative social work research', in I. Shaw and N. Gould (eds) *Qualitative research in social work*, London: Sage Publications, pp 179-202.

Sheridan, D. and Holland, C. (2003) 'A day in the life: interpreting first hand accounts from the Mass-Observation Archive', in B. Bytheway (ed) *Everyday living in later life*, London: Centre for Policy on Ageing, pp 20-33.

Sidell, M. (1995) *Health in old age: Myth, mystery and management*, Buckingham: Open University Press.

Sidenvall, B., Nydahl, M. and Fjellstrom, C. (2001) 'Managing food shopping and cooking: the experiences of older Swedish women', *Ageing & Society*, vol 21, no 2, pp 151-68.

Silverman, D. (1993) *Interpreting qualitative data: Methods for analysing talk, text and interaction*, London: Sage Publications.

Silverstein, M., Chen, X. and Heller, K. (1996) 'Too much of a good thing? Intergenerational social support and the psychological well-being of older parents', *Journal of Marriage and the Family*, vol 58, no 4, pp 970-82.

SSI (Social Services Inspectorate)/DH (Department of Health) (1991) *Care management and assessment: Practitioners' guide*, London: DH.

Stafford, M., Chandola, T. and Marmot, M. (2007) 'Association between fear of crime and mental health and physical functioning', *American Journal of Public Health*, vol 97, no 11, pp 2076-81.

Stainton, T. and Boyce, S. (2004) '"I have got my life back": users' experience of direct payments', *Disability and Society*, vol 19, no 5, pp 443-54.

Stanley, L. and Wise, S. (1993) *Breaking out again: Feminist ontology and epistemology* (2nd edn), London: Routledge.

Stanley, N. (1999) 'User-practitioner transactions in the new culture of community care', *British Journal of Social Work*, vol 29, pp 417-35.

Stevens, N. (2001) 'Combating loneliness: a friendship enrichment programme for older women', *Ageing & Society*, vol 21, pp 183-202.

Steverink, N., Lindenberg, S. and Ormel, J. (1998) 'Towards understanding successful ageing: patterned change in resources and goals', *Ageing & Society*, vol 18, pp 441-67.

Strauss, A. and Corbin, J. (1990) *Basics of qualitative research: Grounded theory procedures and techniques*, Newbury Park, CA: Sage Publications.

Strauss, A. and Corbin, J. (eds) (1997) *Grounded theory in practice*, Thousand Oaks, CA: Sage Publications.

Strauss, A. and Corbin, J. (1998) 'Grounded theory methodology: an overview', in N. Denzin and Y. Lincoln (eds) *Strategies of qualitative inquiry*, London: Sage Publications.

Sullivan, M. (2009) 'Social workers in community care practice: ideologies and interactions with older people', *British Journal of Social Work*, vol 39, pp 1306-25.

Swain, J. and French, S. (eds) (2008) *Disability on equal terms*, London: Sage Publications.

Sword, W. (1999) 'Accounting for presence of self: reflections on doing qualitative research', *Qualitative Health Research*, vol 9, no 2, pp 270-8.

Symonds, A. (1998) 'The social reconstruction of care: from the state to the "community"', in A. Symonds and A. Kelly (eds) *The social construction of community care*, Basingstoke: Macmillan, pp 33-50.

Tanner, D. (2009) 'Modernisation and the delivery of user-centred services', in J. Harris and V. White (eds) *Modernising social work: Critical considerations*, Bristol: The Policy Press, pp 107-126.

Taylor, D. (1998) 'Social identity and social policy: engagements with postmodern theory', *Journal of Social Policy*, vol 27, no 3, pp 329-50.

Thompson, P., Itzin, C. and Abendstern, M. (1990) '"*I don't feel old": The experience of later life*, Oxford: Oxford University Press.

Thornton, P. and Tozer, R. (1994) *Involving older people in planning and evaluating community care: A review of initiatives*, York: Joseph Rowntree Foundation.

Tilse, C., Setterland, D., Wilson, J. and Rosenman, L. (2007) 'Managing the financial assets of older people: balancing independence and protection', *British Journal of Social Work*, vol 37, pp 565-72.

Titley, M. and Chasey, B. (1996) 'Across differences of age: young women speaking of and with old women', in C. Kitzinger and S. Wilkinson (eds) *Representing the other: A feminism and psychology reader*, London: Sage Publications, pp 147-151.

Townsend, J., Godfrey, M. and Denby, T. (2006) 'Heroines, villains and victims: older people's perceptions of others', *Ageing & Society*, vol 26 pp 883-900.

Townsend, P. (1981) 'The structured dependency of the elderly: the creation of social policy in the twentieth century', *Ageing & Society*, vol 1, no 1, pp 5-28.

Tulle-Winton, E. (1999) 'Growing old and resistance: towards a new cultural economy of old age?', *Ageing & Society*, vol 19, pp 281-99.

Twigg, J. (1997) 'Deconstructing the "social bath": help with bathing at home for older and disabled people', *Journal of Social Policy*, vol 26, no 2, pp 211-32.

Vernon, A. (2002) *User-defined outcomes of community care for Asian disabled people*, Bristol: The Policy Press.

Villarreal, M. (1992) 'The poverty of practice: power, gender and intervention from an actor-oriented perspective', in N. Long and A. Long (eds) *Battlegrounds of knowledge: The interlocking of theory and practice in social research and development*, London: Routledge, pp 247-67.

Walker, A. (1981) 'Towards a political economy of old age', *Ageing & Society*, vol 1, no 1, pp 73-94.

Walker, A. (1993) 'Community care policy: from consensus to conflict', in J. Bornat, J. Johnson, C. Pereira, D. Pilgrim and F. Williams (eds) *Community care: A reader*, Basingstoke: Macmillan.

Wallcraft, J. (2005) 'Recovery from mental breakdown', in J. Tew (ed) *Social perspectives in mental health: Developing social models to understand and work with mental distress*, London: Jessica Kingsley Publishers, pp 200-15.

Wanless, D. (2006) *Securing good care for older people: Taking a long-term view*, London: The King's Fund.

Ware, T., Matasevic, T., Hardy, B., Knapp, M., Kendall, J. and Farder, J. (2003) 'Commissioning care services for older people in England and Wales: the view from care managers, users and carers', *Ageing & Society*, vol 23, pp 411-28.

Warren, L., Maltby, T. and Cook, J. (2003) *Older women's lives and voices: Participation and policy in Sheffield*, Economic and Social Research Council Growing Older Programme, Findings 21, Sheffield: University of Sheffield (www.shef.ac.uk/uni/projects/gop).

Watt, P., Blair, I., Davis, H. and Ritters, K. (2007) *Towards a business case for LinkAge Plus*, Working Paper No 42, London: Department for Work and Pensions (www.dwp.gov.uk/asd/asd5/WP42.pdf).

Wenger, G.C. (1984) *The supportive network: Coping with old age*, London: George Allen and Unwin.

Wenger, G.C. (1994) *Understanding support networks and community care*, Aldershot: Avebury, Ashgate.

Wenger, G.C. (1997) 'Social networks and the prediction of elderly people at risk', *Ageing and Mental Health*, vol 1, no 4, pp 311-20.

Wenger, G.C. (2001) 'Myths and realities of ageing in rural Britain', *Ageing & Society*, vol 21, no 1, pp 117-30.

Wilkin, D. (1990) 'Dependency', in S. Peace (ed) *Researching social gerontology: Concepts, methods and issues*, London: Sage Publications, pp 19-31.

Williams, F. (1999) 'Good enough principles for welfare', *Journal of Social Policy*, vol 28, no 4, pp 667-87.

Williams, F. (2000) 'Principles of recognition and respect in welfare', in G. Lewis, S. Gewirtz and J. Clarke (eds) *Rethinking social policy*, London: Sage Publications, pp 338-52.

Wilson, G. (1995) 'Low expectations reinforced: experiences of health services in advanced old age', in G. Wilson (ed) *Community care: Asking the user*, London: Chapman Hall, pp 69-82.

Wilson, G. (2001) 'Conceptual frameworks and emancipatory research in social gerontology', *Ageing & Society*, vol 21, pp 471-87.

Windle, K., Wagland, R., Forder, J., D'Amico, F., Janssen, D. and Wistow, G. (2009) *National evaluation of Partnerships for Older People Projects: Final evaluation*, Canterbury: Personal Social Services Research Unit.

Wistow, G. and Lewis, H. (1997) *Preventative services for older people: Current approaches and future opportunities*, Oxford: Anchor Trust.

Wistow, G., Knapp, M., Hardy, B., Forder, J., Kendall, J. and Manning, R. (1996) *Social care markets: Progress and prospects*, Buckingham: Open University Press.

Withnall, A. (2004) *Older people and lifelong learning: Choices and experiences*, Economic and Social Research Council Growing Older Programme, Findings 13, Sheffield: University of Sheffield (www.shef.ac.uk/uni/projects/gop).

Wolcott, H. (1994) *Transforming qualitative data: Description, analysis and interpretation*, Thousand Oaks, CA: Sage Publications.

Woods, P. (1999) *Successful writing for qualitative researchers*, London: Routledge.

Yeandle, S. and Buckner, L. (2005) *Older carers in the UK*, London/Sheffield: Carers UK/Sheffield Hallam University.

Index

Note: The letter f following a page number indicates a figure